HARROW

DARK TIMES A'COMING

COUNTY

HARROW

DARK TIMES A'COMING

COUNTY

Script
CULLEN BUNN

Art and Lettering
TYLER CROOK

DARK HORSE BOOKS

President and Publisher
MIKE RICHARDSON

Editor
DANIEL CHABON

Associate Editor
CARDNER CLARK

Assistant Editor
BRETT ISRAEL

Designer
KEITH WOOD

Digital Art Technician
CHRISTIANNE GOUDREAU

NEIL HANKERSON Executive Vice President · **TOM WEDDLE** Chief Financial Officer · **RANDY STRADLEY** Vice President of Publishing
MATT PARKINSON Vice President of Marketing · **DAVID SCROGGY** Vice President of Product Development
DALE LaFOUNTAIN Vice President of Information Technology · **CARA NIECE** Vice President of Production and Scheduling
NICK McWHORTER Vice President of Media Licensing · **MARK BERNARDI** Vice President of Book Trade and Digital Sales
KEN LIZZI General Counsel · **DAVE MARSHALL** Editor in Chief · **DAVEY ESTRADA** Editorial Director
CHRIS WARNER Senior Books Editor · **CARY GRAZZINI** Director of Specialty Projects · **LIA RIBACCHI** Art Director
VANESSA TODD Director of Print Purchasing · **MATT DRYER** Director of Digital Art and Prepress
MICHAEL GOMBOS Director of International Publishing and Licensing

Published by Dark Horse Books
A division of Dark Horse Comics, Inc.
10956 SE Main Street
Milwaukie, OR 97222

First edition: March 2018
ISBN 978-1-50670-397-8

International Licensing: (503) 905-2377 · Comic Shop Locator Service: comicshoplocator.com

Harrow County Volume 7: Dark Times A'Coming

This volume collects *Harrow County* #25–#28.

10 9 8 7 6 5 4 3 2 1
Printed in China

DarkHorse.com

Library of Congress Cataloging-in-Publication Data

Names: Bunn, Cullen, author. | Crook, Tyler, artist, letterer.

Title: Dark times a'coming / script, Cullen Bunn ; art and lettering, Tyler Crook.

Description: First edition. | Milwaukie, OR : Dark Horse Books, March 2018. |
  Series: Harrow County ; Volume 7 | "This volume collects Harrow County
  #25-#28"

Identifiers: LCCN 2017045316 | ISBN 9781506703978 (paperback)

Subjects: LCSH: Comic books, strips, etc. | BISAC: COMICS & GRAPHIC NOVELS / Horror.
COMICS & GRAPHIC NOVELS / Fantasy. | COMICS & GRAPHIC NOVELS / General.

Classification: LCC PN6728.H369 B856 2018 | DDC 741.5/973--dc23

LC record available at https://lccn.loc.gov/2017045316

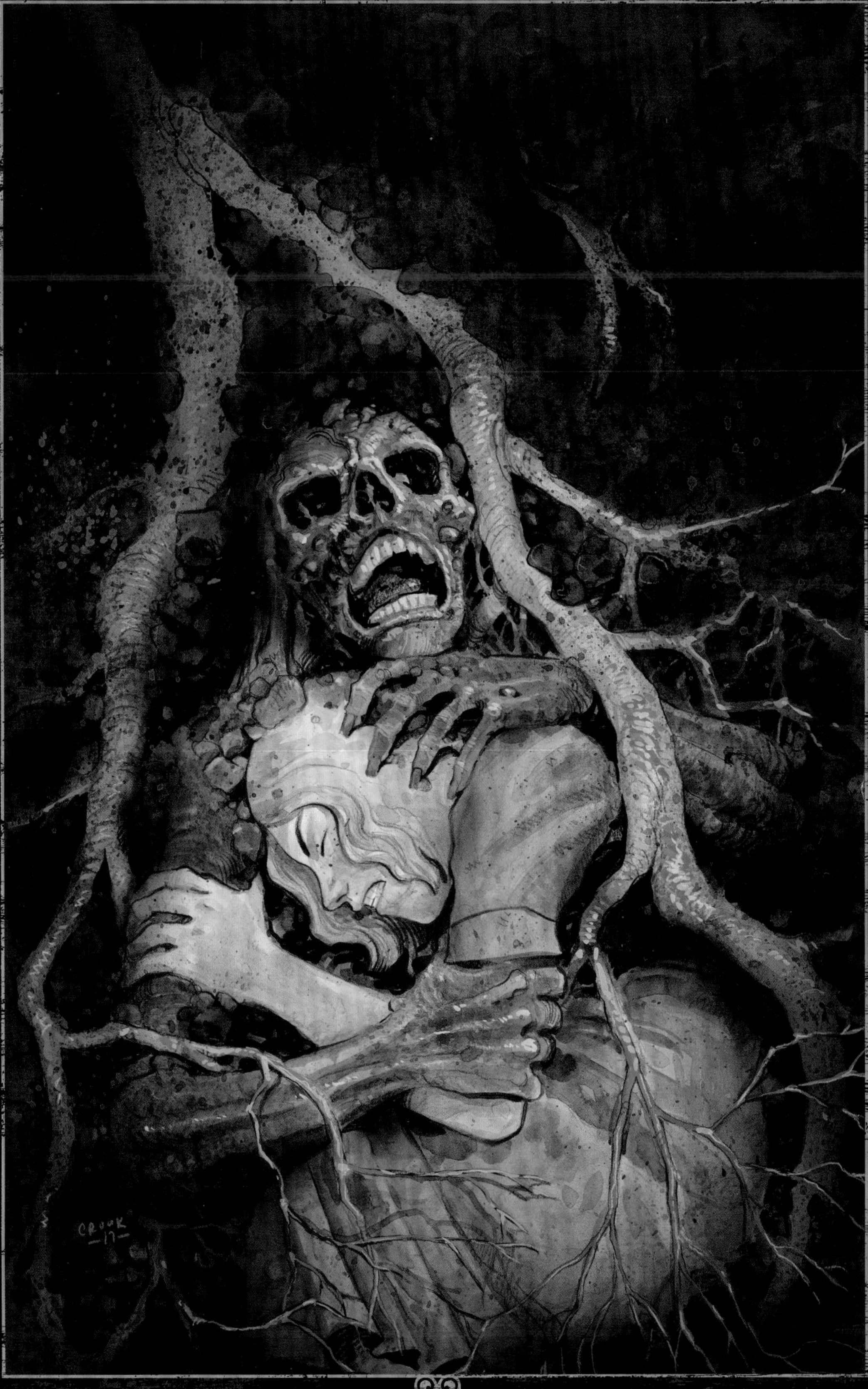
CROOK
-17-

ONE

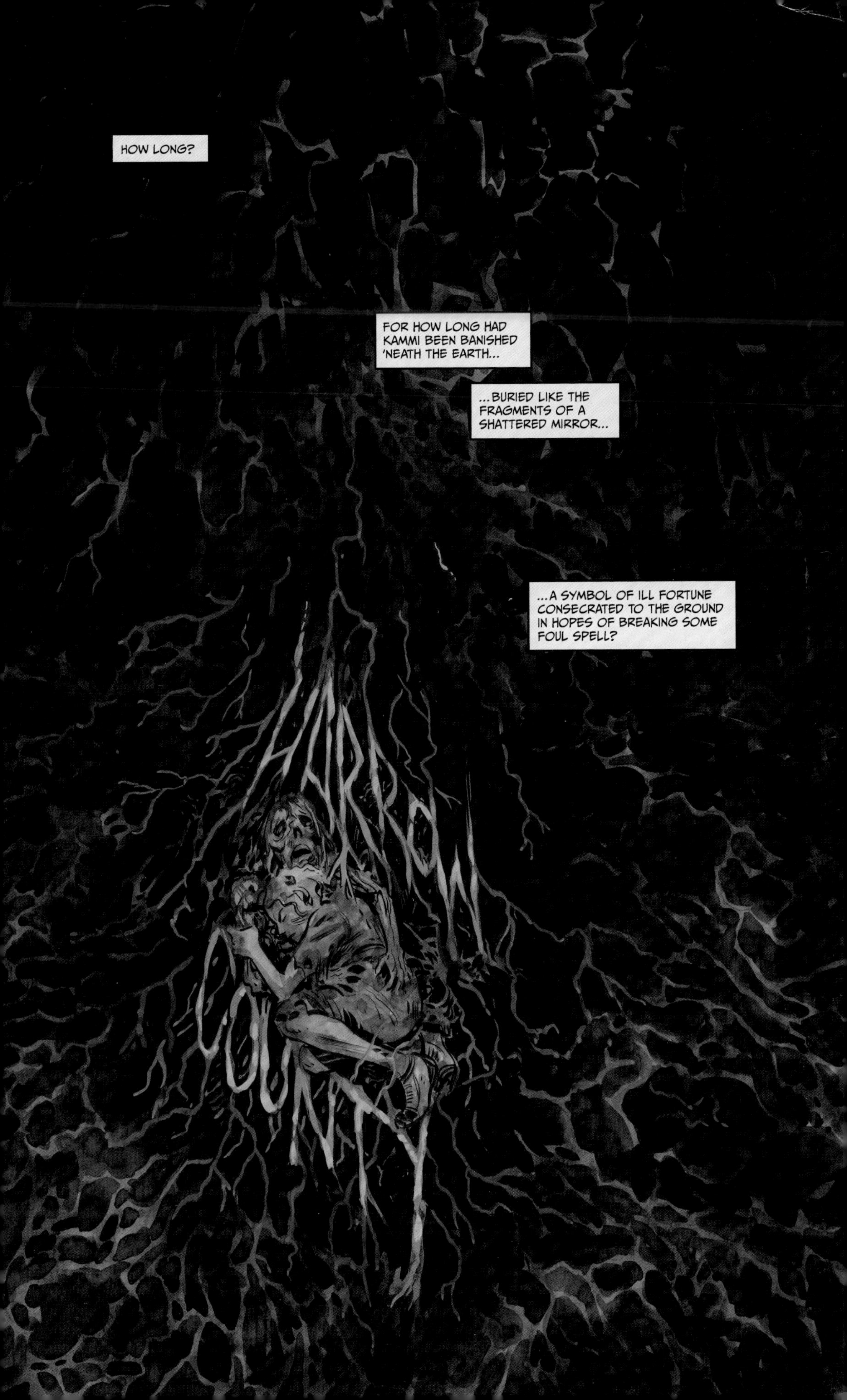
HOW LONG?
FOR HOW LONG HAD KAMMI BEEN BANISHED 'NEATH THE EARTH...
...BURIED LIKE THE FRAGMENTS OF A SHATTERED MIRROR...
...A SYMBOL OF ILL FORTUNE CONSECRATED TO THE GROUND IN HOPES OF BREAKING SOME FOUL SPELL?
HARROW COUNTY

HOW LONG?

IF THE GIRL COULD OPEN HER MOUTH WITHOUT GAGGING ON THE DIRT AND WORMS...

...SHE WOULD HAVE SCREAMED THE QUESTION 'TIL HER THROAT WAS RAW.

IT MIGHT HAVE BEEN YEARS.

IT MIGHT HAVE BEEN ONLY A FEW MINUTES.

IT FELT LIKE *FOREVER.*

SHE HAD ONLY WANTED TO KNOW THE SISTER FROM WHOM SHE HAD BEEN ESTRANGED FOR SO LONG.

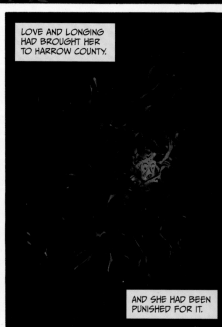

LOVE AND LONGING HAD BROUGHT HER TO HARROW COUNTY.

AND SHE HAD BEEN PUNISHED FOR IT.

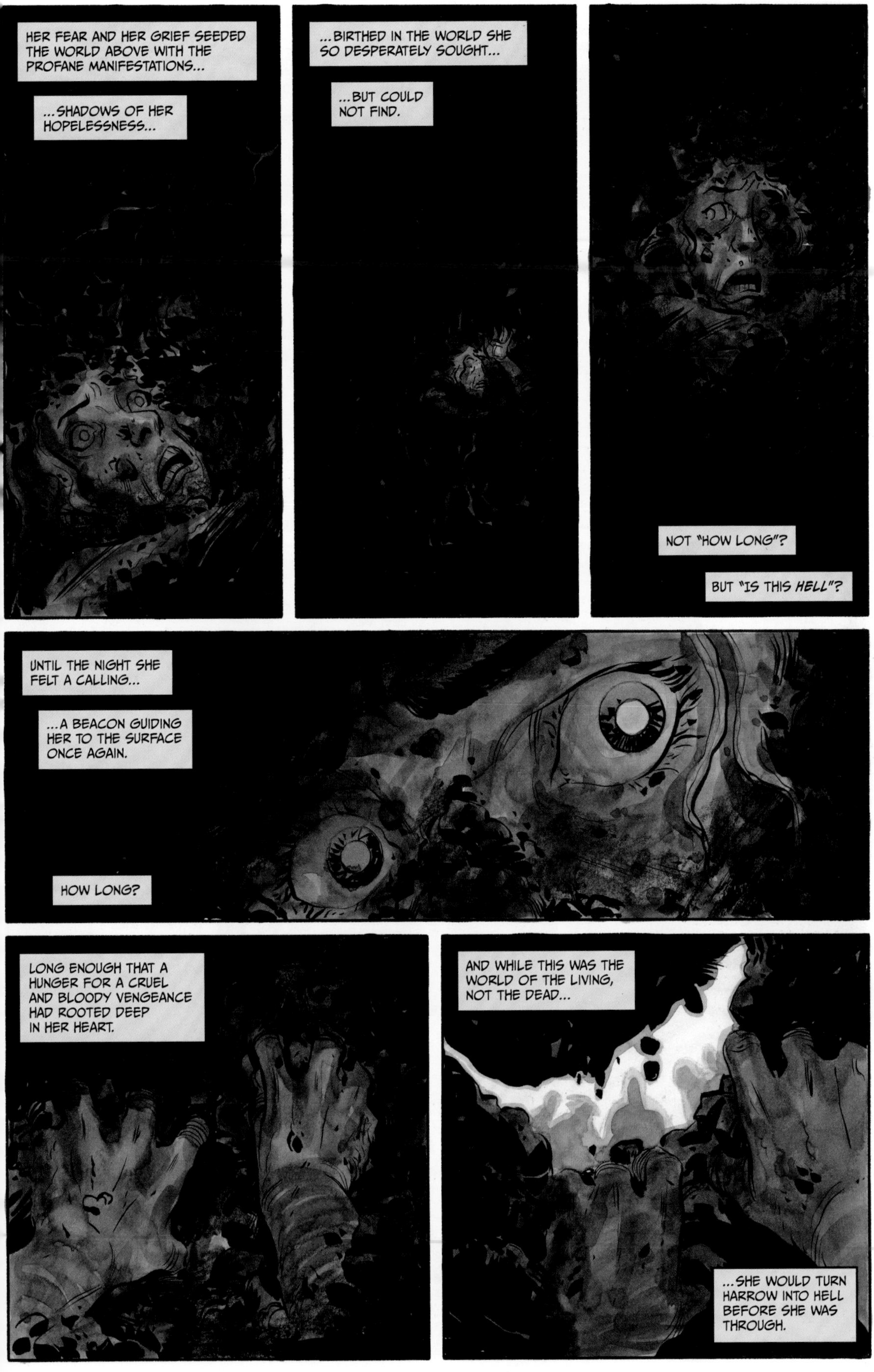
HER FEAR AND HER GRIEF SEEDED THE WORLD ABOVE WITH THE PROFANE MANIFESTATIONS...
...SHADOWS OF HER HOPELESSNESS...
...BIRTHED IN THE WORLD SHE SO DESPERATELY SOUGHT...
...BUT COULD NOT FIND.
NOT "HOW LONG"?
BUT "IS THIS HELL"?
UNTIL THE NIGHT SHE FELT A CALLING...
...A BEACON GUIDING HER TO THE SURFACE ONCE AGAIN.
HOW LONG?
LONG ENOUGH THAT A HUNGER FOR A CRUEL AND BLOODY VENGEANCE HAD ROOTED DEEP IN HER HEART.
AND WHILE THIS WAS THE WORLD OF THE LIVING, NOT THE DEAD...
...SHE WOULD TURN HARROW INTO HELL BEFORE SHE WAS THROUGH.

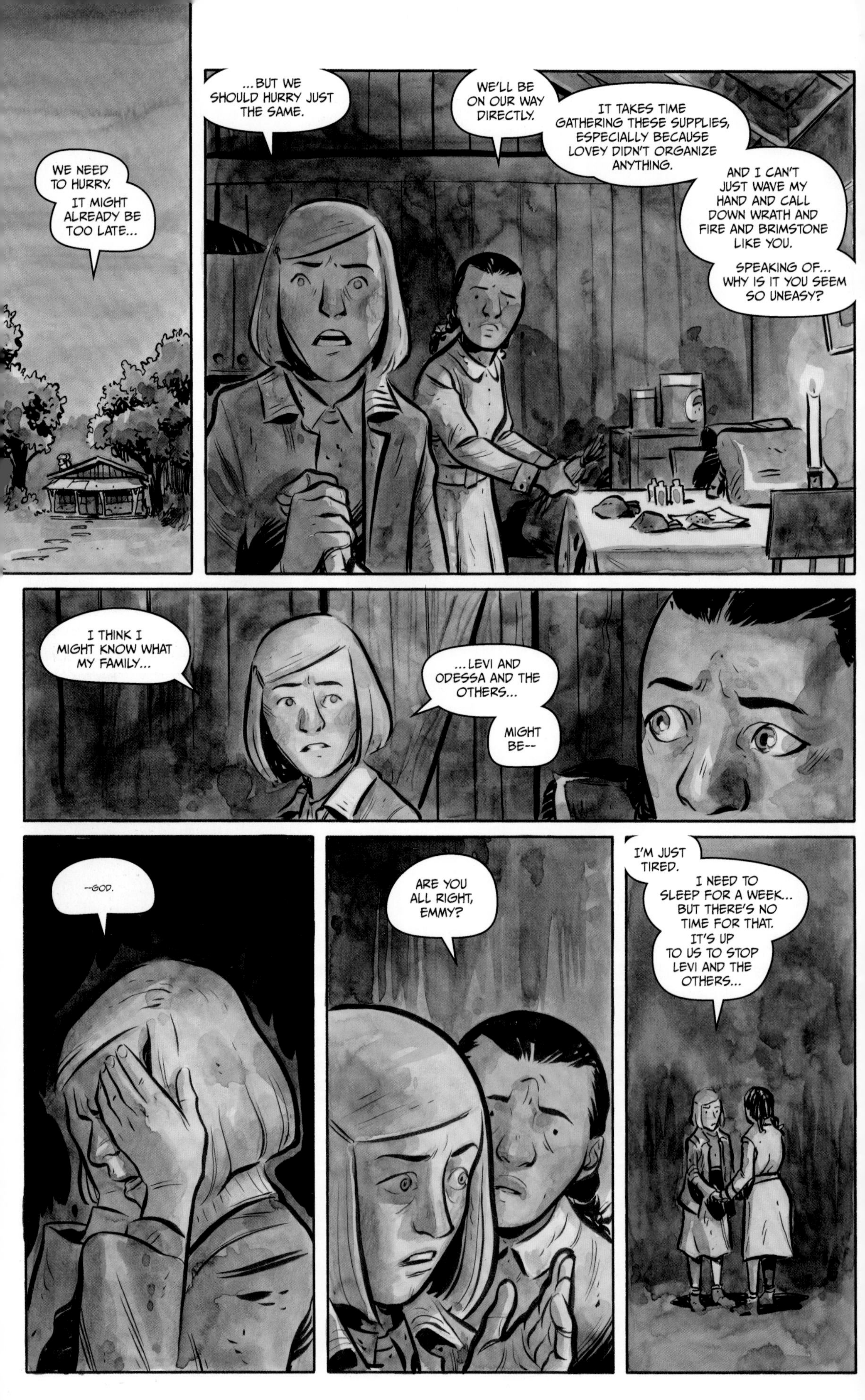
WE NEED TO HURRY.
IT MIGHT ALREADY BE TOO LATE...
...BUT WE SHOULD HURRY JUST THE SAME.
WE'LL BE ON OUR WAY DIRECTLY.
IT TAKES TIME GATHERING THESE SUPPLIES, ESPECIALLY BECAUSE LOVEY DIDN'T ORGANIZE ANYTHING.
AND I CAN'T JUST WAVE MY HAND AND CALL DOWN WRATH AND FIRE AND BRIMSTONE LIKE YOU.
SPEAKING OF... WHY IS IT YOU SEEM SO UNEASY?
I THINK I MIGHT KNOW WHAT MY FAMILY...
...LEVI AND ODESSA AND THE OTHERS...
MIGHT BE--
--GOD.
ARE YOU ALL RIGHT, EMMY?
I'M JUST TIRED.
I NEED TO SLEEP FOR A WEEK... BUT THERE'S NO TIME FOR THAT.
IT'S UP TO US TO STOP LEVI AND THE OTHERS...

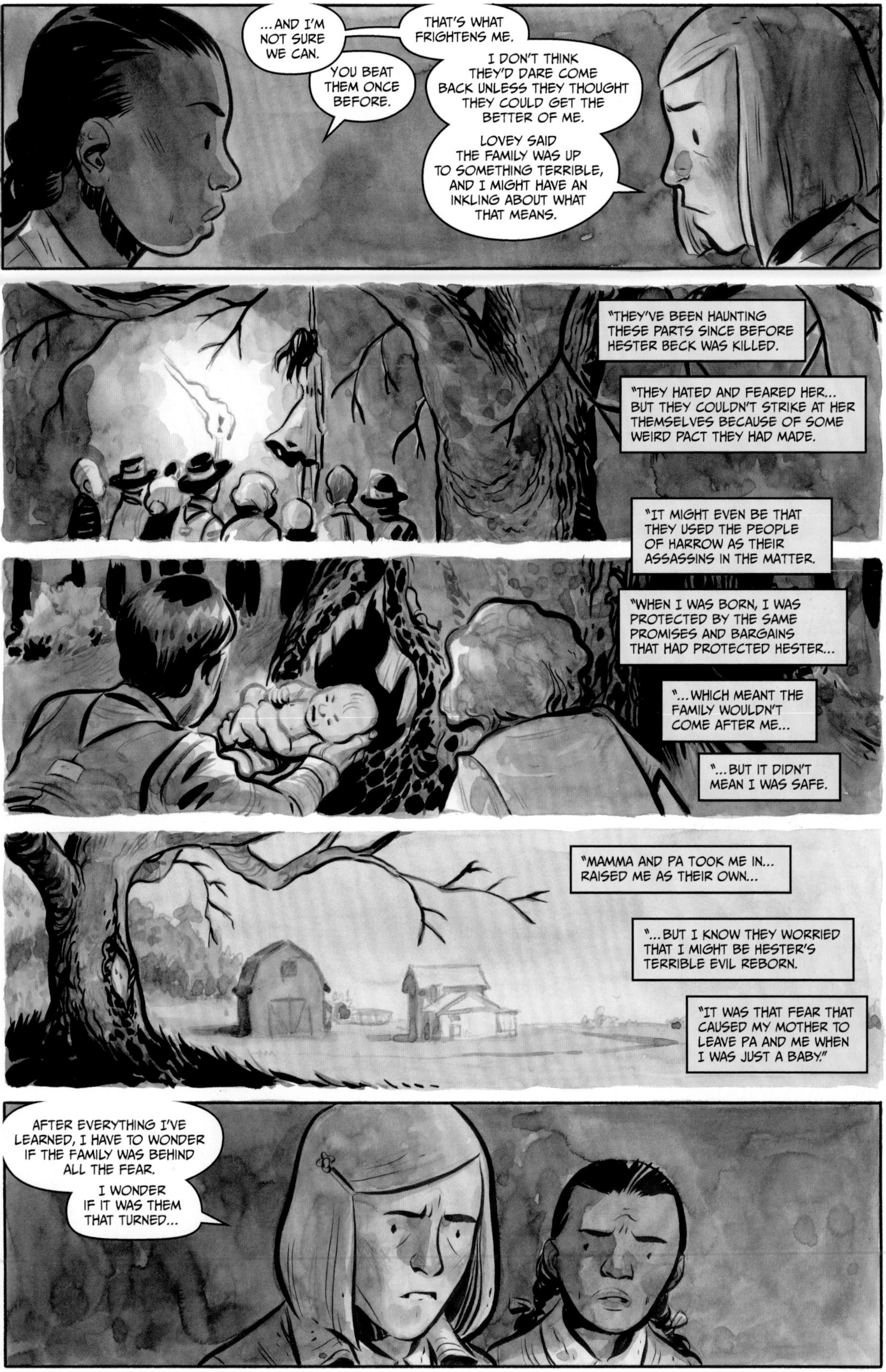
...AND I'M NOT SURE WE CAN.
THAT'S WHAT FRIGHTENS ME.
YOU BEAT THEM ONCE BEFORE.
I DON'T THINK THEY'D DARE COME BACK UNLESS THEY THOUGHT THEY COULD GET THE BETTER OF ME.
LOVEY SAID THE FAMILY WAS UP TO SOMETHING TERRIBLE, AND I MIGHT HAVE AN INKLING ABOUT WHAT THAT MEANS.
"THEY'VE BEEN HAUNTING THESE PARTS SINCE BEFORE HESTER BECK WAS KILLED.
"THEY HATED AND FEARED HER... BUT THEY COULDN'T STRIKE AT HER THEMSELVES BECAUSE OF SOME WEIRD PACT THEY HAD MADE.
"IT MIGHT EVEN BE THAT THEY USED THE PEOPLE OF HARROW AS THEIR ASSASSINS IN THE MATTER.
"WHEN I WAS BORN, I WAS PROTECTED BY THE SAME PROMISES AND BARGAINS THAT HAD PROTECTED HESTER...
"...WHICH MEANT THE FAMILY WOULDN'T COME AFTER ME...
"...BUT IT DIDN'T MEAN I WAS SAFE.
"MAMMA AND PA TOOK ME IN... RAISED ME AS THEIR OWN...
"...BUT I KNOW THEY WORRIED THAT I MIGHT BE HESTER'S TERRIBLE EVIL REBORN.
"IT WAS THAT FEAR THAT CAUSED MY MOTHER TO LEAVE PA AND ME WHEN I WAS JUST A BABY."
AFTER EVERYTHING I'VE LEARNED, I HAVE TO WONDER IF THE FAMILY WAS BEHIND ALL THE FEAR.
I WONDER IF IT WAS THEM THAT TURNED...

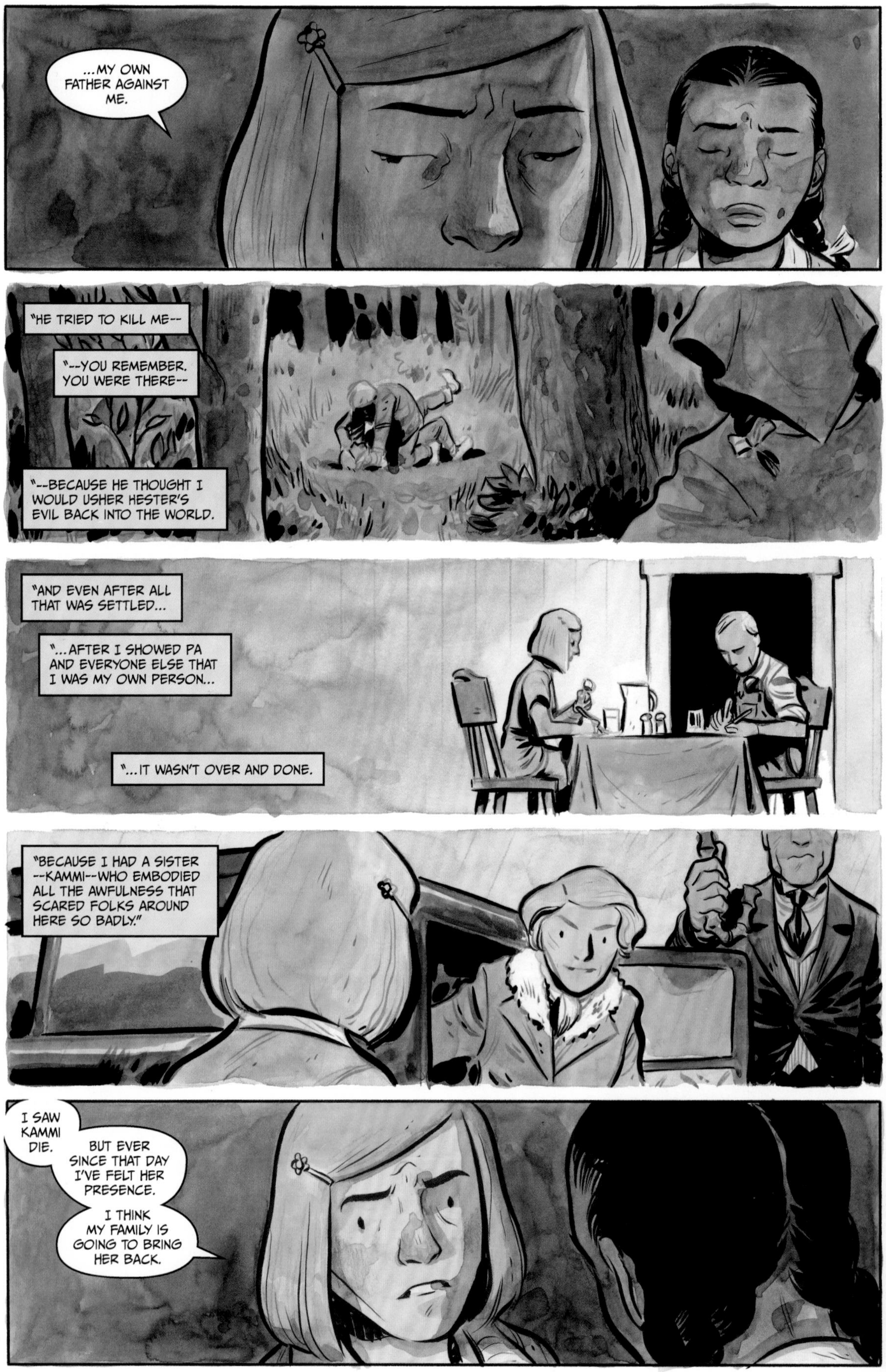
...MY OWN FATHER AGAINST ME.
"HE TRIED TO KILL ME--
"--YOU REMEMBER. YOU WERE THERE--
"--BECAUSE HE THOUGHT I WOULD USHER HESTER'S EVIL BACK INTO THE WORLD.
"AND EVEN AFTER ALL THAT WAS SETTLED...
"...AFTER I SHOWED PA AND EVERYONE ELSE THAT I WAS MY OWN PERSON...
"...IT WASN'T OVER AND DONE.
"BECAUSE I HAD A SISTER --KAMMI--WHO EMBODIED ALL THE AWFULNESS THAT SCARED FOLKS AROUND HERE SO BADLY."
I SAW KAMMI DIE.
BUT EVER SINCE THAT DAY I'VE FELT HER PRESENCE.
I THINK MY FAMILY IS GOING TO BRING HER BACK.

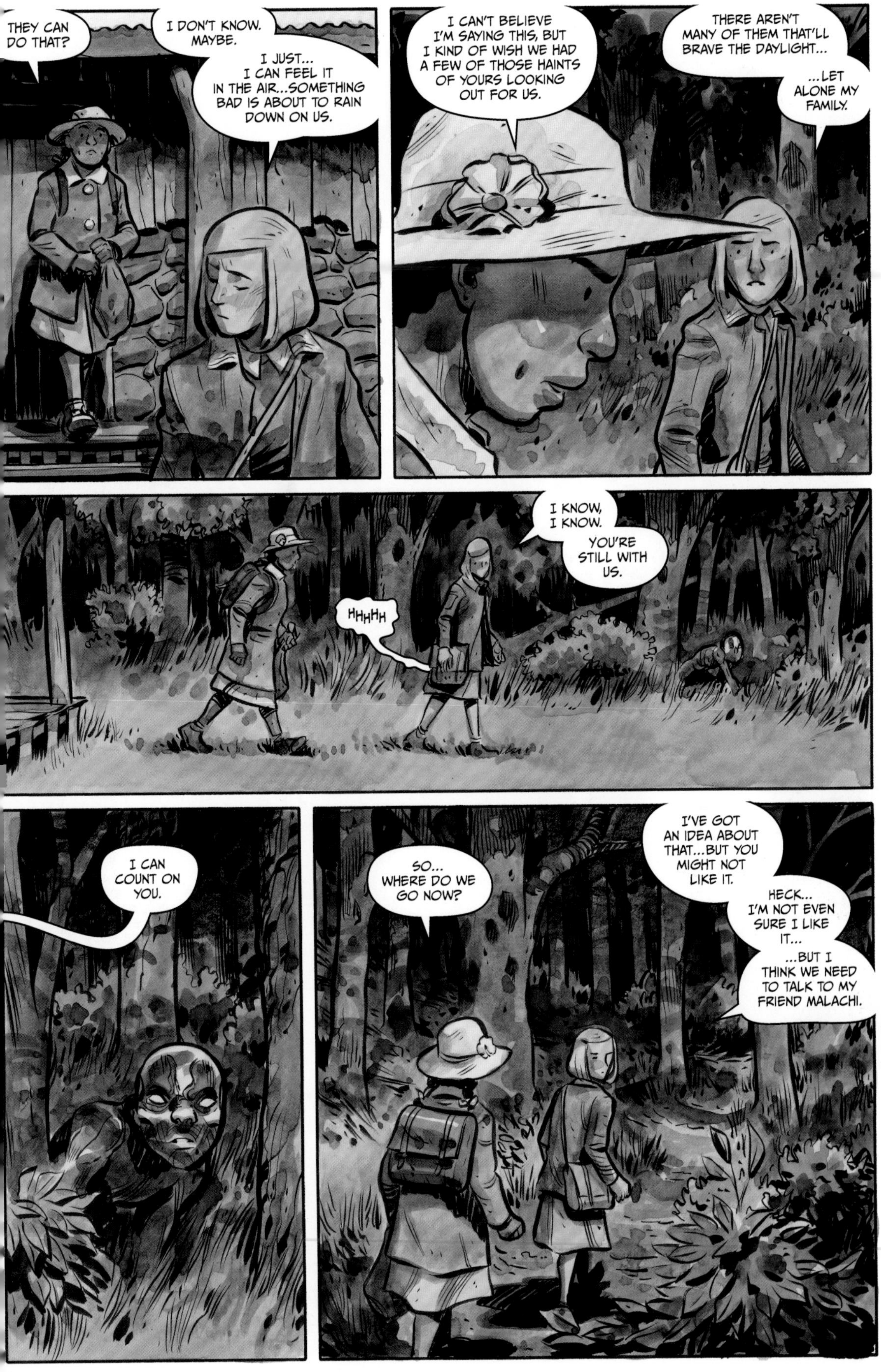
THEY CAN DO THAT?
I DON'T KNOW. MAYBE.
I JUST... I CAN FEEL IT IN THE AIR...SOMETHING BAD IS ABOUT TO RAIN DOWN ON US.
I CAN'T BELIEVE I'M SAYING THIS, BUT I KIND OF WISH WE HAD A FEW OF THOSE HAINTS OF YOURS LOOKING OUT FOR US.
THERE AREN'T MANY OF THEM THAT'LL BRAVE THE DAYLIGHT...
...LET ALONE MY FAMILY.
I KNOW, I KNOW.
YOU'RE STILL WITH US.
HHHHH
I CAN COUNT ON YOU.
SO... WHERE DO WE GO NOW?
I'VE GOT AN IDEA ABOUT THAT...BUT YOU MIGHT NOT LIKE IT.
HECK... I'M NOT EVEN SURE I LIKE IT...
...BUT I THINK WE NEED TO TALK TO MY FRIEND MALACHI.

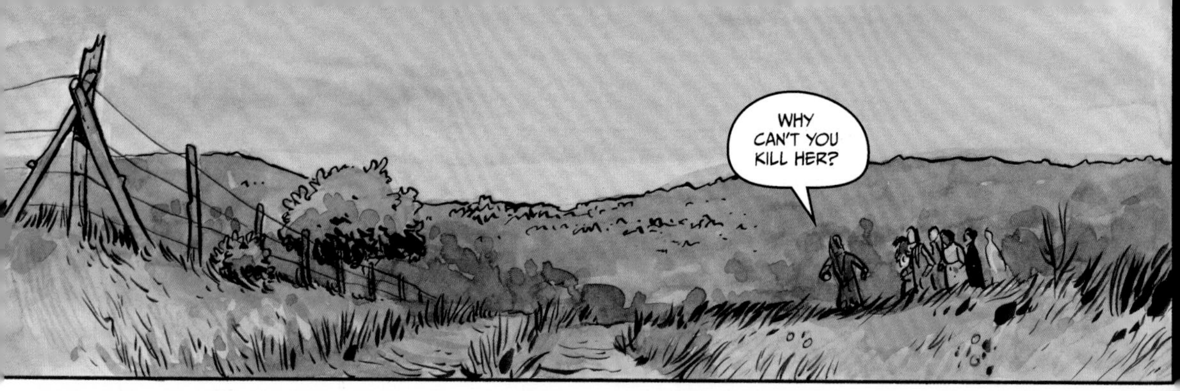
WHY CAN'T YOU KILL HER?

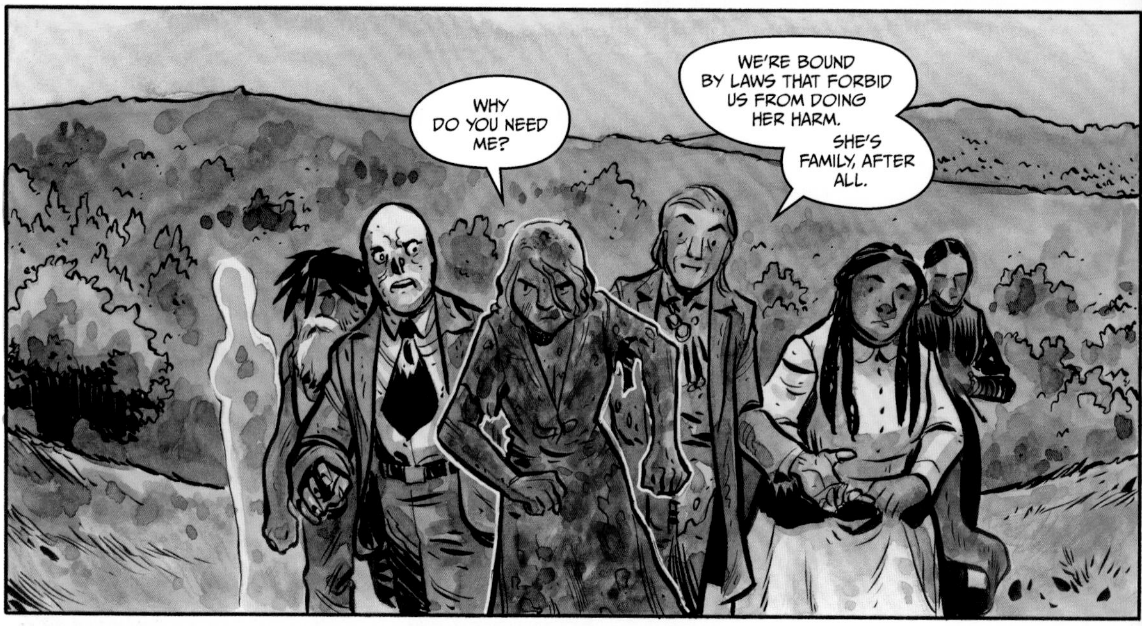
WHY DO YOU NEED ME?
WE'RE BOUND BY LAWS THAT FORBID US FROM DOING HER HARM.
SHE'S FAMILY, AFTER ALL.

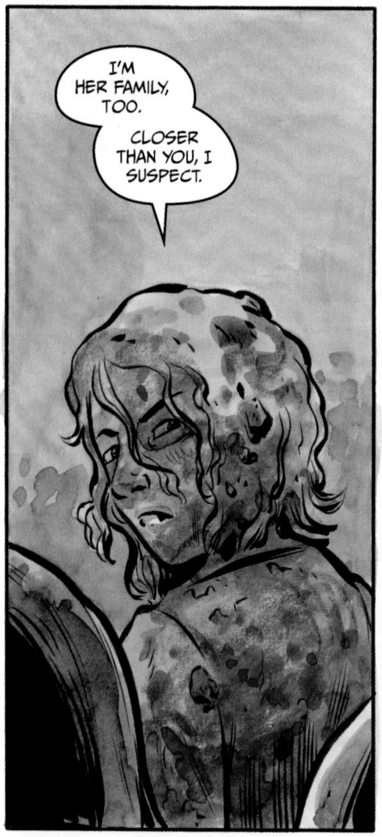
I'M HER FAMILY, TOO.
CLOSER THAN YOU, I SUSPECT.

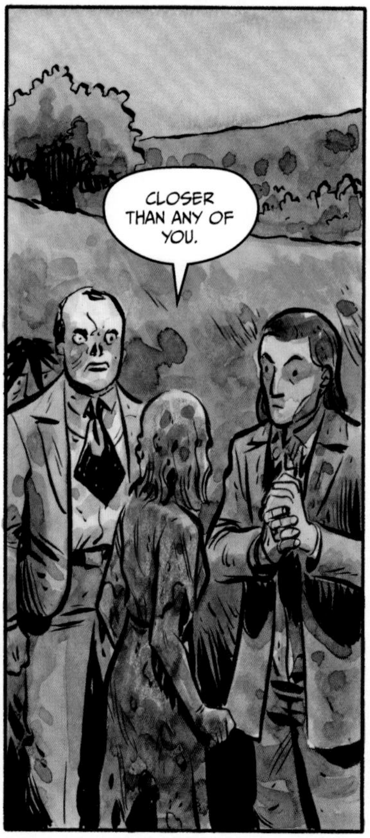
CLOSER THAN ANY OF YOU.

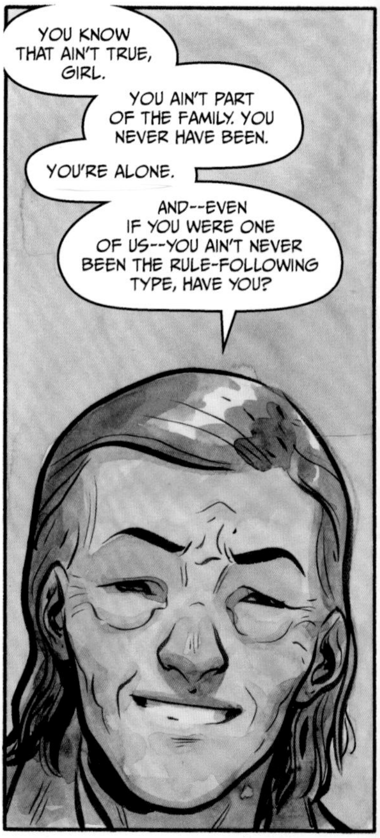
YOU KNOW THAT AIN'T TRUE, GIRL.
YOU AIN'T PART OF THE FAMILY. YOU NEVER HAVE BEEN.
YOU'RE ALONE.
AND--EVEN IF YOU WERE ONE OF US--YOU AIN'T NEVER BEEN THE RULE-FOLLOWING TYPE, HAVE YOU?

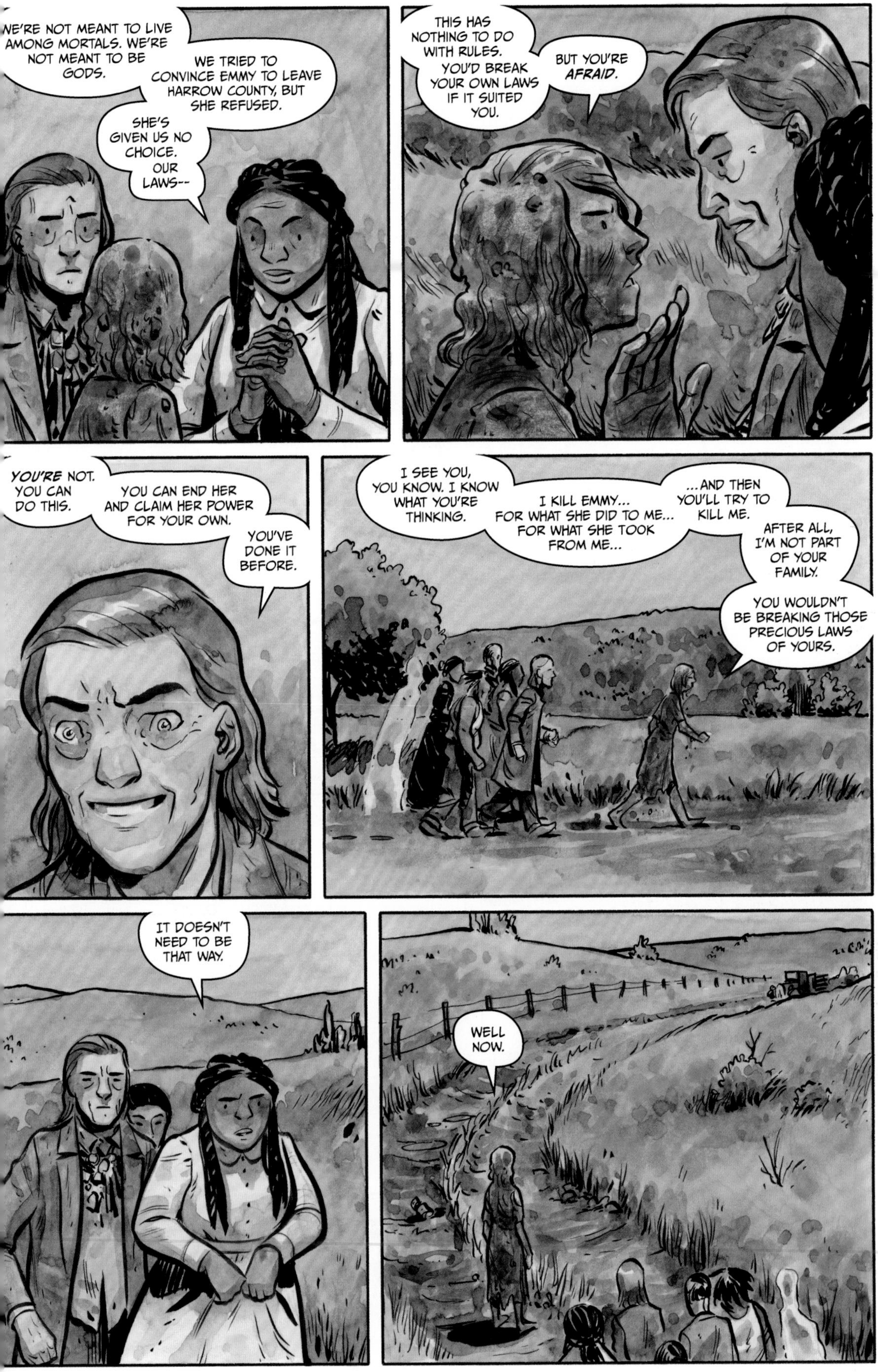
WE'RE NOT MEANT TO LIVE AMONG MORTALS. WE'RE NOT MEANT TO BE GODS.
WE TRIED TO CONVINCE EMMY TO LEAVE HARROW COUNTY, BUT SHE REFUSED.
SHE'S GIVEN US NO CHOICE.
OUR LAWS--
THIS HAS NOTHING TO DO WITH RULES.
YOU'D BREAK YOUR OWN LAWS IF IT SUITED YOU.
BUT YOU'RE *AFRAID.*
YOU'RE NOT. YOU CAN DO THIS.
YOU CAN END HER AND CLAIM HER POWER FOR YOUR OWN.
YOU'VE DONE IT BEFORE.
I SEE YOU, YOU KNOW. I KNOW WHAT YOU'RE THINKING.
I KILL EMMY... FOR WHAT SHE DID TO ME... FOR WHAT SHE TOOK FROM ME...
...AND THEN YOU'LL TRY TO KILL ME.
AFTER ALL, I'M NOT PART OF YOUR FAMILY.
YOU WOULDN'T BE BREAKING THOSE PRECIOUS LAWS OF YOURS.
IT DOESN'T NEED TO BE THAT WAY.
WELL NOW.

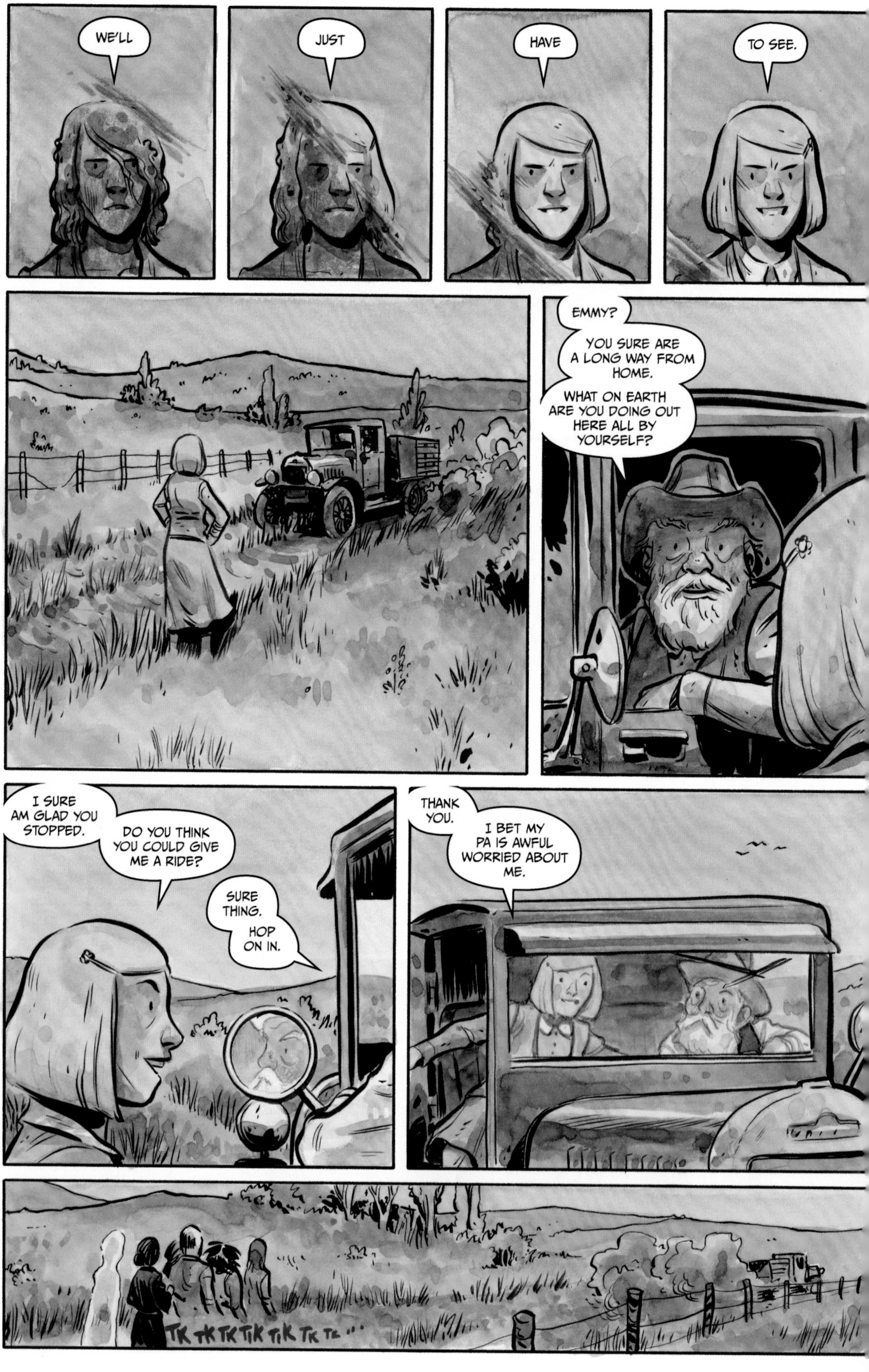
WE'LL
JUST
HAVE
TO SEE.
EMMY?
YOU SURE ARE A LONG WAY FROM HOME.
WHAT ON EARTH ARE YOU DOING OUT HERE ALL BY YOURSELF?
I SURE AM GLAD YOU STOPPED.
DO YOU THINK YOU COULD GIVE ME A RIDE?
SURE THING.
HOP ON IN.
THANK YOU.
I BET MY PA IS AWFUL WORRIED ABOUT ME.
TK TK TK TIK TIK TK TK ...

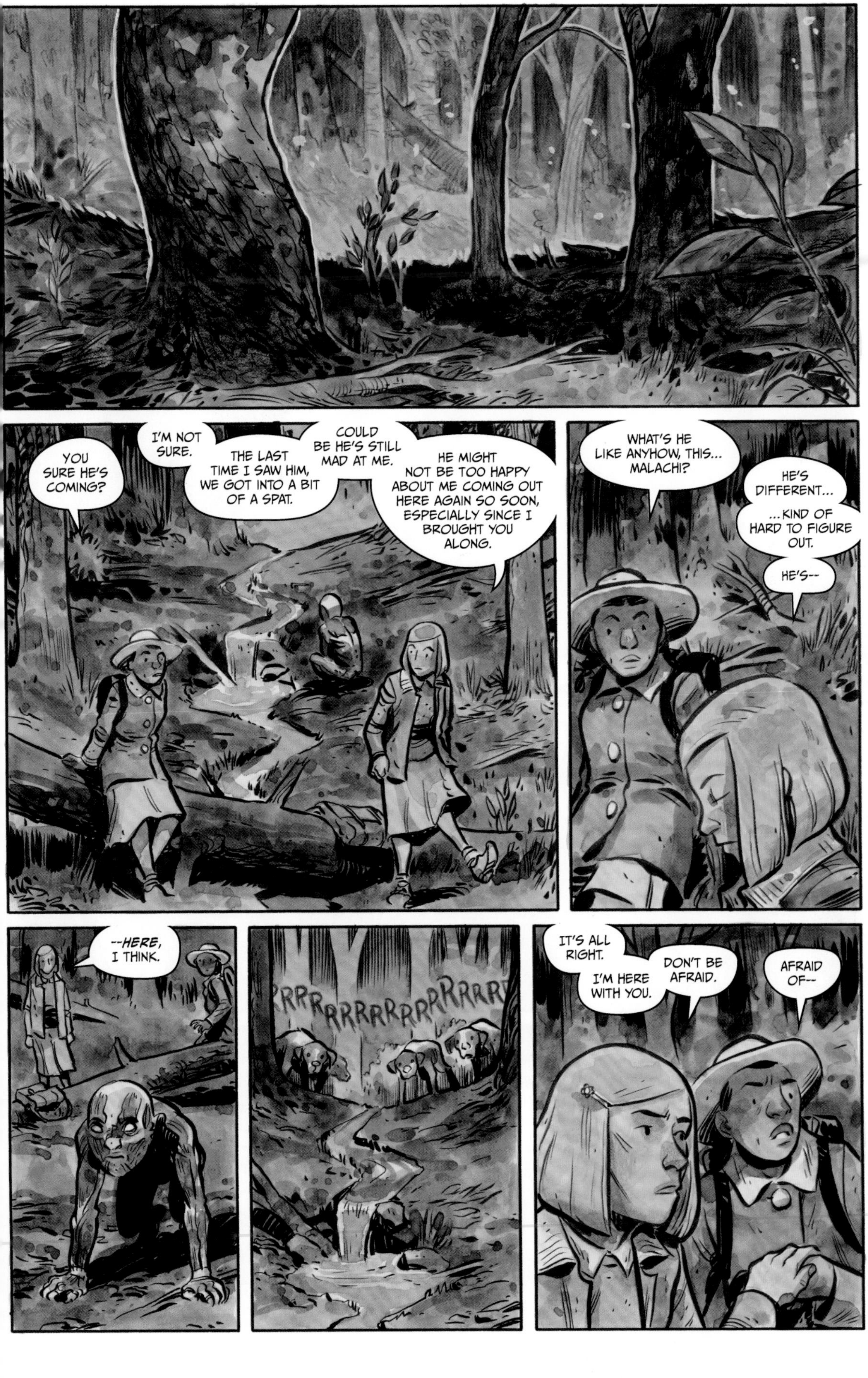
YOU SURE HE'S COMING?
I'M NOT SURE.
THE LAST TIME I SAW HIM, WE GOT INTO A BIT OF A SPAT.
COULD BE HE'S STILL MAD AT ME.
HE MIGHT NOT BE TOO HAPPY ABOUT ME COMING OUT HERE AGAIN SO SOON, ESPECIALLY SINCE I BROUGHT YOU ALONG.
WHAT'S HE LIKE ANYHOW, THIS... MALACHI?
HE'S DIFFERENT...
...KIND OF HARD TO FIGURE OUT.
HE'S--
--HERE, I THINK.
RRRRRRRRRRRRRRRRR
IT'S ALL RIGHT.
I'M HERE WITH YOU.
DON'T BE AFRAID.
AFRAID OF--

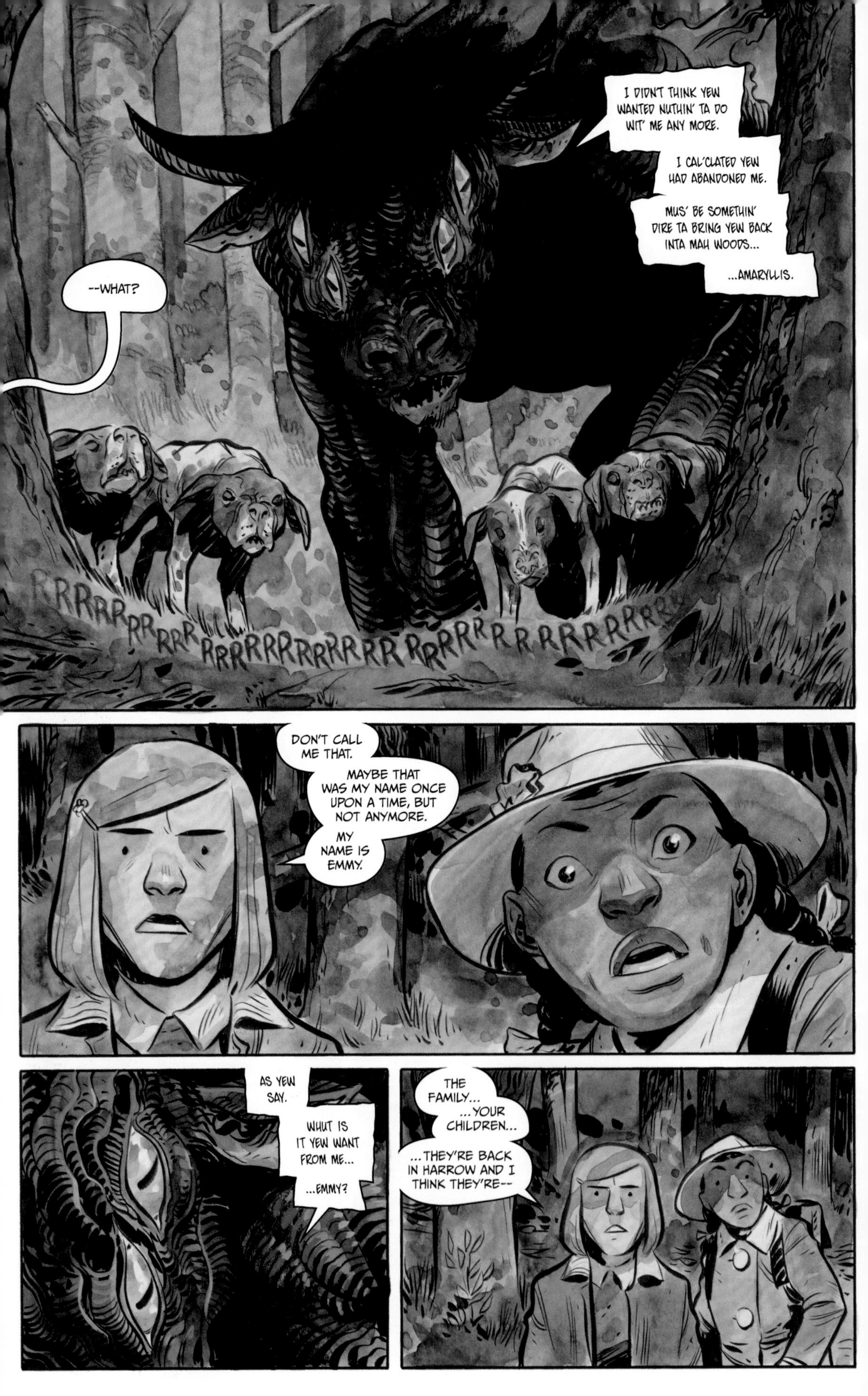
I DIDN'T THINK YEW WANTED NUTHIN' TA DO WIT' ME ANY MORE.
I CAL'CLATED YEW HAD ABANDONED ME.
MUS' BE SOMETHIN' DIRE TA BRING YEW BACK INTA MAH WOODS...
...AMARYLLIS.
--WHAT?
RRRRRRRRRRRRRRRRRRRRRRRRRRRRRRR
DON'T CALL ME THAT.
MAYBE THAT WAS MY NAME ONCE UPON A TIME, BUT NOT ANYMORE.
MY NAME IS EMMY.
AS YEW SAY.
WHUT IS IT YEW WANT FROM ME...
...EMMY?
THE FAMILY...
...YOUR CHILDREN...
...THEY'RE BACK IN HARROW AND I THINK THEY'RE--

YEW DON' THINK NUTHIN'. YEW KNOW WHUT THEY'RE ABOUT.

YEW KNOW WHUT THEY'VE DUN.

THEY BRUNG BACK YER SISTER.

THEY BRUNG HER BACK TA DO AWAY WIT' YEW.

MORE'N LIKELY WIT' ME, TOO.

ARE YOU SAYING YOU ALREADY KNEW?

ARE YOU SAYING THEY'VE ALREADY CALLED HER UP?

I BURIED HER. IT CAN'T BE THAT EASY TO--

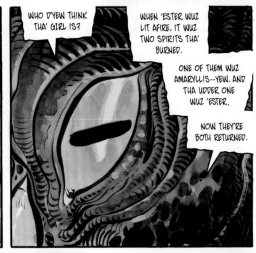

WHO D'YEW THINK THA' GIRL IS?

WHEN 'ESTER WUZ LIT AFIRE, IT WUZ TWO SPIRITS THA' BURNED.

ONE OF THEM WUZ AMARYLLIS--YEW. AND THA UDDER ONE WUZ 'ESTER.

NOW THEY'RE BOTH RETURNED.

HESTER CONSUMED AMARYLLIS...CONSUMED HER POWER.

WHEN SHE DIED...

...OH LORD...

...BOTH WOMEN WERE REBORN.

EMMY--WHAT IS HE SAYING?

WHAT DOES IT MEAN?

IS KAMMI COMING FOR YOU?

NOT YET.

BUT I C'N SMELL 'ER ON THA AIR.

SHE'S ALREADY MOVIN'...MOVIN' AGAINST YEW, EMMY.

SHE WANTS TA 'URT YEW.

SNIF

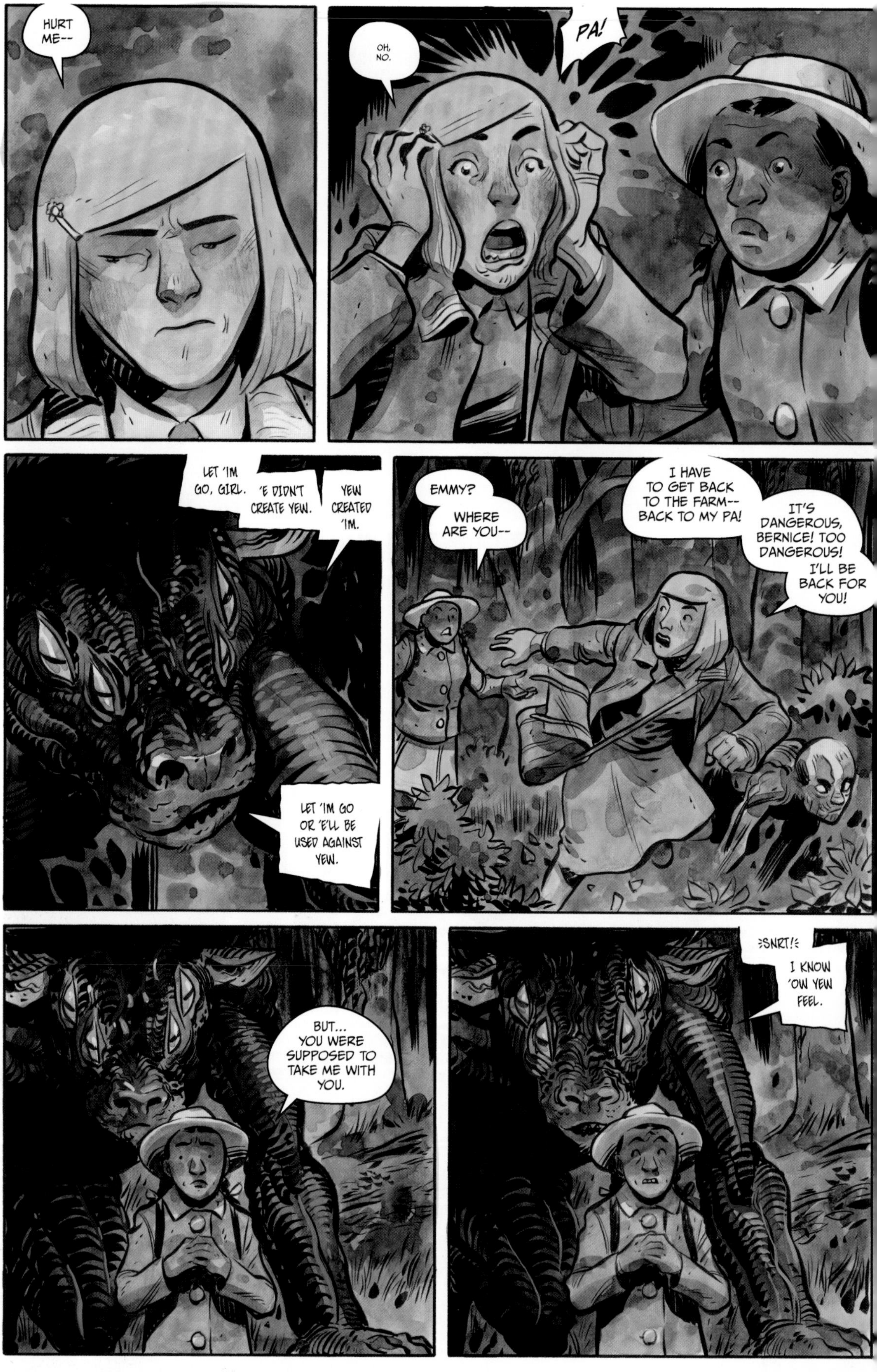
HURT ME--
OH, NO.
PA!
LET 'IM GO, GIRL.
'E DIDN'T CREATE YEW.
YEW CREATED 'IM.
LET 'IM GO OR 'E'LL BE USED AGAINST YEW.
EMMY?
WHERE ARE YOU--
I HAVE TO GET BACK TO THE FARM-- BACK TO MY PA!
IT'S DANGEROUS, BERNICE! TOO DANGEROUS!
I'LL BE BACK FOR YOU!
BUT... YOU WERE SUPPOSED TO TAKE ME WITH YOU.
SNRT!
I KNOW 'OW YEW FEEL.

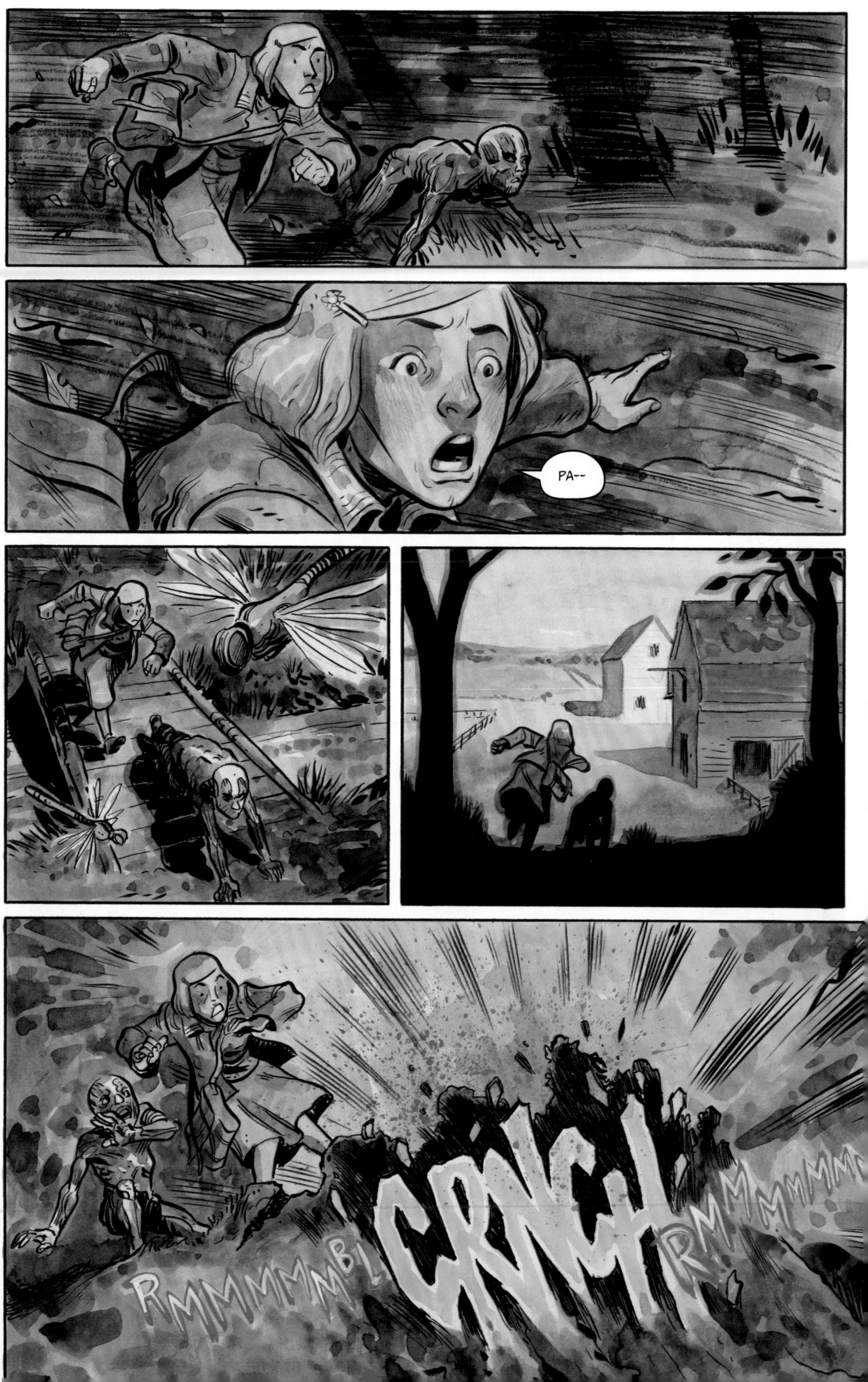
PA--
RMMMMMBL
CRNCH
RMMMMMMM

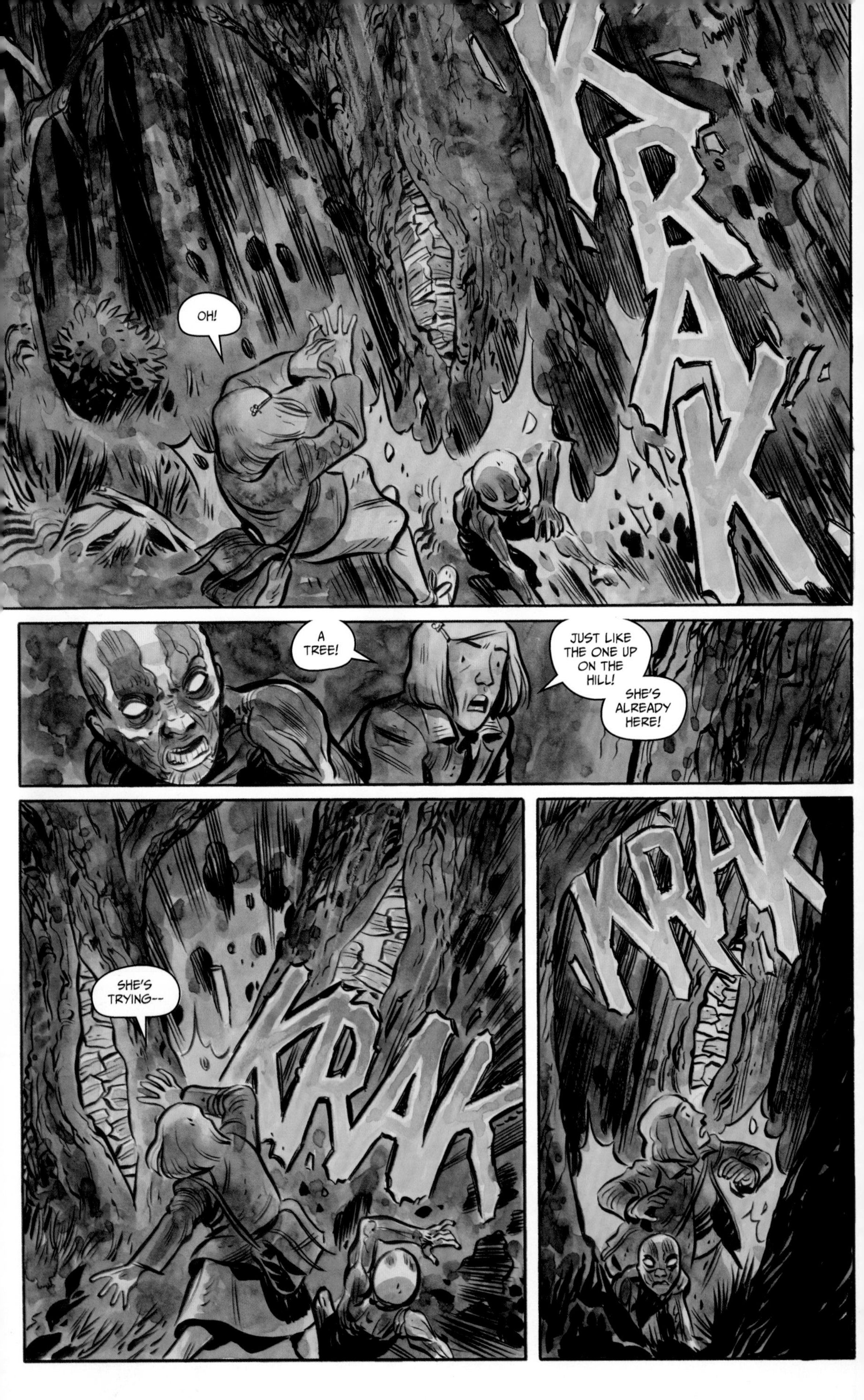
OH!
KRAK!
A TREE!
JUST LIKE THE ONE UP ON THE HILL!
SHE'S ALREADY HERE!
SHE'S TRYING--
KRAK
KRAK

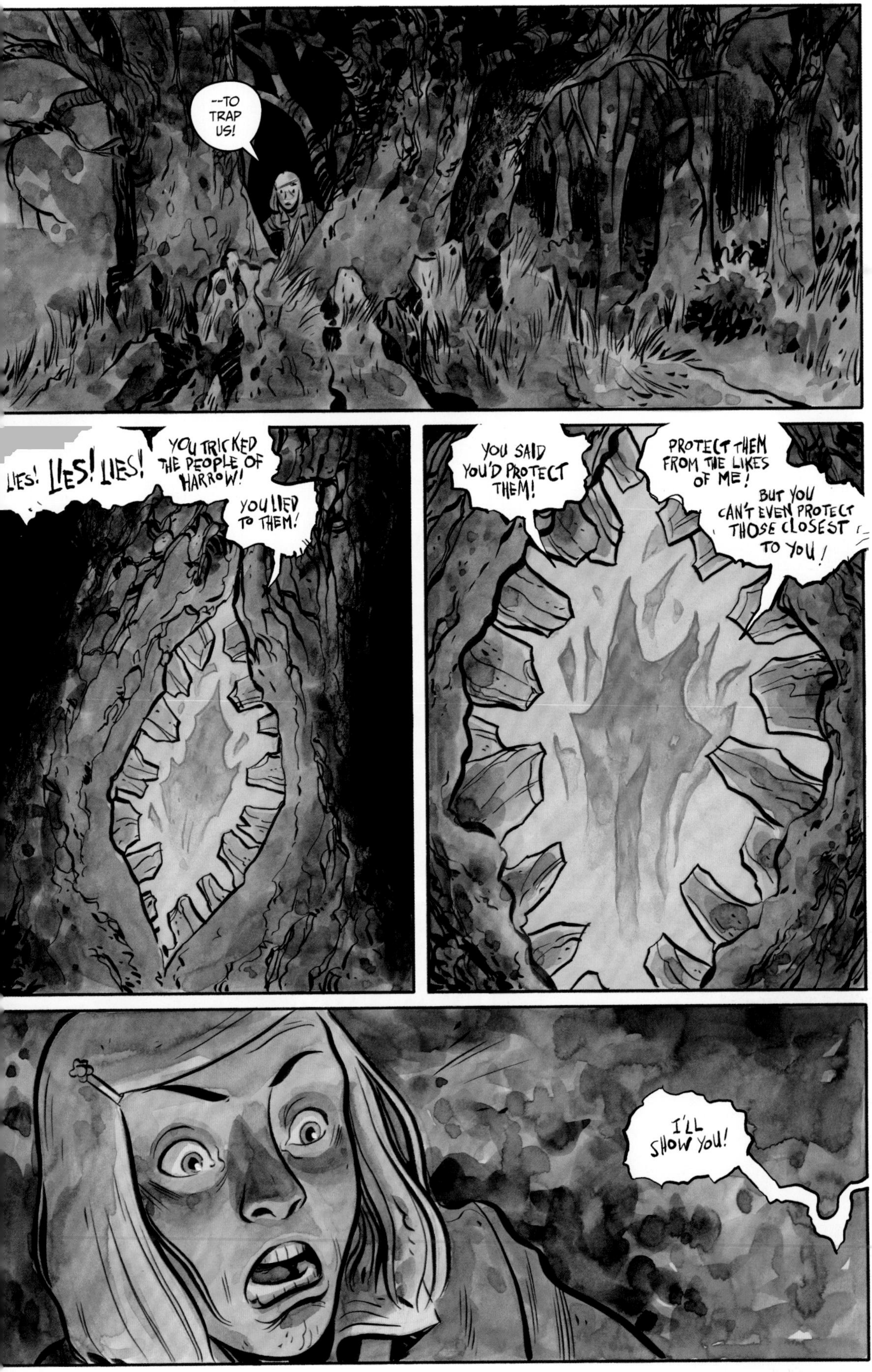
--TO TRAP US!
LIES! LIES! LIES!
YOU TRICKED THE PEOPLE OF HARROW!
YOU LIED TO THEM!
YOU SAID YOU'D PROTECT THEM!
PROTECT THEM FROM THE LIKES OF ME!
BUT YOU CAN'T EVEN PROTECT THOSE CLOSEST TO YOU!
I'LL SHOW YOU!

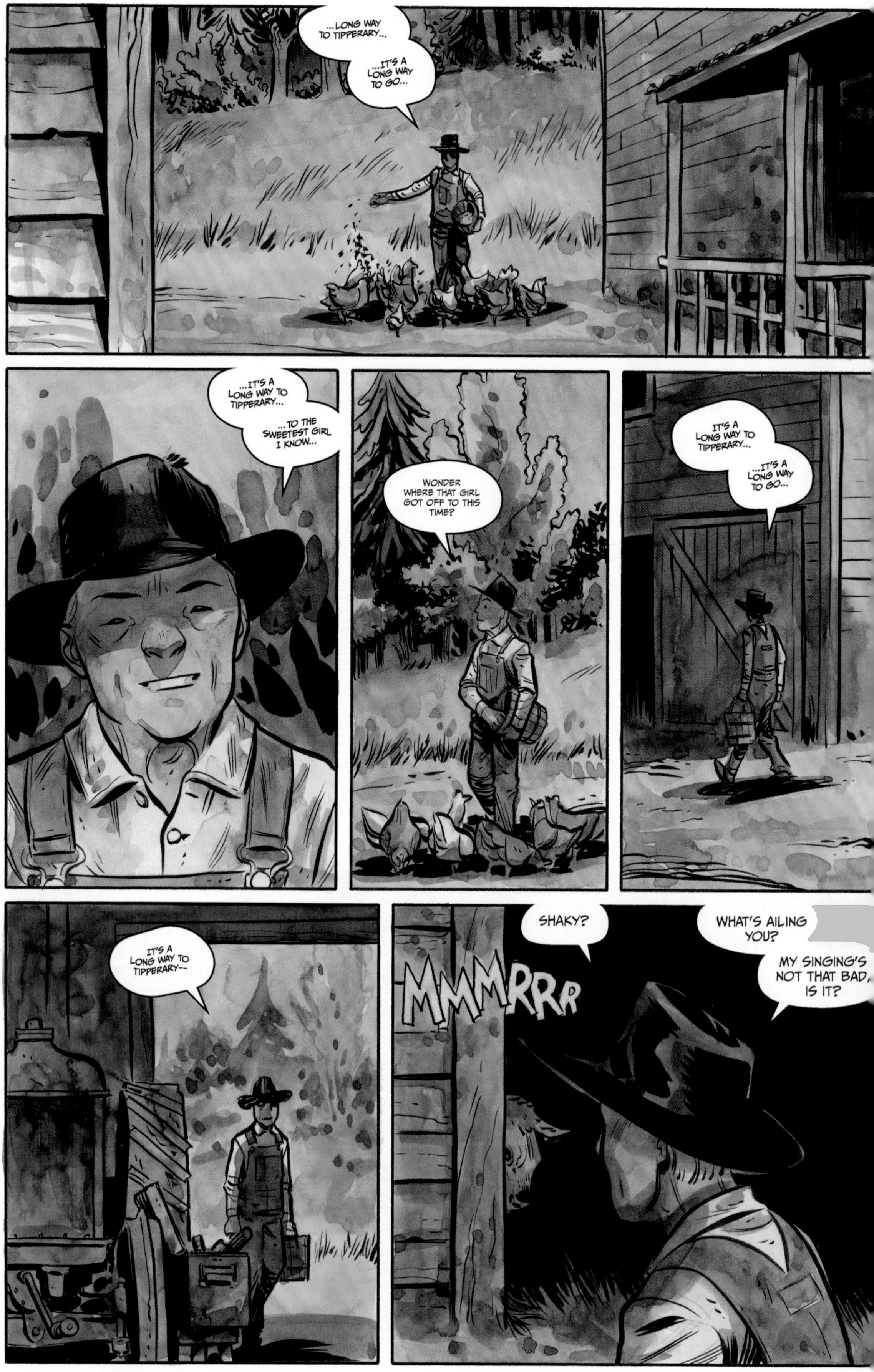
...LONG WAY TO TIPPERARY...
...IT'S A LONG WAY TO GO...
...IT'S A LONG WAY TO TIPPERARY...
...TO THE SWEETEST GIRL I KNOW...
WONDER WHERE THAT GIRL GOT OFF TO THIS TIME?
IT'S A LONG WAY TO TIPPERARY...
...IT'S A LONG WAY TO GO...
IT'S A LONG WAY TO TIPPERARY--
MMMRRR
SHAKY?
WHAT'S AILING YOU?
MY SINGING'S NOT THAT BAD, IS IT?

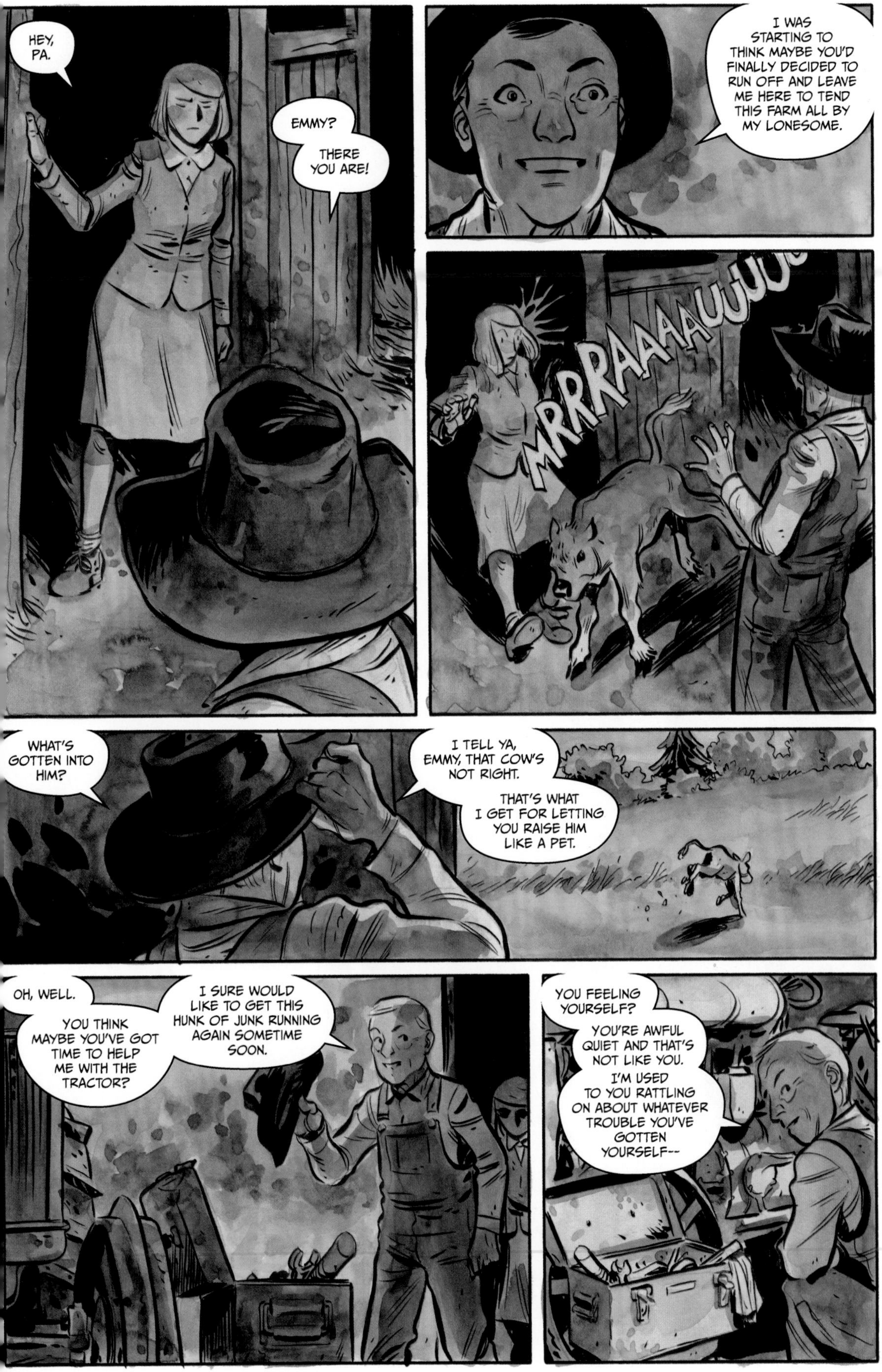
HEY, PA.
EMMY?
THERE YOU ARE!
I WAS STARTING TO THINK MAYBE YOU'D FINALLY DECIDED TO RUN OFF AND LEAVE ME HERE TO TEND THIS FARM ALL BY MY LONESOME.
MRRRAAAAUUUU
WHAT'S GOTTEN INTO HIM?
I TELL YA, EMMY, THAT COW'S NOT RIGHT.
THAT'S WHAT I GET FOR LETTING YOU RAISE HIM LIKE A PET.
OH, WELL.
YOU THINK MAYBE YOU'VE GOT TIME TO HELP ME WITH THE TRACTOR?
I SURE WOULD LIKE TO GET THIS HUNK OF JUNK RUNNING AGAIN SOMETIME SOON.
YOU FEELING YOURSELF?
YOU'RE AWFUL QUIET AND THAT'S NOT LIKE YOU.
I'M USED TO YOU RATTLING ON ABOUT WHATEVER TROUBLE YOU'VE GOTTEN YOURSELF--

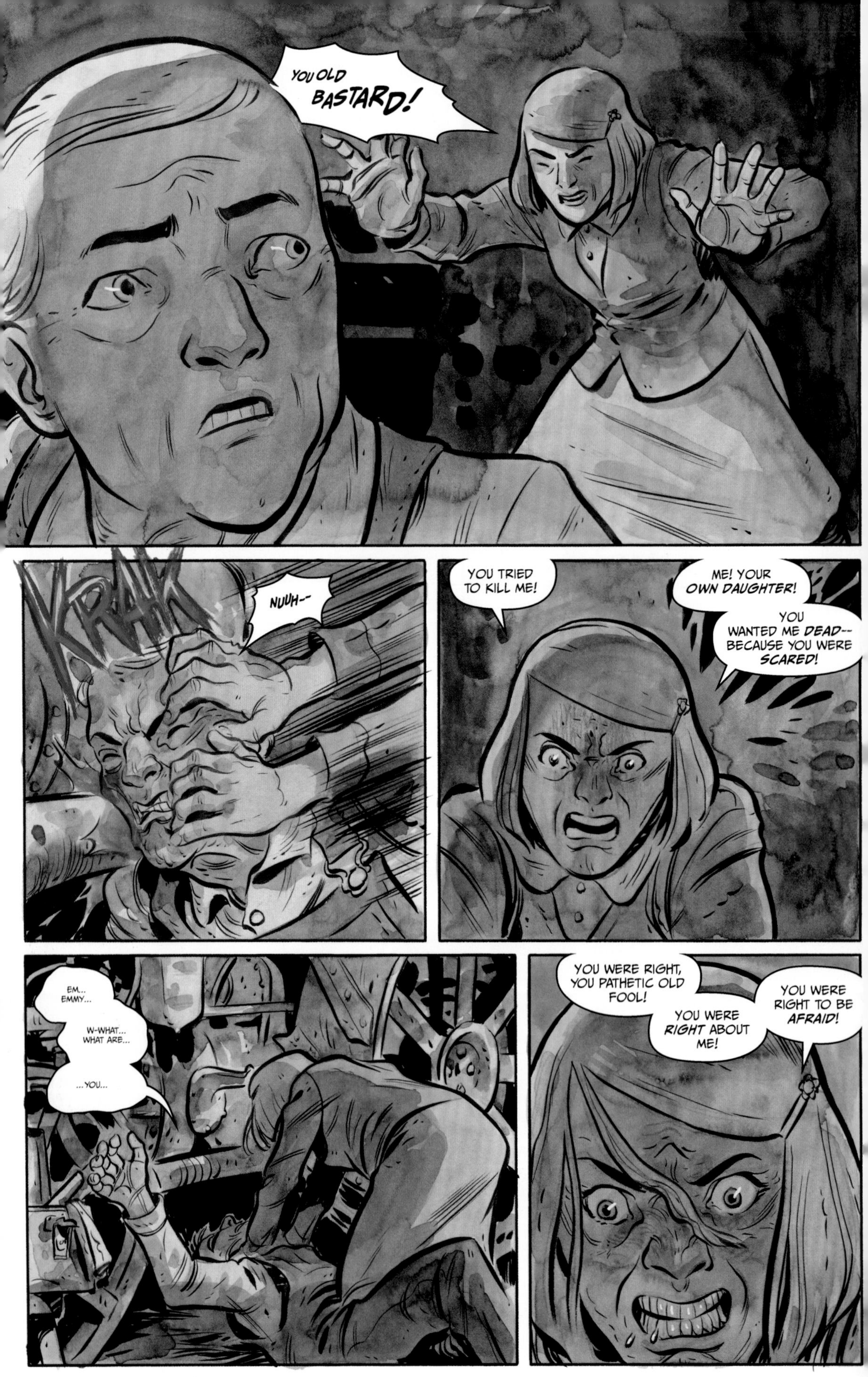
YOU OLD BASTARD!
KRAK
NUUH--
YOU TRIED TO KILL ME!
ME! YOUR OWN DAUGHTER!
YOU WANTED ME DEAD-- BECAUSE YOU WERE SCARED!
EM... EMMY...
W-WHAT... WHAT ARE...
...YOU...
YOU WERE RIGHT, YOU PATHETIC OLD FOOL!
YOU WERE RIGHT ABOUT ME!
YOU WERE RIGHT TO BE AFRAID!

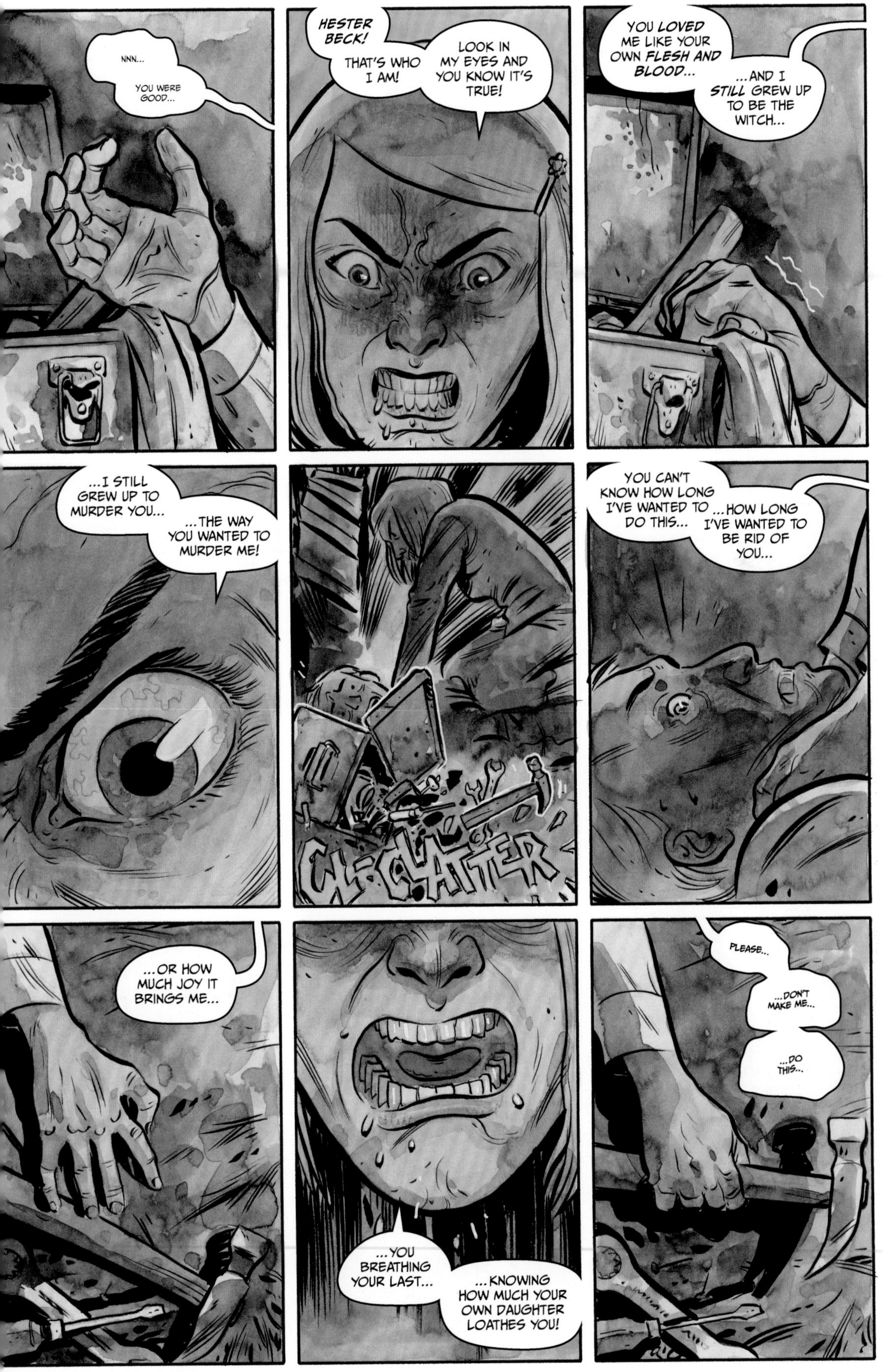
NNN...
YOU WERE GOOD...
HESTER BECK!
THAT'S WHO I AM!
LOOK IN MY EYES AND YOU KNOW IT'S TRUE!
YOU LOVED ME LIKE YOUR OWN FLESH AND BLOOD...
...AND I STILL GREW UP TO BE THE WITCH...
...I STILL GREW UP TO MURDER YOU...
...THE WAY YOU WANTED TO MURDER ME!
CL-CLATTER
YOU CAN'T KNOW HOW LONG I'VE WANTED TO DO THIS...
...HOW LONG I'VE WANTED TO BE RID OF YOU...
...OR HOW MUCH JOY IT BRINGS ME...
...YOU BREATHING YOUR LAST...
...KNOWING HOW MUCH YOUR OWN DAUGHTER LOATHES YOU!
PLEASE...
...DON'T MAKE ME...
...DO THIS...

GO AHEAD, PA.

GO AHEAD, IF THAT'S WHAT YOU WANT TO DO.

IF YOU NEED TO BASH MY HEAD IN...

...SPATTER MY BRAINS ALL OVER THE GROUND...

I WON'T HOLD IT AGAINST YOU.

I LOVE YOU.

...EMMY-GIRL...

TMP

...NNGGGH...

...HHRRGGH...

YOU WERE MY CREATION, NOT MY SISTER'S.

ALL OF HARROW COUNTY BELONGS TO ME.

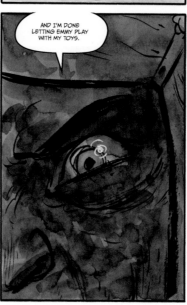

AND I'M DONE LETTING EMMY PLAY WITH MY TOYS.

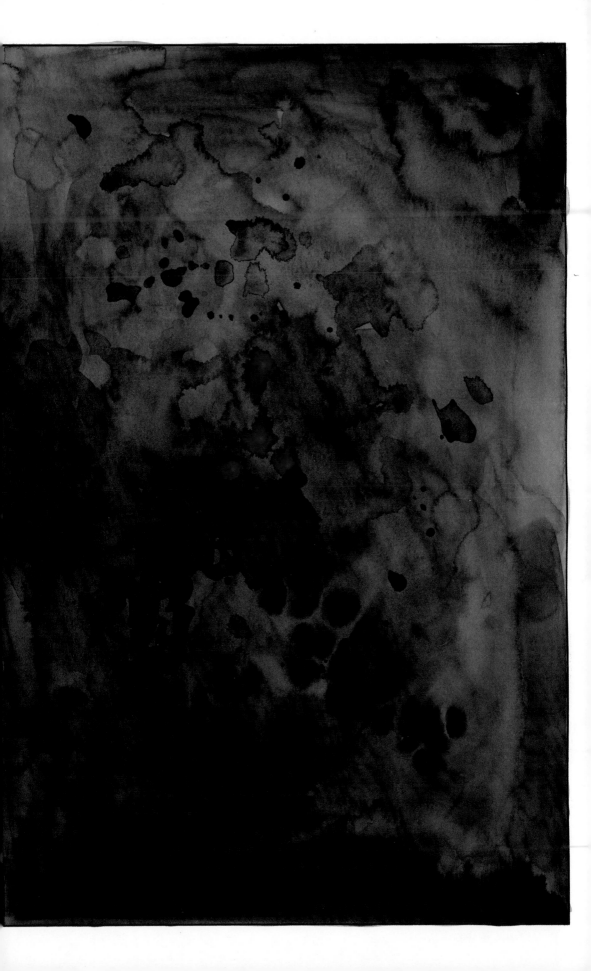

PA!

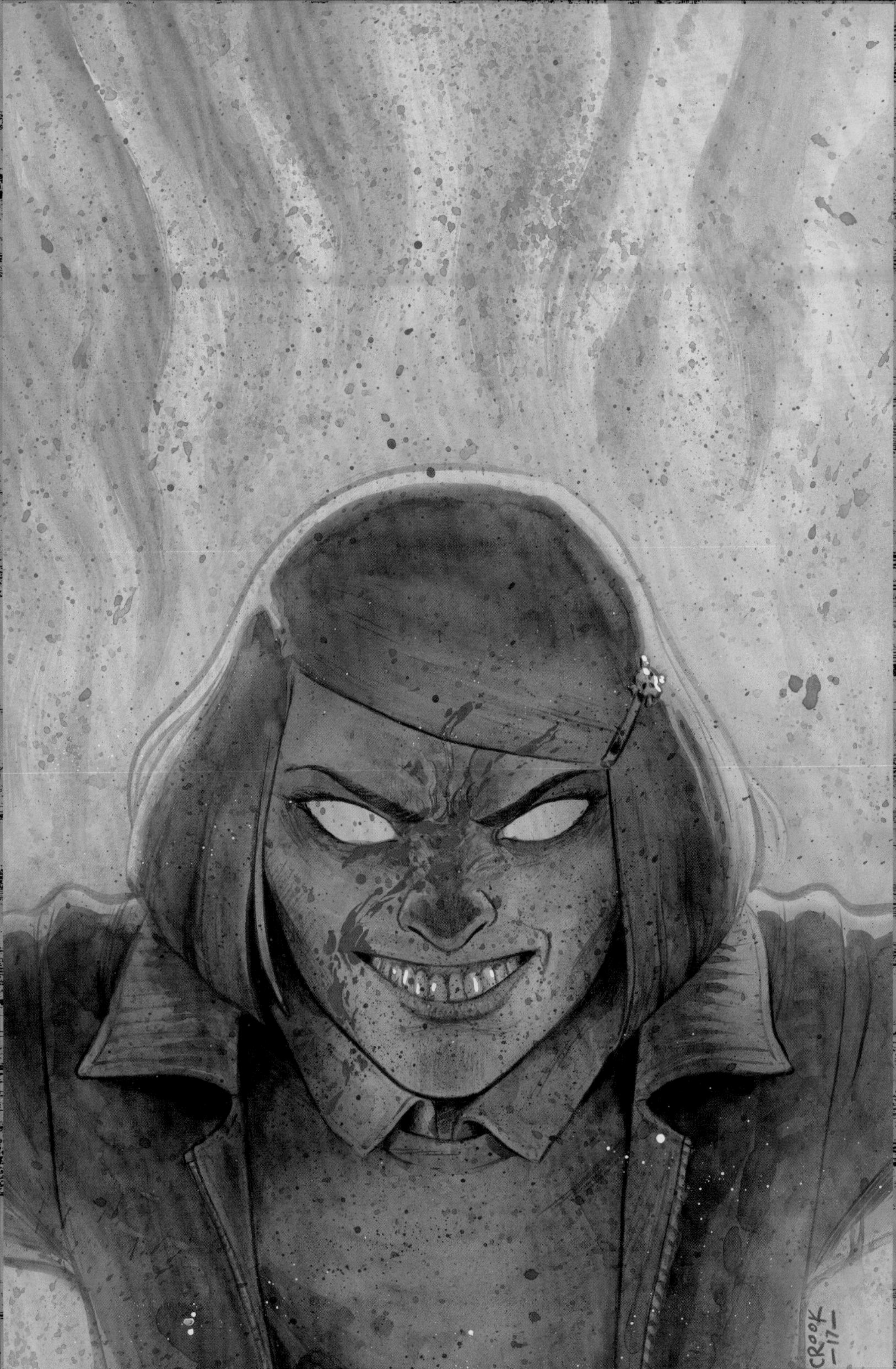
CROOK -17-

TWO

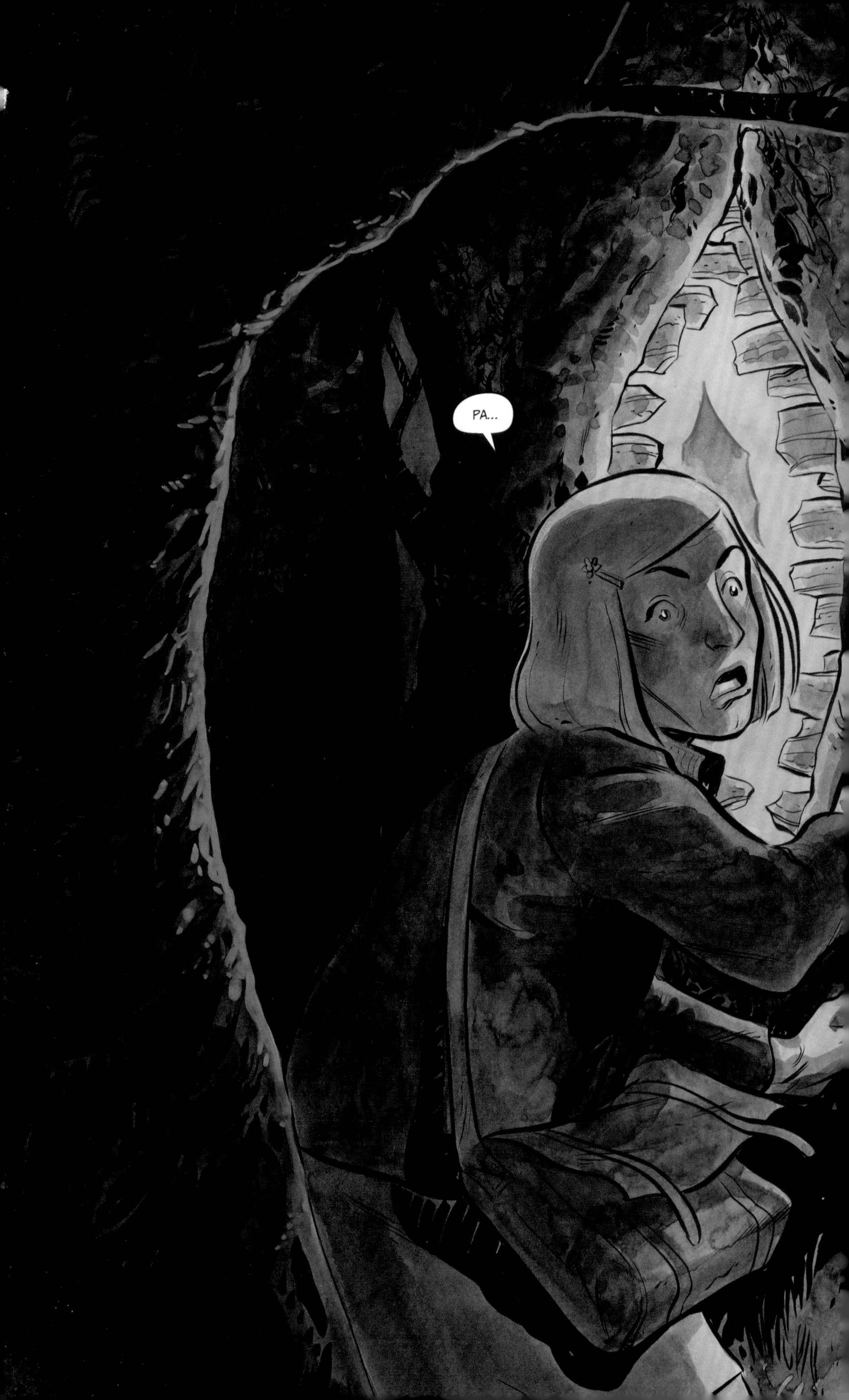
PA...

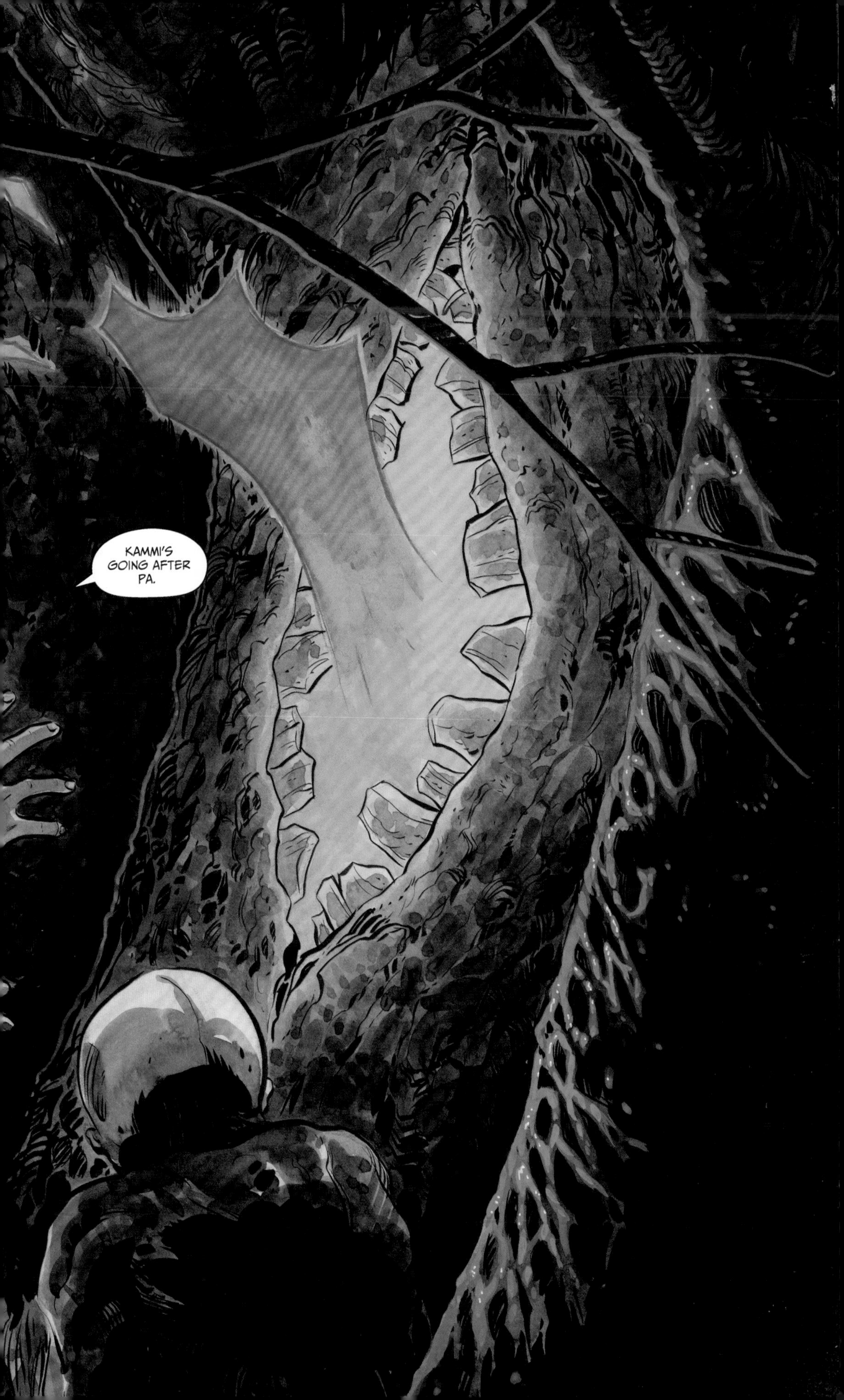
KAMMI'S GOING AFTER PA.

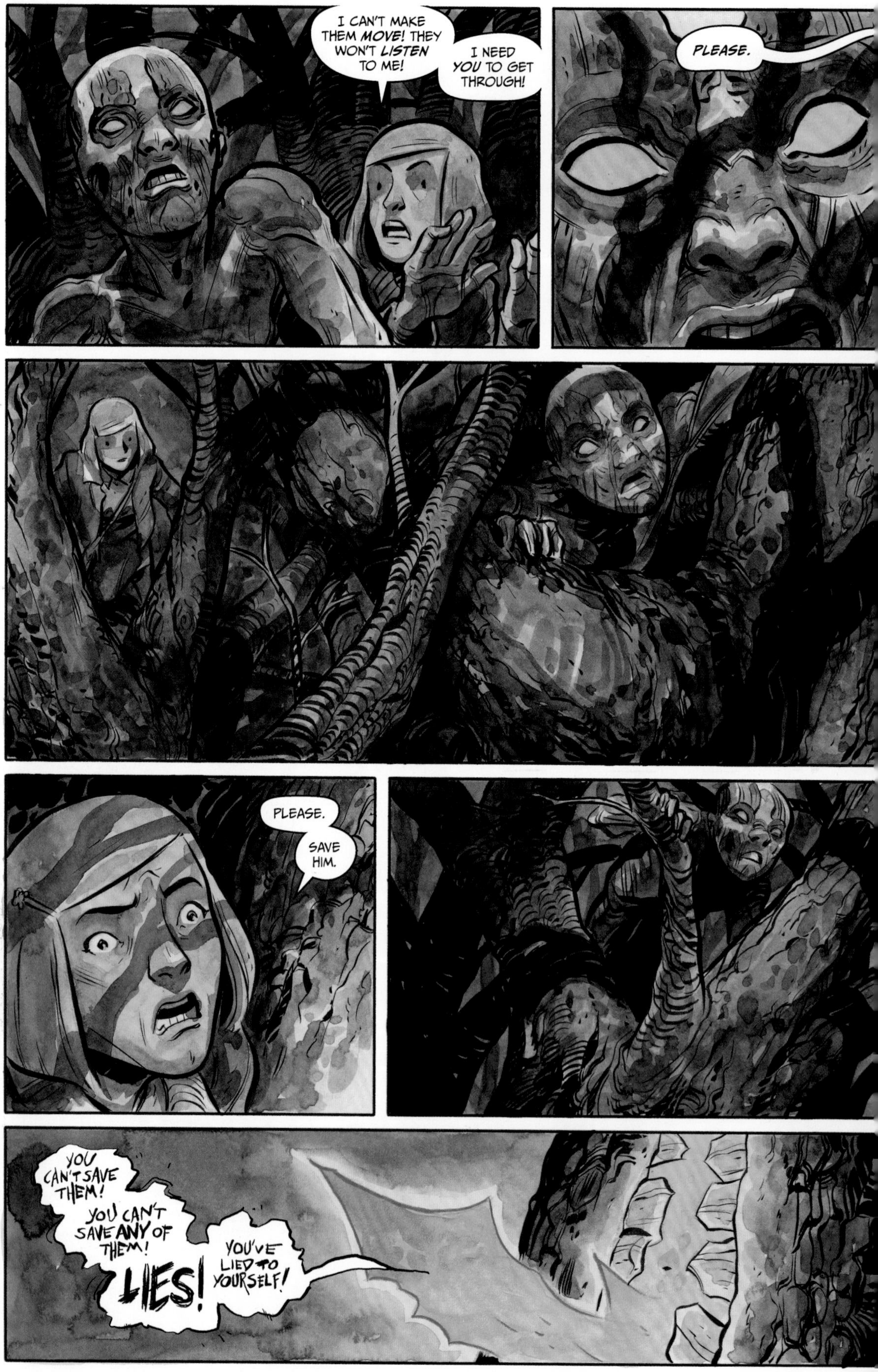
I CAN'T MAKE THEM *MOVE*! THEY WON'T *LISTEN* TO ME!
I NEED *YOU* TO GET THROUGH!
PLEASE.
PLEASE.
SAVE HIM.
YOU CAN'T SAVE THEM!
YOU CAN'T SAVE ANY OF THEM!
LIES!
YOU'VE LIED TO YOURSELF!

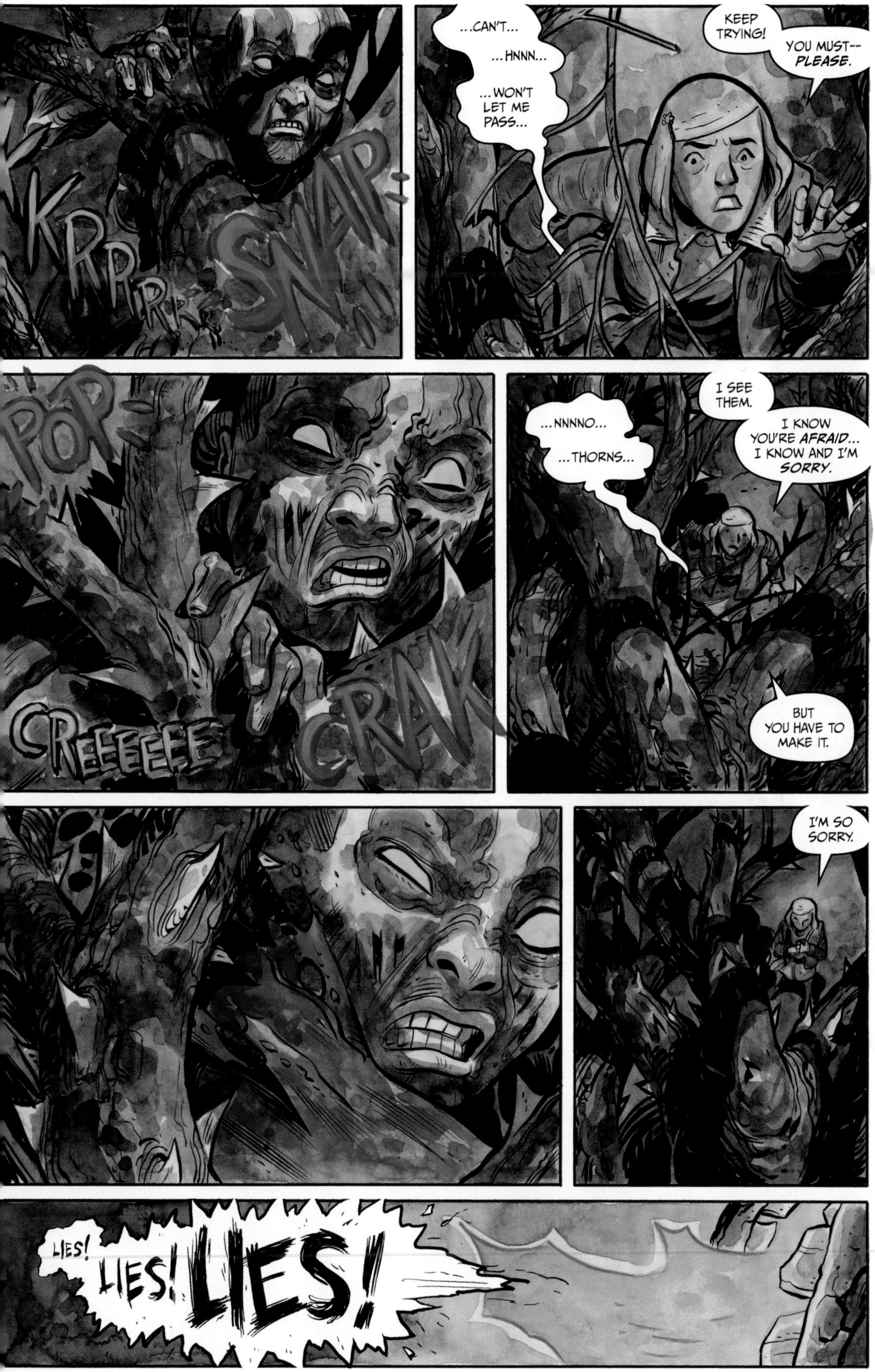
KRRRRRR
SNAP
...CAN'T...
...HNNN...
...WON'T LET ME PASS...
KEEP TRYING!
YOU MUST-- PLEASE.
POP
CREEEEEE
CRAK
...NNNNO...
...THORNS...
I SEE THEM.
I KNOW YOU'RE AFRAID... I KNOW AND I'M SORRY.
BUT YOU HAVE TO MAKE IT.
I'M SO SORRY.
LIES! LIES! LIES!

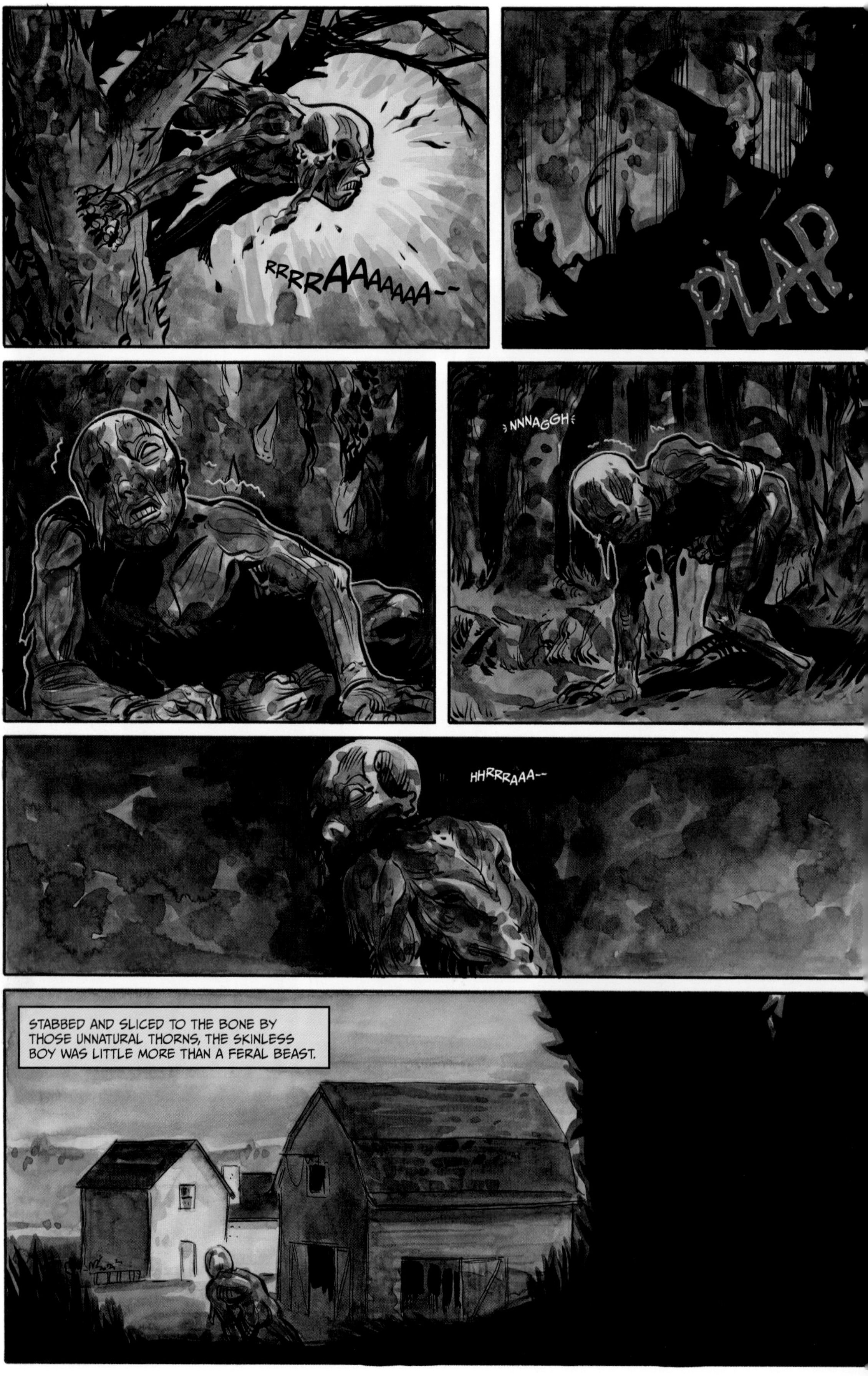
RRRRAAAAAAA--
PLAP
NNNAGGH
HHRRRAAA--
STABBED AND SLICED TO THE BONE BY THOSE UNNATURAL THORNS, THE SKINLESS BOY WAS LITTLE MORE THAN A FERAL BEAST.

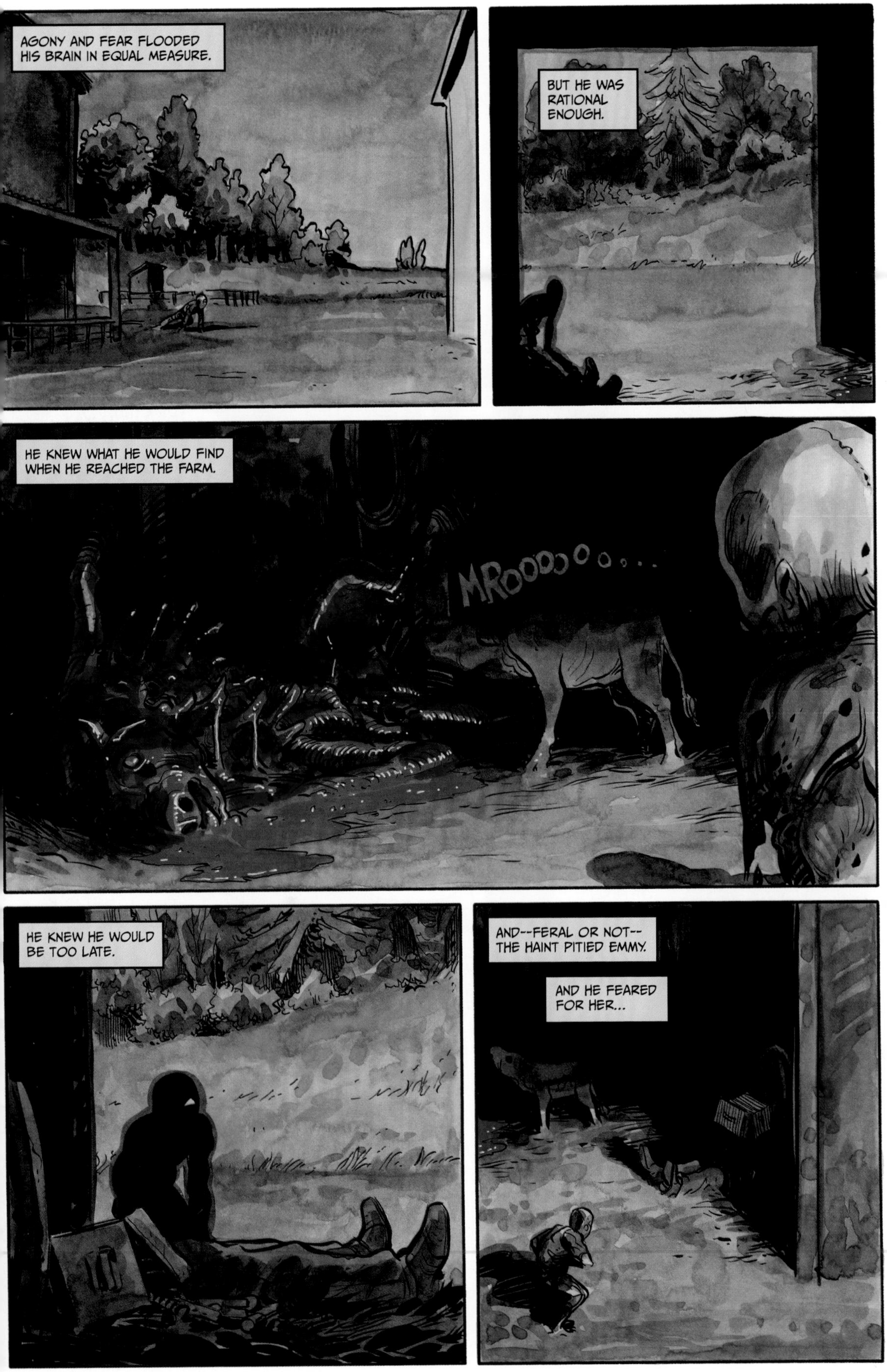
AGONY AND FEAR FLOODED HIS BRAIN IN EQUAL MEASURE.
BUT HE WAS RATIONAL ENOUGH.
HE KNEW WHAT HE WOULD FIND WHEN HE REACHED THE FARM.
MROOOOOO...
HE KNEW HE WOULD BE TOO LATE.
AND--FERAL OR NOT--THE HAINT PITIED EMMY.
AND HE FEARED FOR HER...

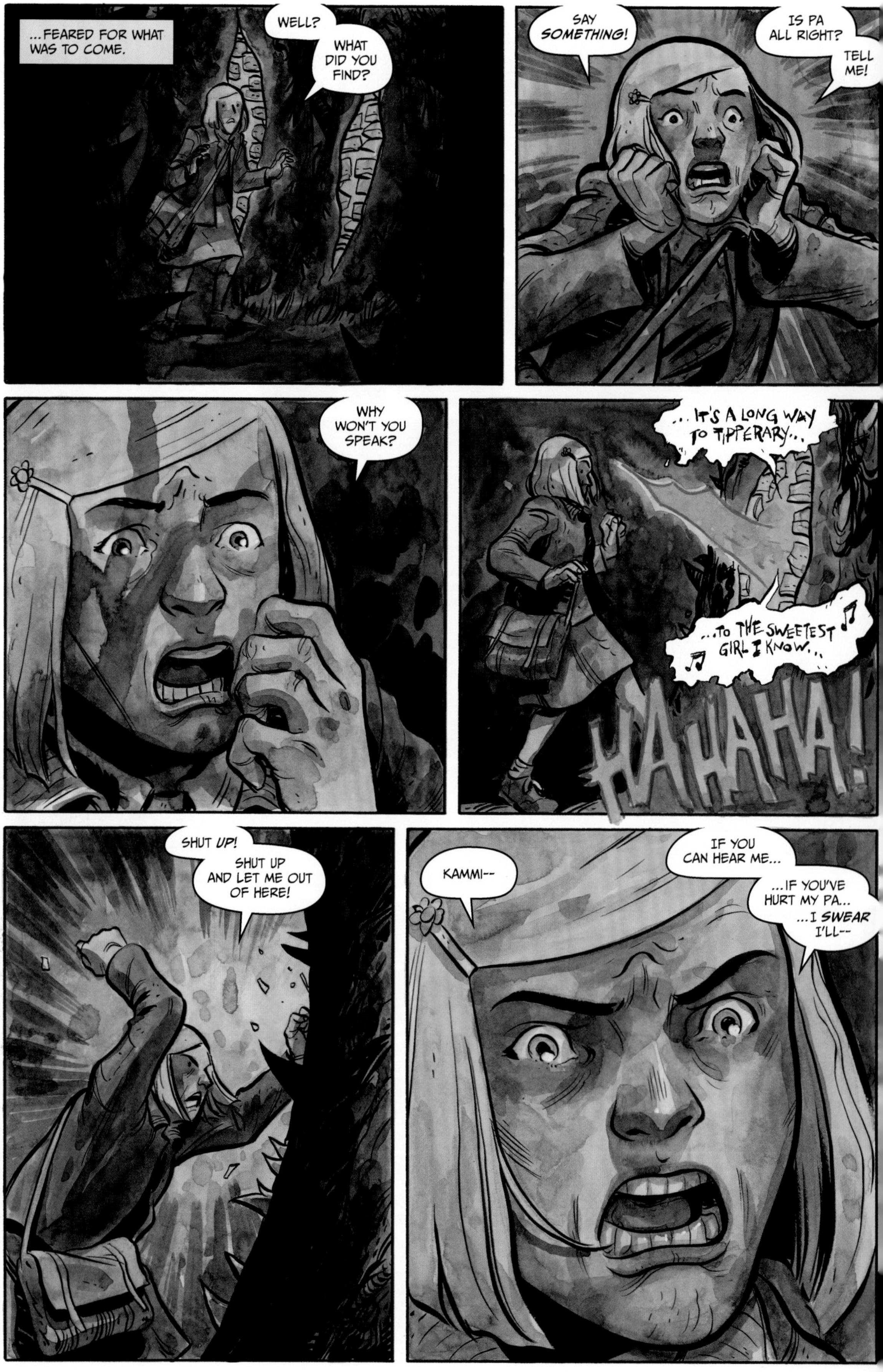
...FEARED FOR WHAT WAS TO COME.
WELL?
WHAT DID YOU FIND?
SAY SOMETHING!
IS PA ALL RIGHT?
TELL ME!
WHY WON'T YOU SPEAK?
...IT'S A LONG WAY TO TIPPERARY...
...TO THE SWEETEST GIRL I KNOW...
HAHAHA!
SHUT UP!
SHUT UP AND LET ME OUT OF HERE!
KAMMI--
IF YOU CAN HEAR ME...
...IF YOU'VE HURT MY PA...
...I SWEAR I'LL--

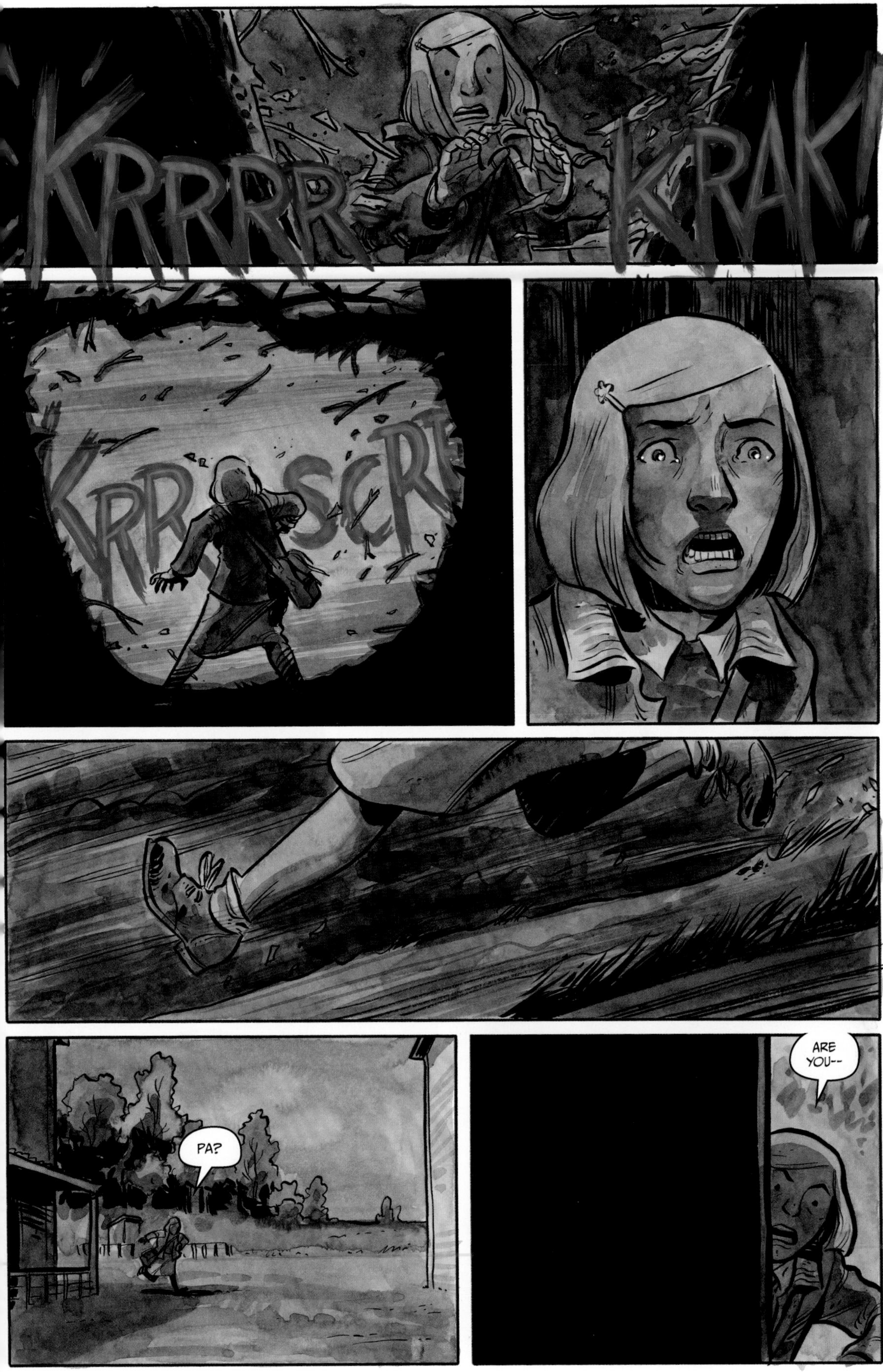
KRRRRR KRAK!
KRR SCRE
PA?
ARE YOU--

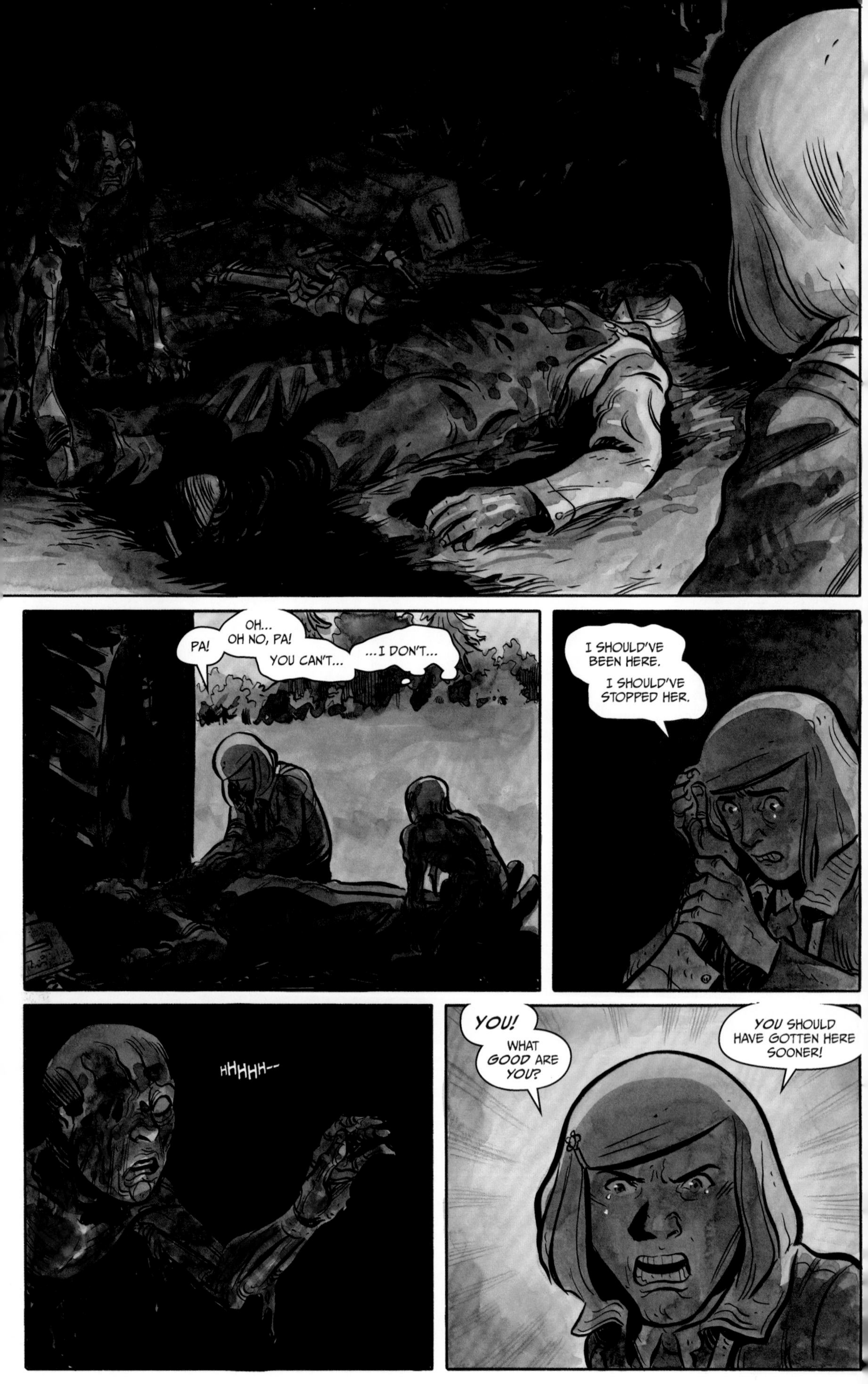
PA!
OH... OH NO, PA!
YOU CAN'T...
...I DON'T...
I SHOULD'VE BEEN HERE.
I SHOULD'VE STOPPED HER.
HHHHH--
YOU! WHAT GOOD ARE YOU?
YOU SHOULD HAVE GOTTEN HERE SOONER!

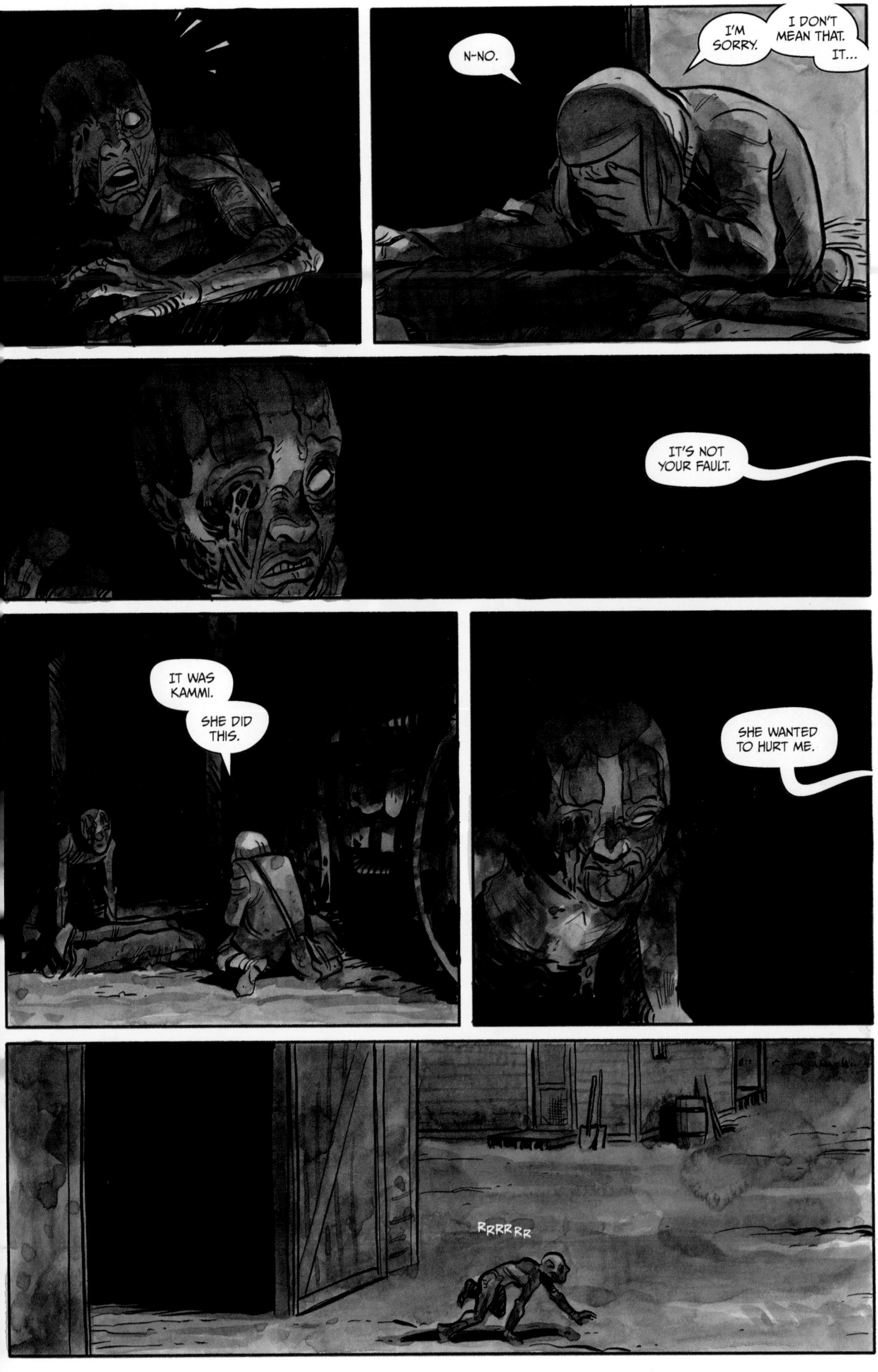
N-NO.
I'M SORRY.
I DON'T MEAN THAT. IT...
IT'S NOT YOUR FAULT.
IT WAS KAMMI.
SHE DID THIS.
SHE WANTED TO HURT ME.
RRRRRR

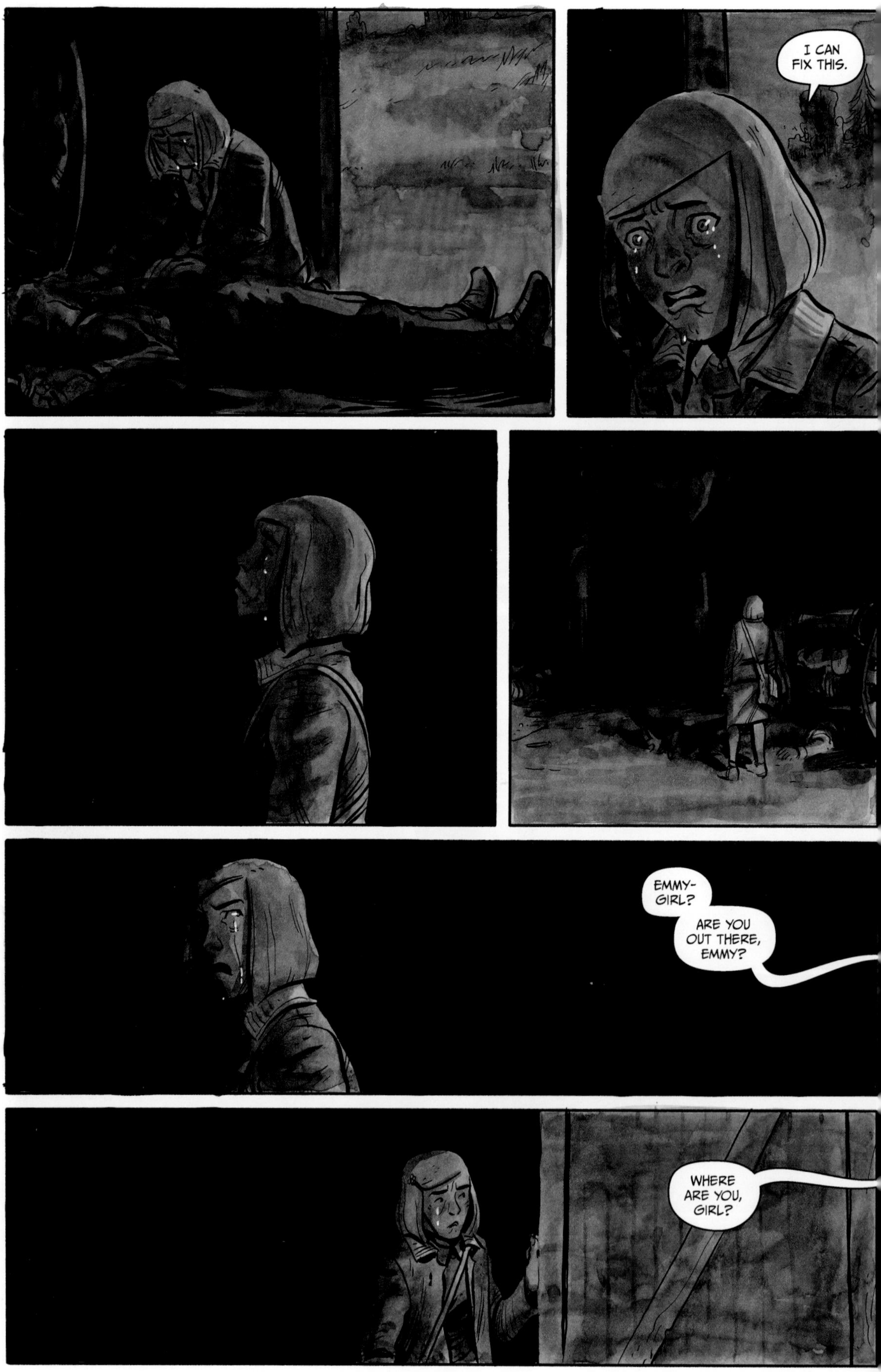
I CAN FIX THIS.
EMMY-GIRL?
ARE YOU OUT THERE, EMMY?
WHERE ARE YOU, GIRL?

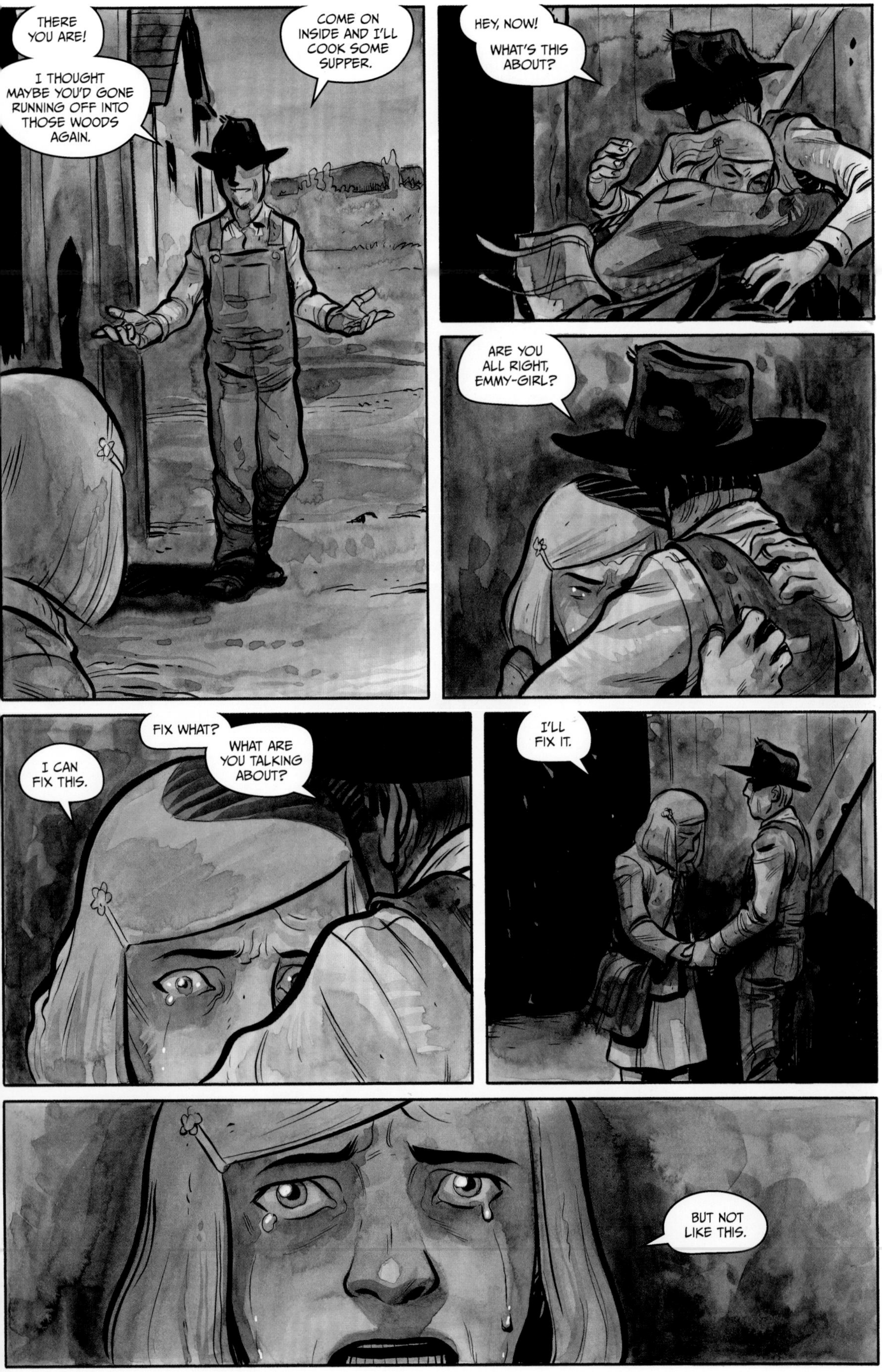
THERE YOU ARE!
I THOUGHT MAYBE YOU'D GONE RUNNING OFF INTO THOSE WOODS AGAIN.
COME ON INSIDE AND I'LL COOK SOME SUPPER.
HEY, NOW!
WHAT'S THIS ABOUT?
ARE YOU ALL RIGHT, EMMY-GIRL?
I CAN FIX THIS.
FIX WHAT?
WHAT ARE YOU TALKING ABOUT?
I'LL FIX IT.
BUT NOT LIKE THIS.

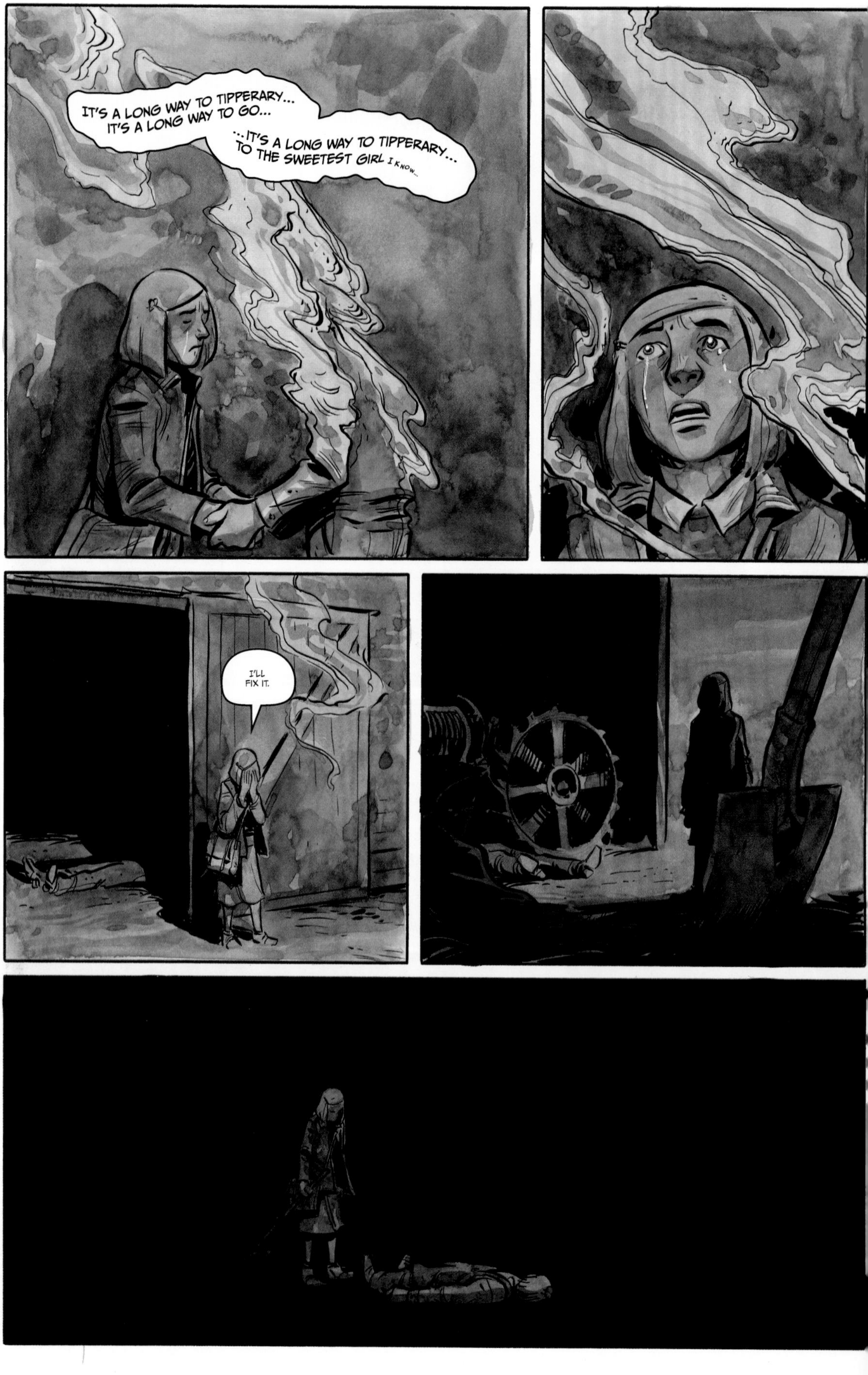
IT'S A LONG WAY TO TIPPERARY... IT'S A LONG WAY TO GO...
...IT'S A LONG WAY TO TIPPERARY... TO THE SWEETEST GIRL I KNOW...
I'LL FIX IT.

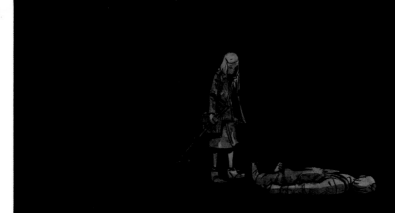

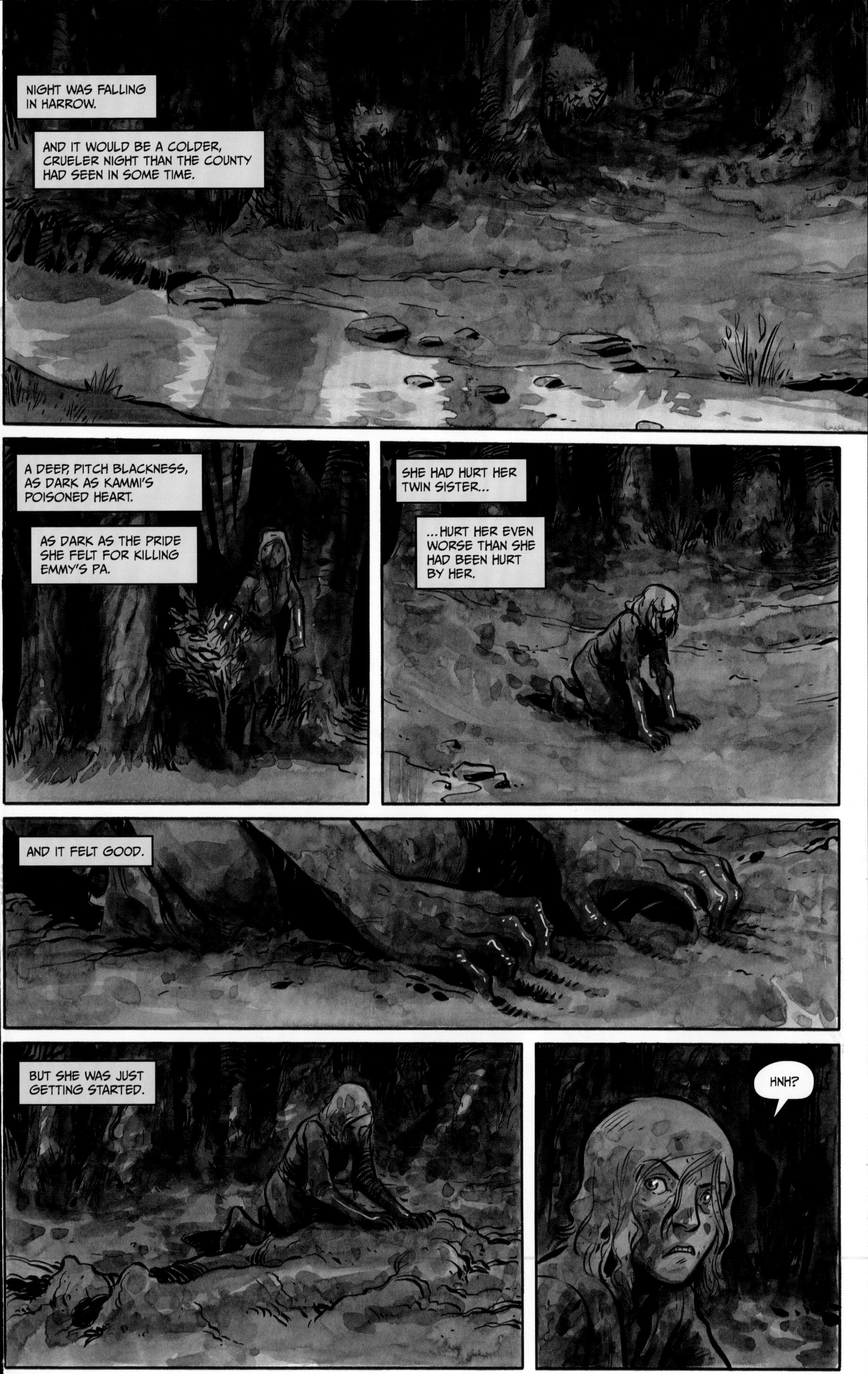
NIGHT WAS FALLING IN HARROW.
AND IT WOULD BE A COLDER, CRUELER NIGHT THAN THE COUNTY HAD SEEN IN SOME TIME.
A DEEP, PITCH BLACKNESS, AS DARK AS KAMMI'S POISONED HEART.
AS DARK AS THE PRIDE SHE FELT FOR KILLING EMMY'S PA.
SHE HAD HURT HER TWIN SISTER...
...HURT HER EVEN WORSE THAN SHE HAD BEEN HURT BY HER.
AND IT FELT GOOD.
BUT SHE WAS JUST GETTING STARTED.
HNH?

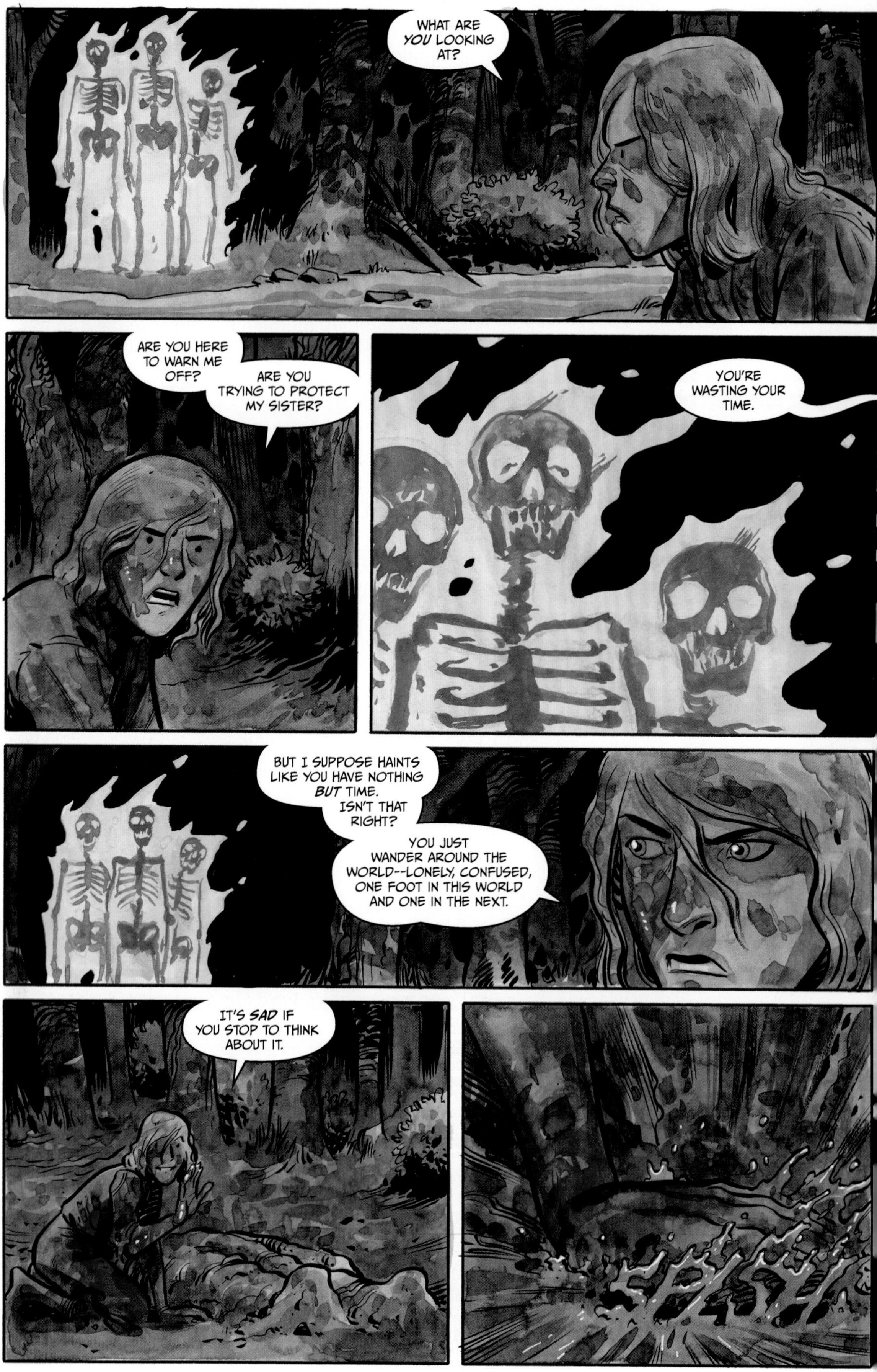
WHAT ARE YOU LOOKING AT?
ARE YOU HERE TO WARN ME OFF?
ARE YOU TRYING TO PROTECT MY SISTER?
YOU'RE WASTING YOUR TIME.
BUT I SUPPOSE HAINTS LIKE YOU HAVE NOTHING BUT TIME. ISN'T THAT RIGHT?
YOU JUST WANDER AROUND THE WORLD--LONELY, CONFUSED, ONE FOOT IN THIS WORLD AND ONE IN THE NEXT.
IT'S SAD IF YOU STOP TO THINK ABOUT IT.

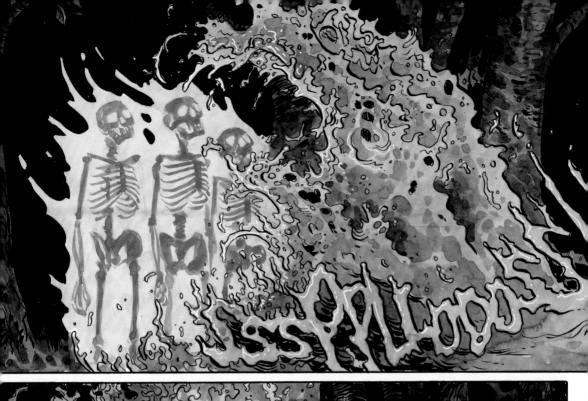

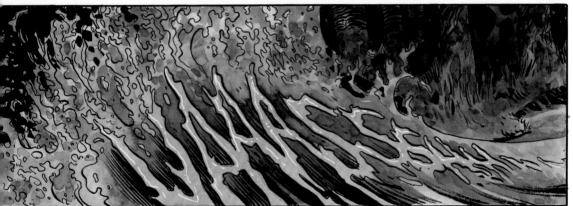

"WHERE IS SHE?"

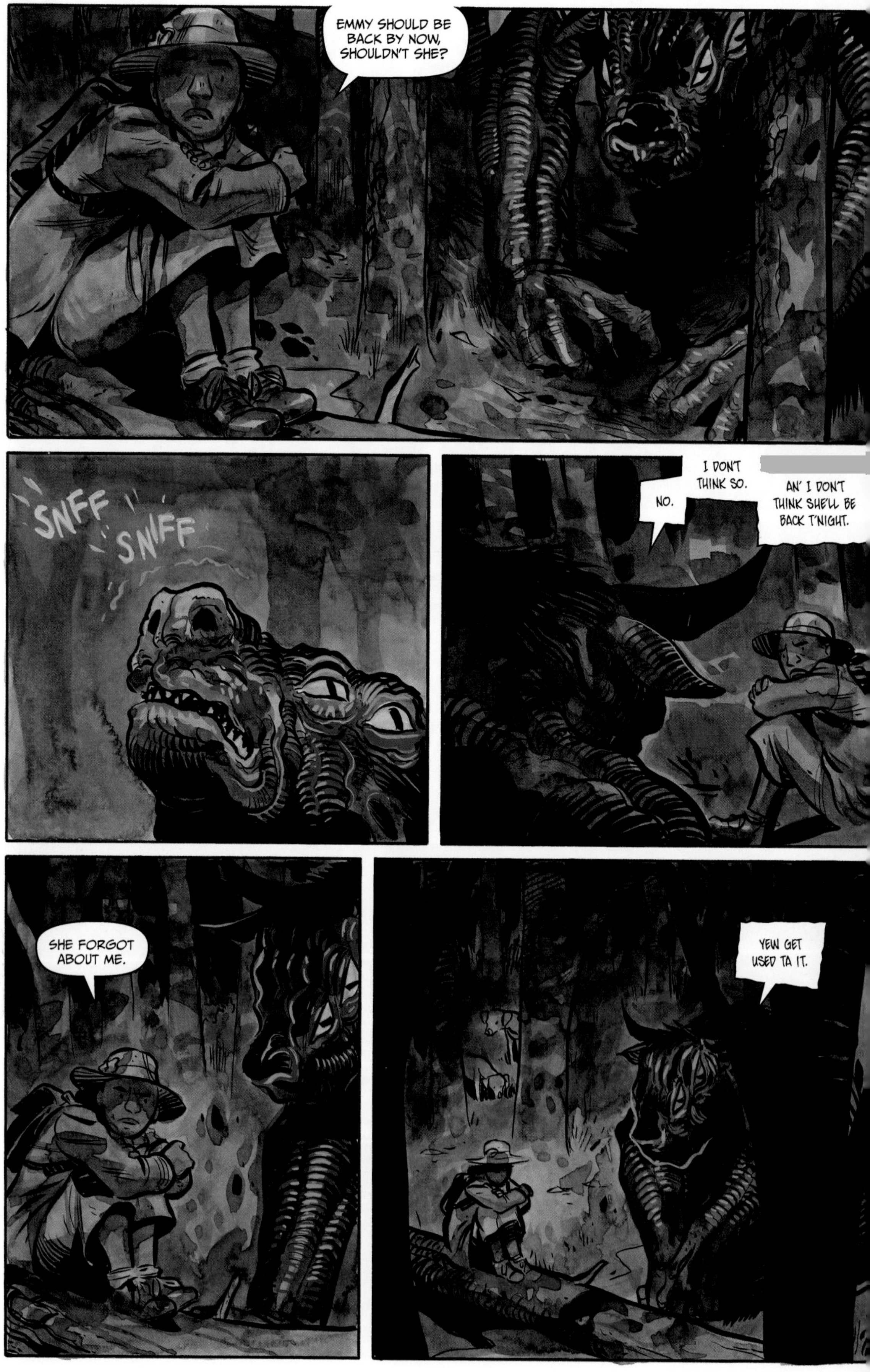
EMMY SHOULD BE BACK BY NOW, SHOULDN'T SHE?
SNFF
SNIFF
NO.
I DON'T THINK SO.
AN' I DON'T THINK SHE'LL BE BACK T'NIGHT.
SHE FORGOT ABOUT ME.
YEW GET USED TA IT.

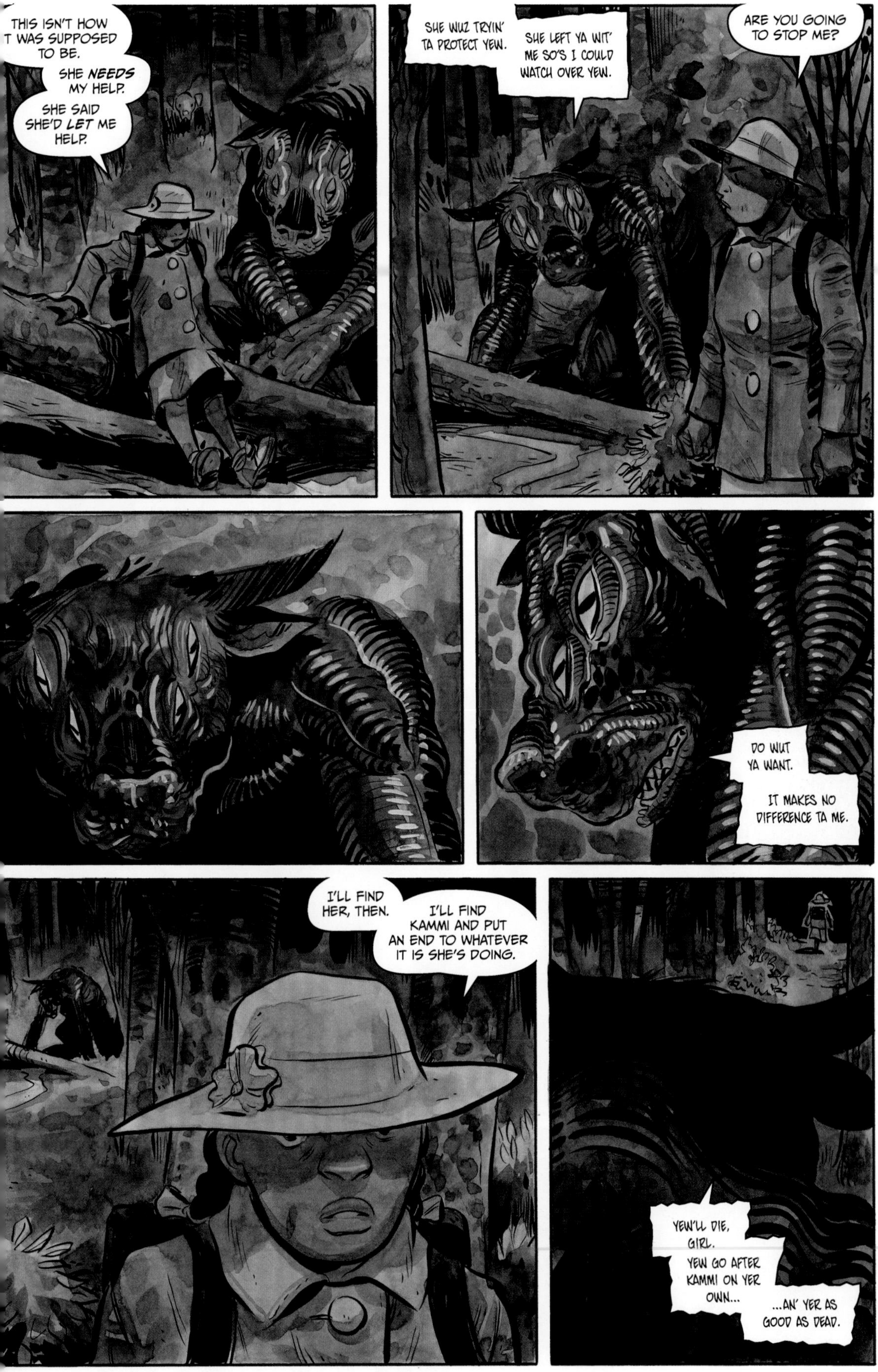
THIS ISN'T HOW
T WAS SUPPOSED TO BE.
SHE NEEDS MY HELP.
SHE SAID SHE'D LET ME HELP.
SHE WUZ TRYIN' TA PROTECT YEW.
SHE LEFT YA WIT' ME SO'S I COULD WATCH OVER YEW.
ARE YOU GOING TO STOP ME?
DO WUT YA WANT.
IT MAKES NO DIFFERENCE TA ME.
I'LL FIND HER, THEN.
I'LL FIND KAMMI AND PUT AN END TO WHATEVER IT IS SHE'S DOING.
YEW'LL DIE, GIRL.
YEW GO AFTER KAMMI ON YER OWN...
...AN' YER AS GOOD AS DEAD.

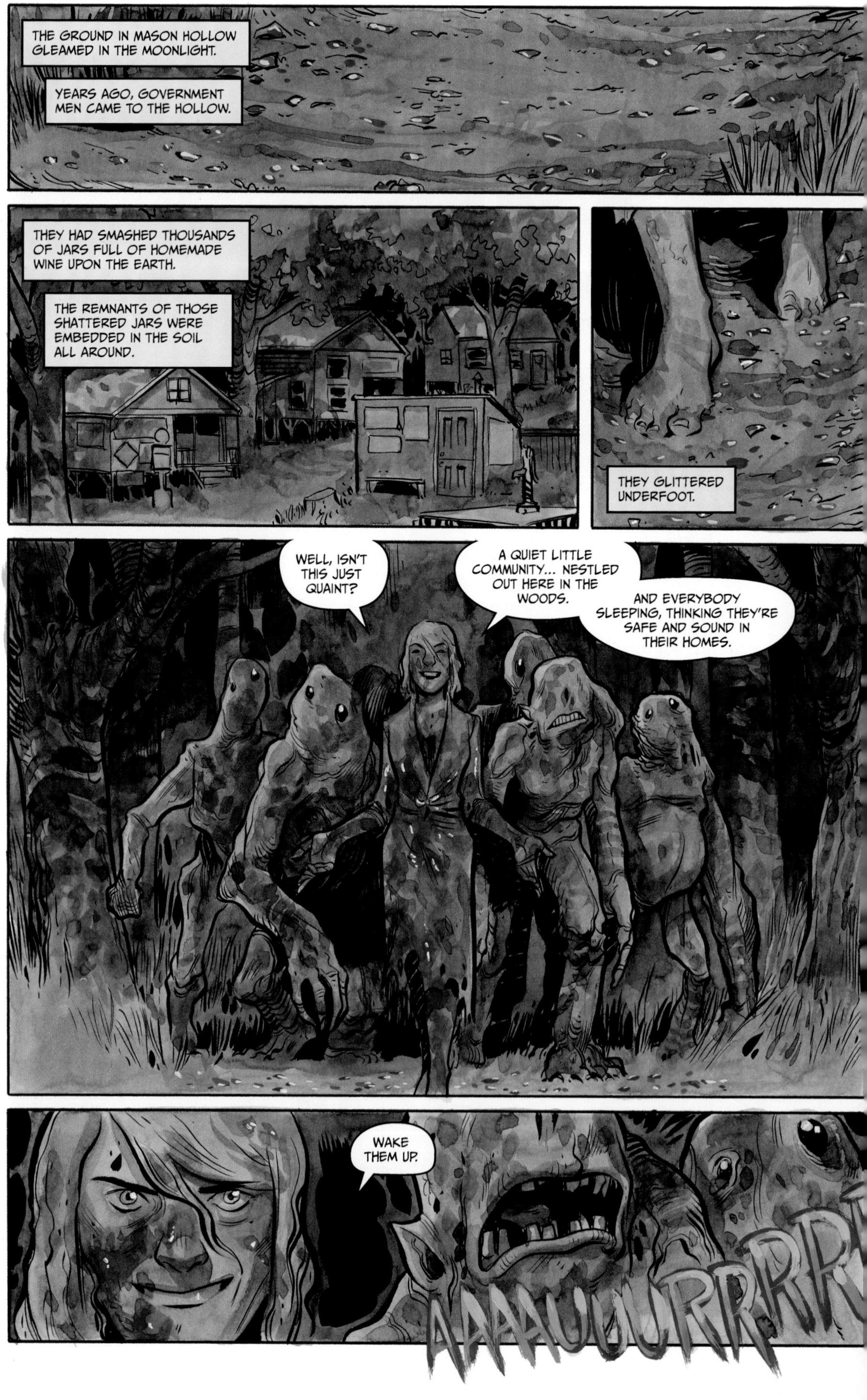
THE GROUND IN MASON HOLLOW GLEAMED IN THE MOONLIGHT.
YEARS AGO, GOVERNMENT MEN CAME TO THE HOLLOW.
THEY HAD SMASHED THOUSANDS OF JARS FULL OF HOMEMADE WINE UPON THE EARTH.
THE REMNANTS OF THOSE SHATTERED JARS WERE EMBEDDED IN THE SOIL ALL AROUND.
THEY GLITTERED UNDERFOOT.
WELL, ISN'T THIS JUST QUAINT?
A QUIET LITTLE COMMUNITY... NESTLED OUT HERE IN THE WOODS.
AND EVERYBODY SLEEPING, THINKING THEY'RE SAFE AND SOUND IN THEIR HOMES.
WAKE THEM UP.
AAAAUUURRRRR

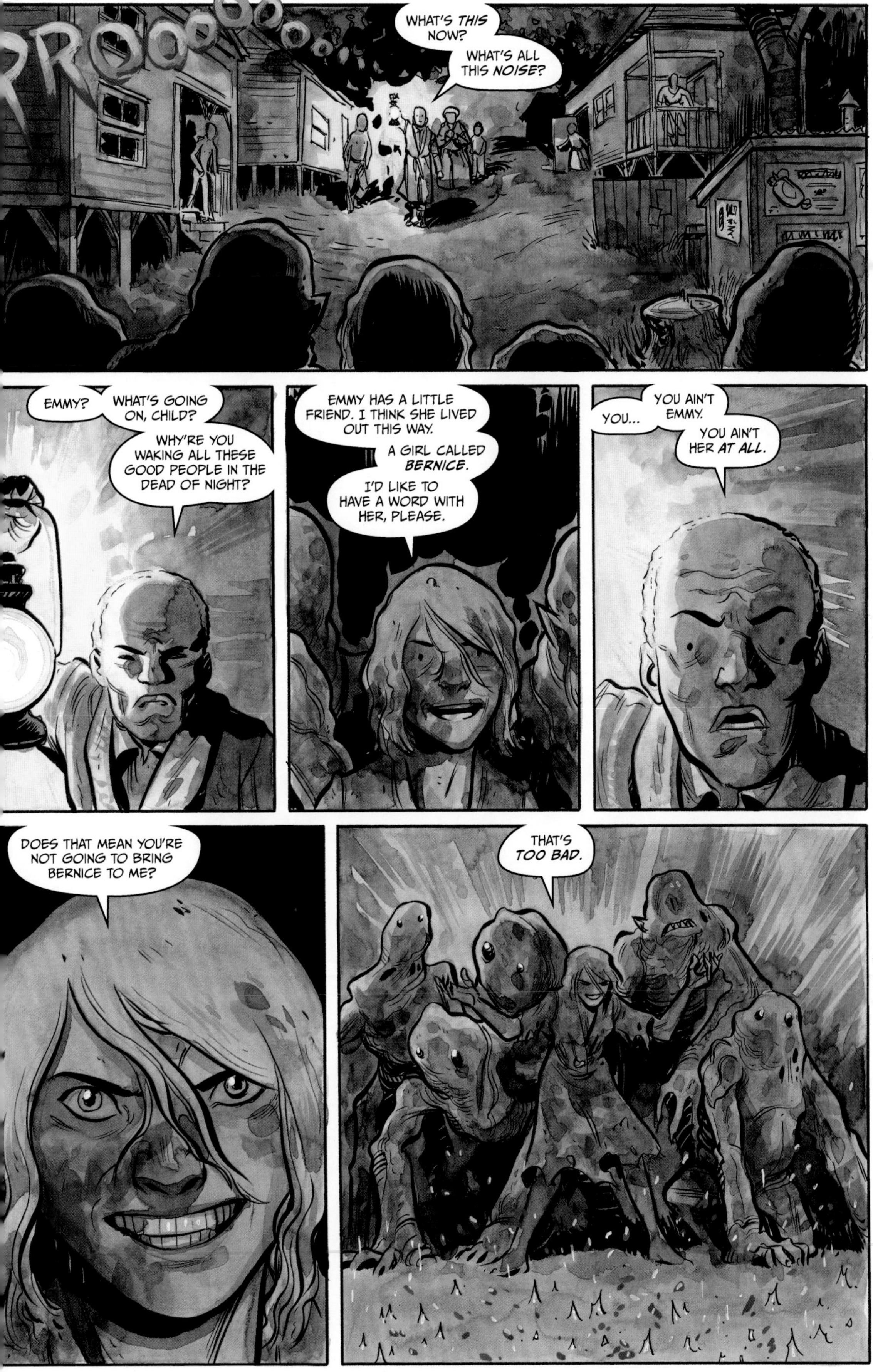
RROOOOOOOO
WHAT'S *THIS* NOW?
WHAT'S ALL THIS *NOISE?*
EMMY?
WHAT'S GOING ON, CHILD?
WHY'RE YOU WAKING ALL THESE GOOD PEOPLE IN THE DEAD OF NIGHT?
EMMY HAS A LITTLE FRIEND. I THINK SHE LIVED OUT THIS WAY.
A GIRL CALLED *BERNICE*.
I'D LIKE TO HAVE A WORD WITH HER, PLEASE.
YOU...
YOU AIN'T EMMY.
YOU AIN'T HER *AT ALL*.
DOES THAT MEAN YOU'RE NOT GOING TO BRING BERNICE TO ME?
THAT'S *TOO BAD*.

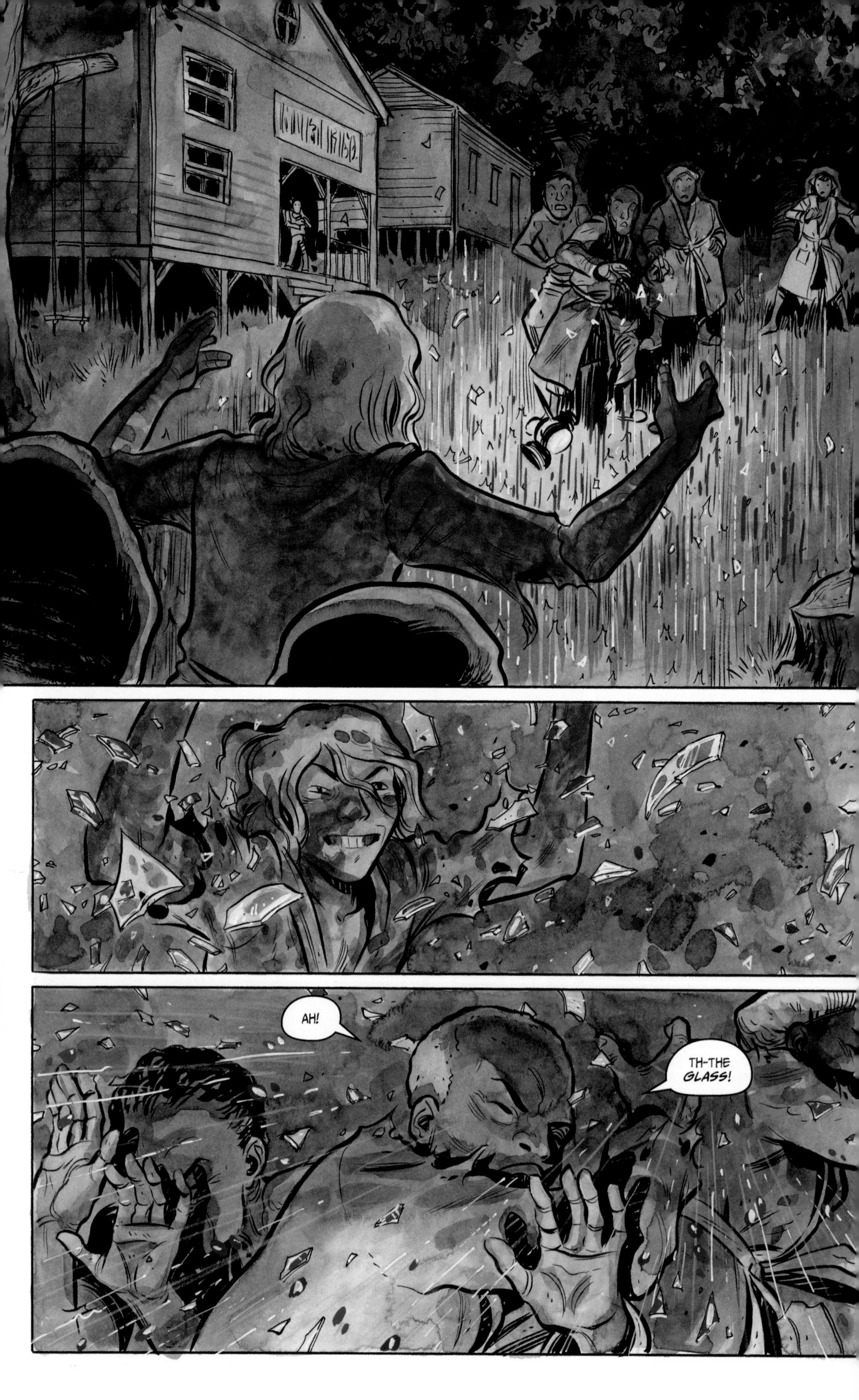
AH!
TH-THE GLASS!

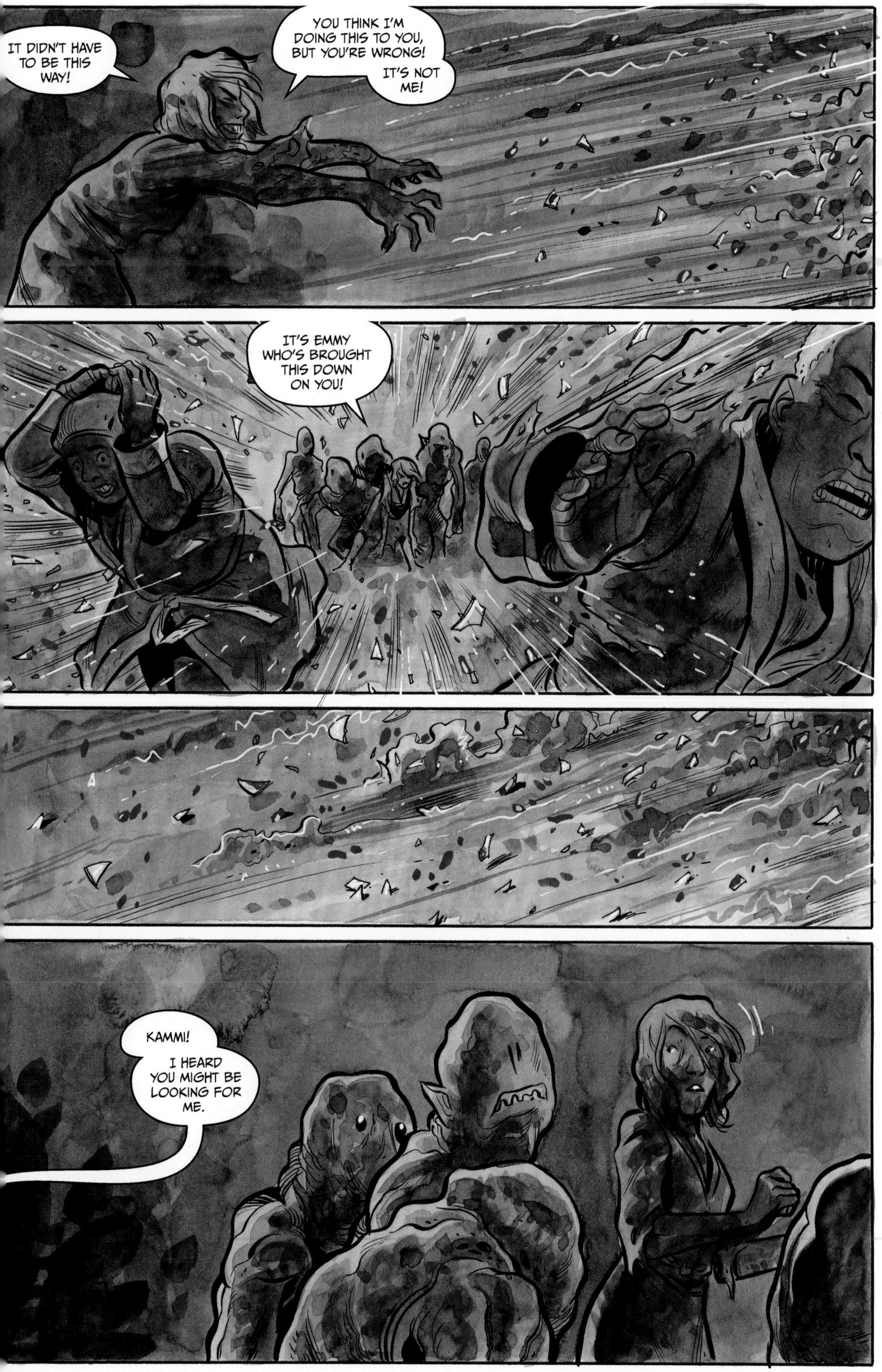
IT DIDN'T HAVE TO BE THIS WAY!
YOU THINK I'M DOING THIS TO YOU, BUT YOU'RE WRONG!
IT'S NOT ME!
IT'S EMMY WHO'S BROUGHT THIS DOWN ON YOU!
KAMMI!
I HEARD YOU MIGHT BE LOOKING FOR ME.

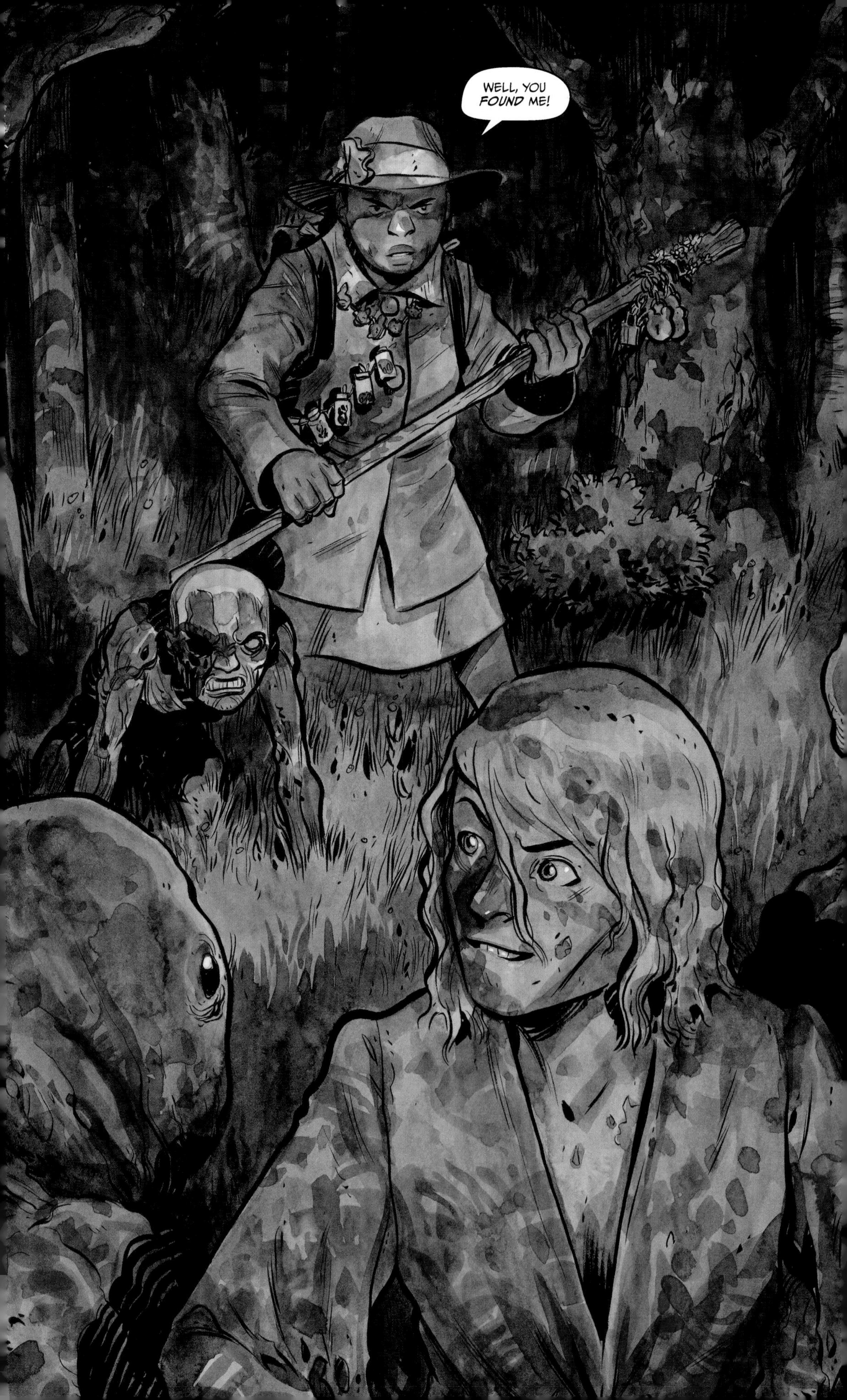
WELL, YOU FOUND ME!

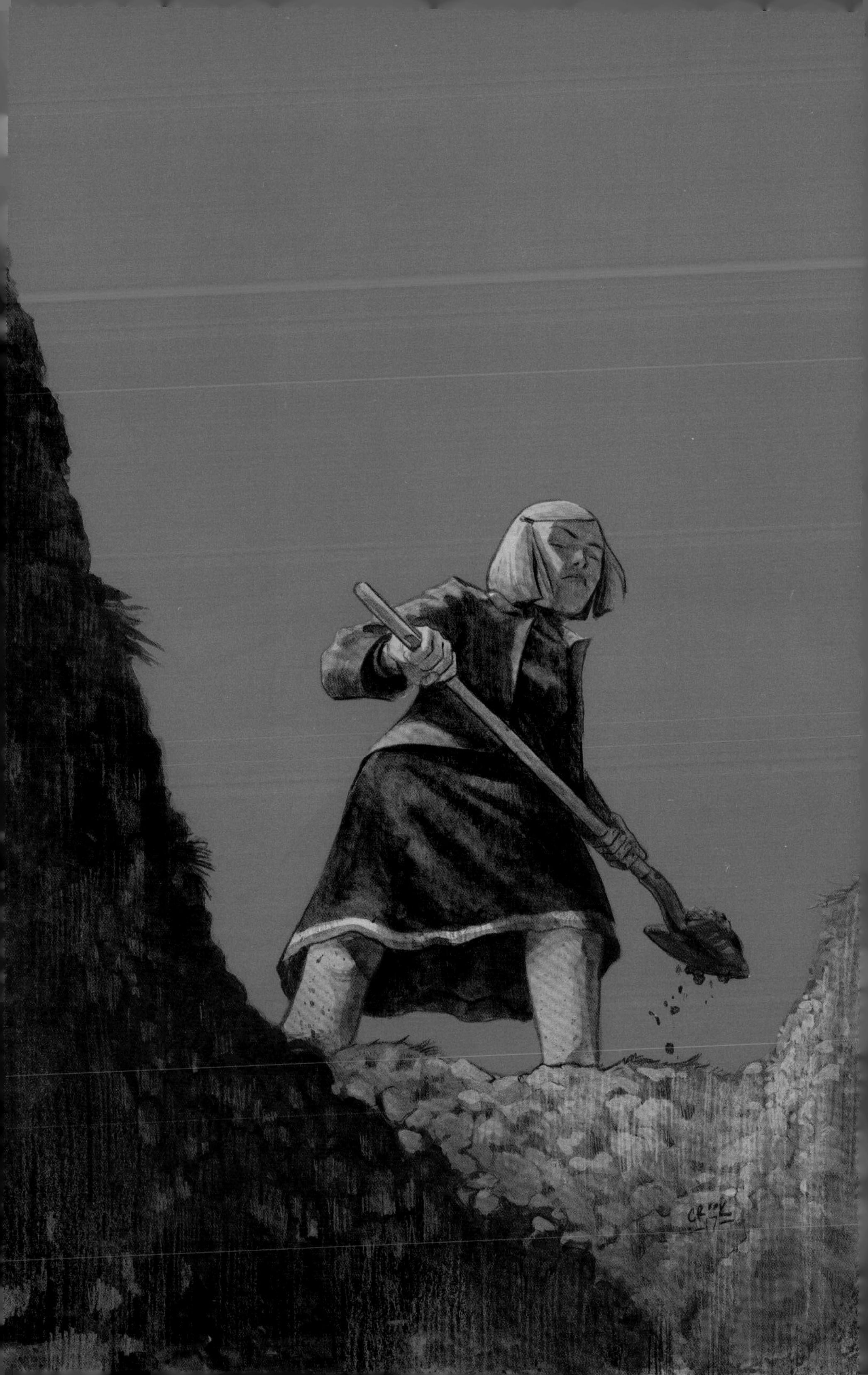

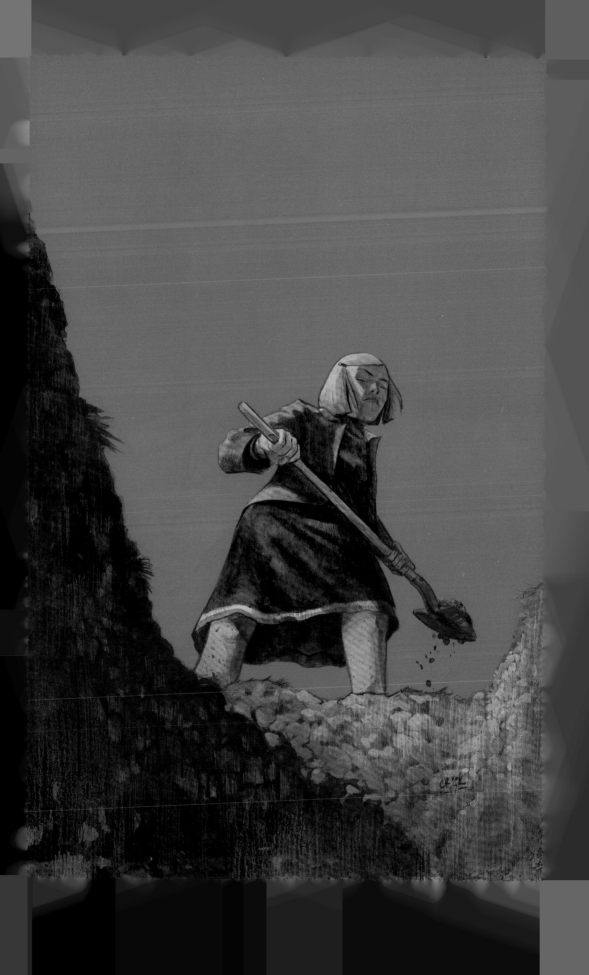

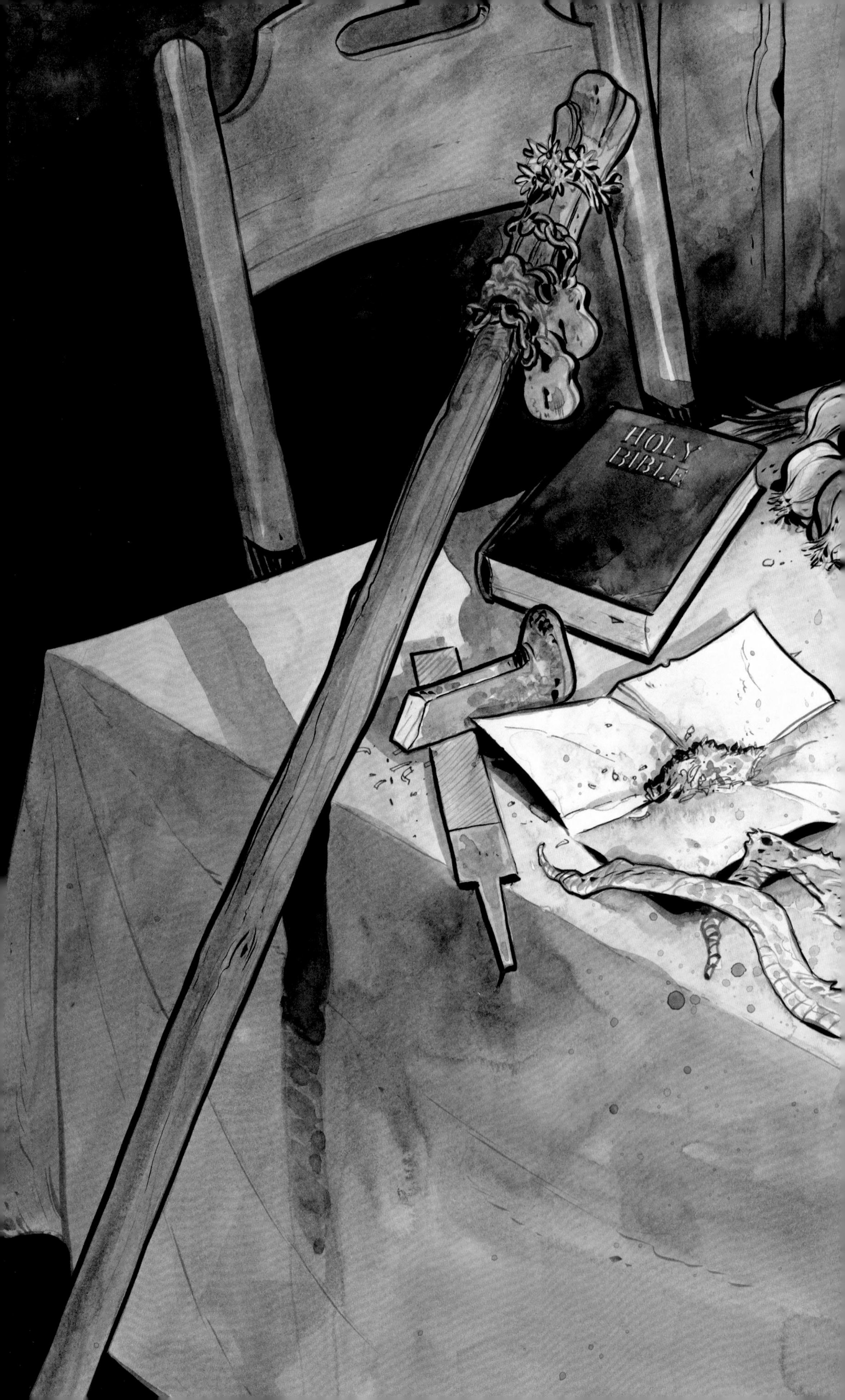
HOLY BIBLE

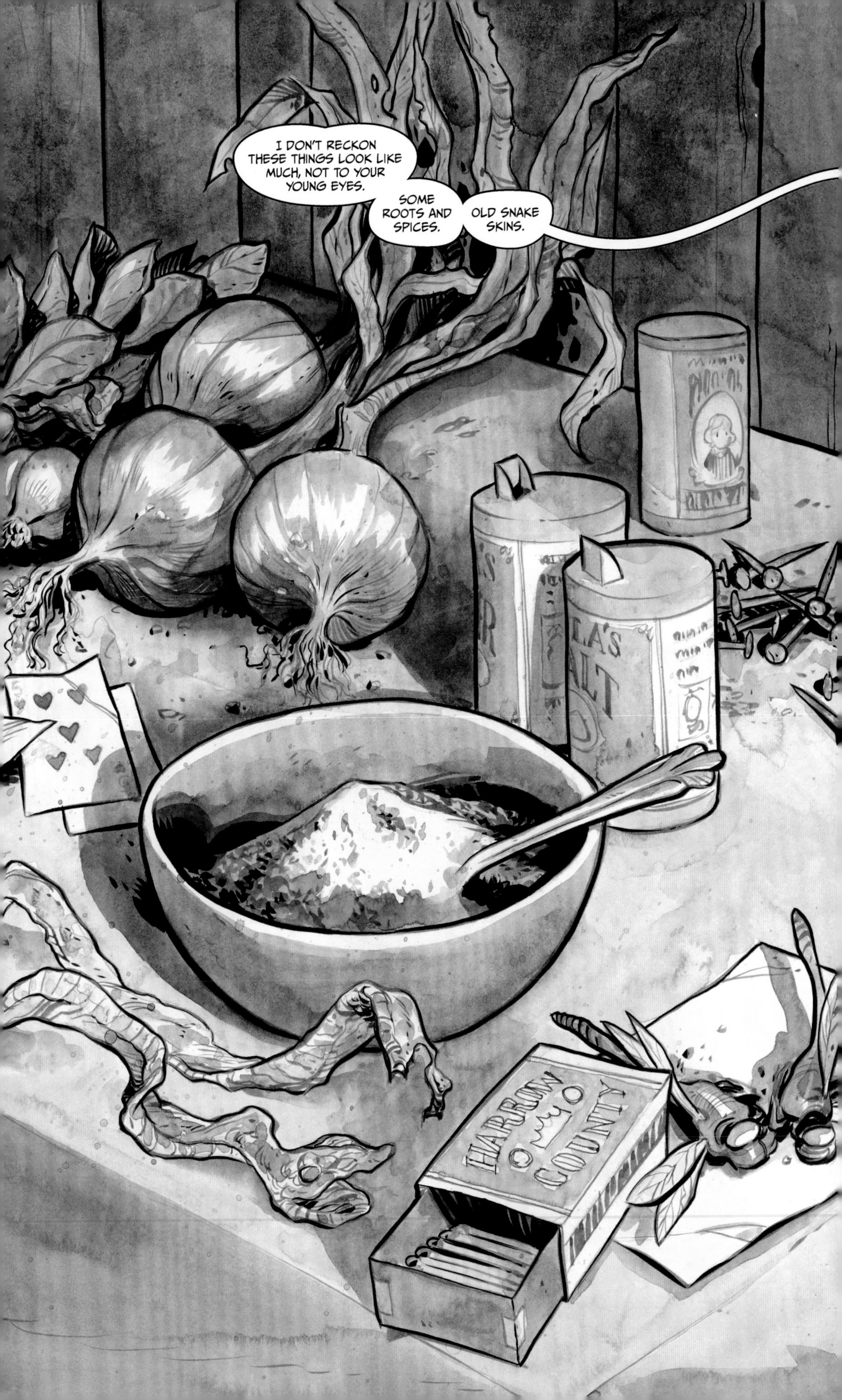
I DON'T RECKON THESE THINGS LOOK LIKE MUCH, NOT TO YOUR YOUNG EYES.
SOME ROOTS AND SPICES.
OLD SNAKE SKINS.
HARROW COUNTY

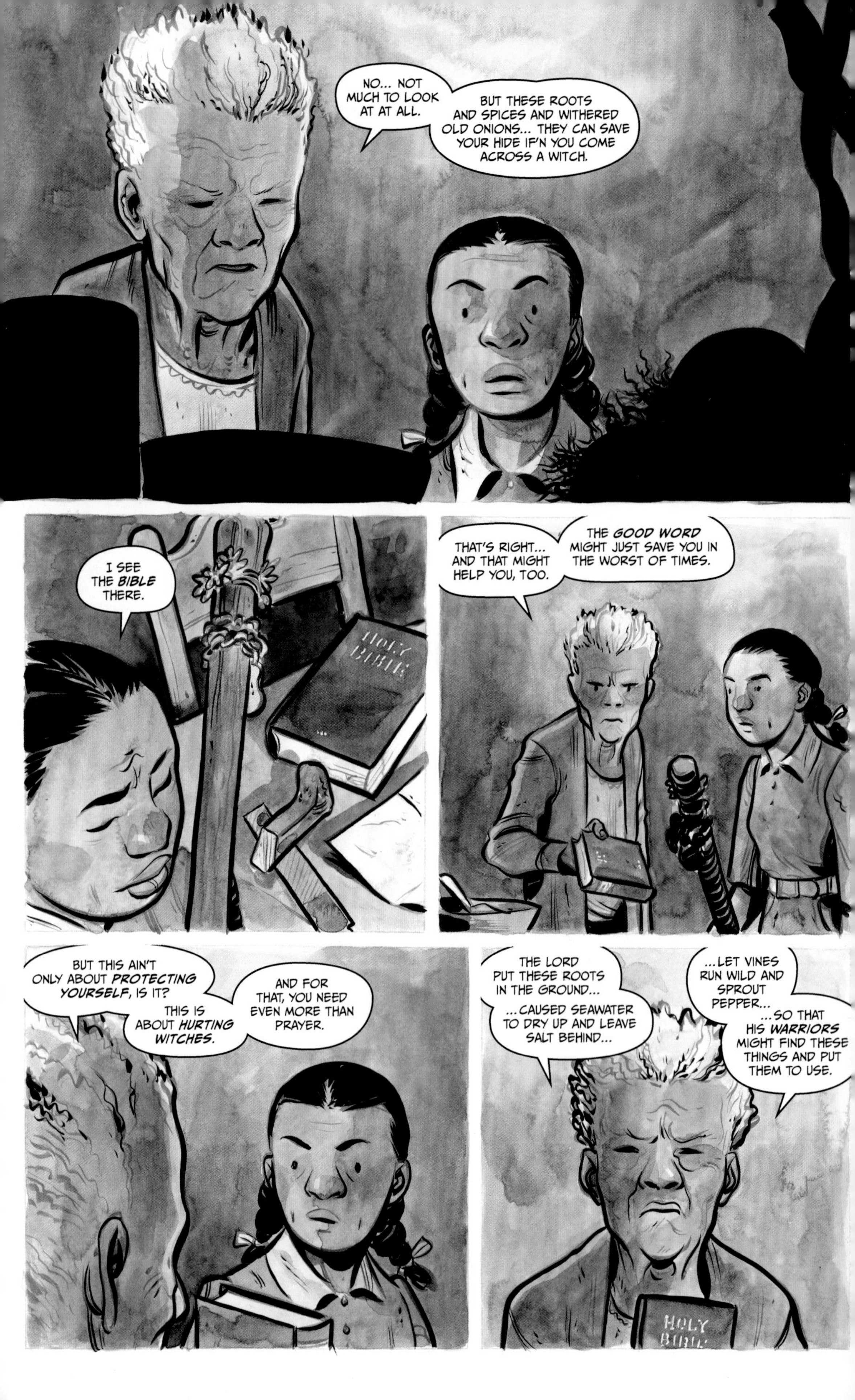
NO... NOT MUCH TO LOOK AT AT ALL.
BUT THESE ROOTS AND SPICES AND WITHERED OLD ONIONS... THEY CAN SAVE YOUR HIDE IF'N YOU COME ACROSS A WITCH.
I SEE THE *BIBLE* THERE.
HOLY BIBLE
THAT'S RIGHT... AND THAT MIGHT HELP YOU, TOO.
THE *GOOD WORD* MIGHT JUST SAVE YOU IN THE WORST OF TIMES.
BUT THIS AIN'T ONLY ABOUT ***PROTECTING YOURSELF***, IS IT?
THIS IS ABOUT ***HURTING WITCHES***.
AND FOR THAT, YOU NEED EVEN MORE THAN PRAYER.
THE LORD PUT THESE ROOTS IN THE GROUND...
...CAUSED SEAWATER TO DRY UP AND LEAVE SALT BEHIND...
...LET VINES RUN WILD AND SPROUT PEPPER...
...SO THAT HIS ***WARRIORS*** MIGHT FIND THESE THINGS AND PUT THEM TO USE.
HOLY BIBLE

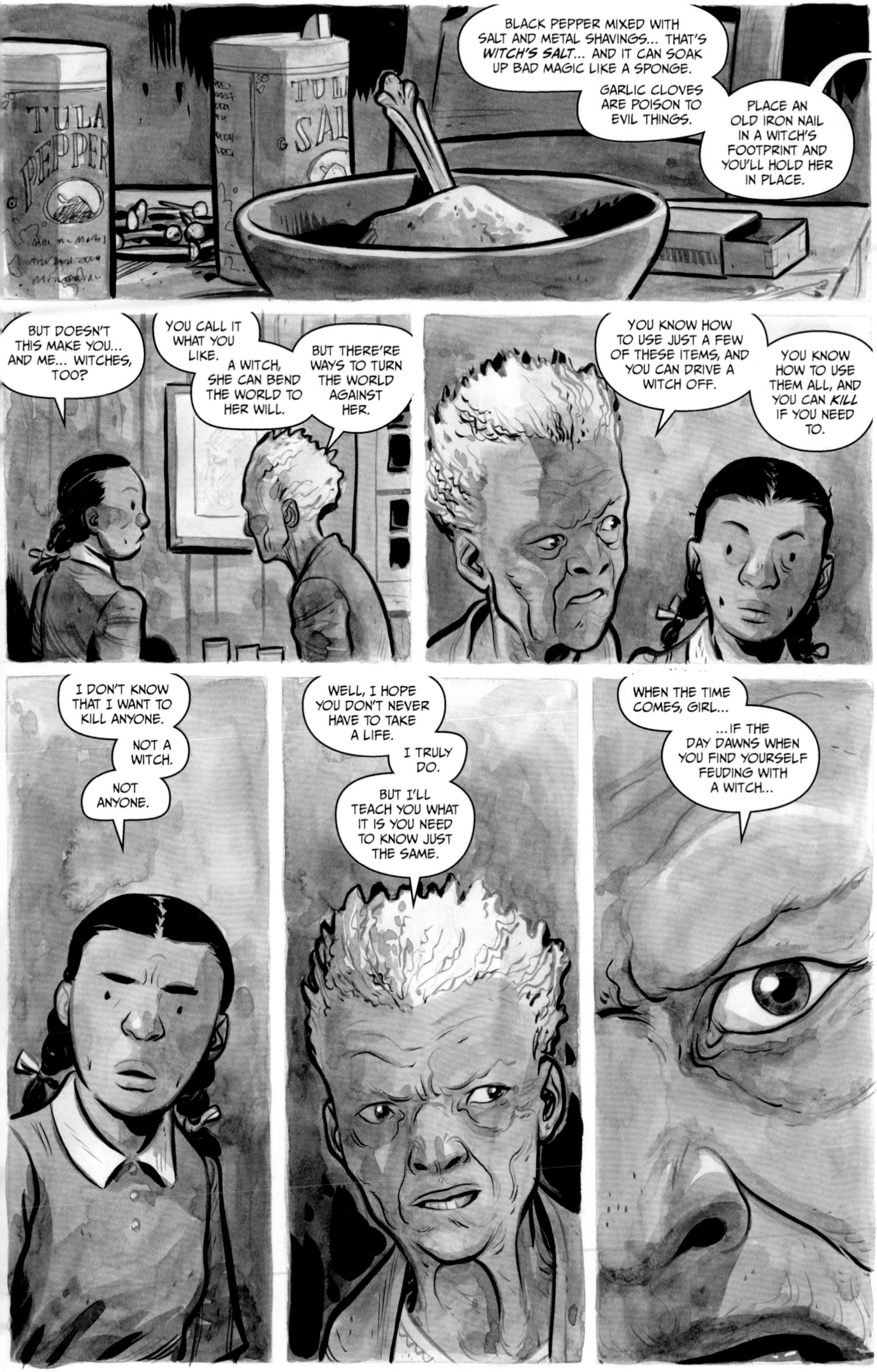
BLACK PEPPER MIXED WITH SALT AND METAL SHAVINGS... THAT'S *WITCH'S SALT*... AND IT CAN SOAK UP BAD MAGIC LIKE A SPONGE.
GARLIC CLOVES ARE POISON TO EVIL THINGS.
PLACE AN OLD IRON NAIL IN A WITCH'S FOOTPRINT AND YOU'LL HOLD HER IN PLACE.
TULA PEPPER
TULA SALT
BUT DOESN'T THIS MAKE YOU... AND ME... WITCHES, TOO?
YOU CALL IT WHAT YOU LIKE.
A WITCH, SHE CAN BEND THE WORLD TO HER WILL.
BUT THERE'RE WAYS TO TURN THE WORLD AGAINST HER.
YOU KNOW HOW TO USE JUST A FEW OF THESE ITEMS, AND YOU CAN DRIVE A WITCH OFF.
YOU KNOW HOW TO USE THEM ALL, AND YOU CAN ***KILL*** IF YOU NEED TO.
I DON'T KNOW THAT I WANT TO KILL ANYONE.
NOT A WITCH.
NOT ANYONE.
WELL, I HOPE YOU DON'T NEVER HAVE TO TAKE A LIFE.
I TRULY DO.
BUT I'LL TEACH YOU WHAT IT IS YOU NEED TO KNOW JUST THE SAME.
WHEN THE TIME COMES, GIRL...
...IF THE DAY DAWNS WHEN YOU FIND YOURSELF FEUDING WITH A WITCH...

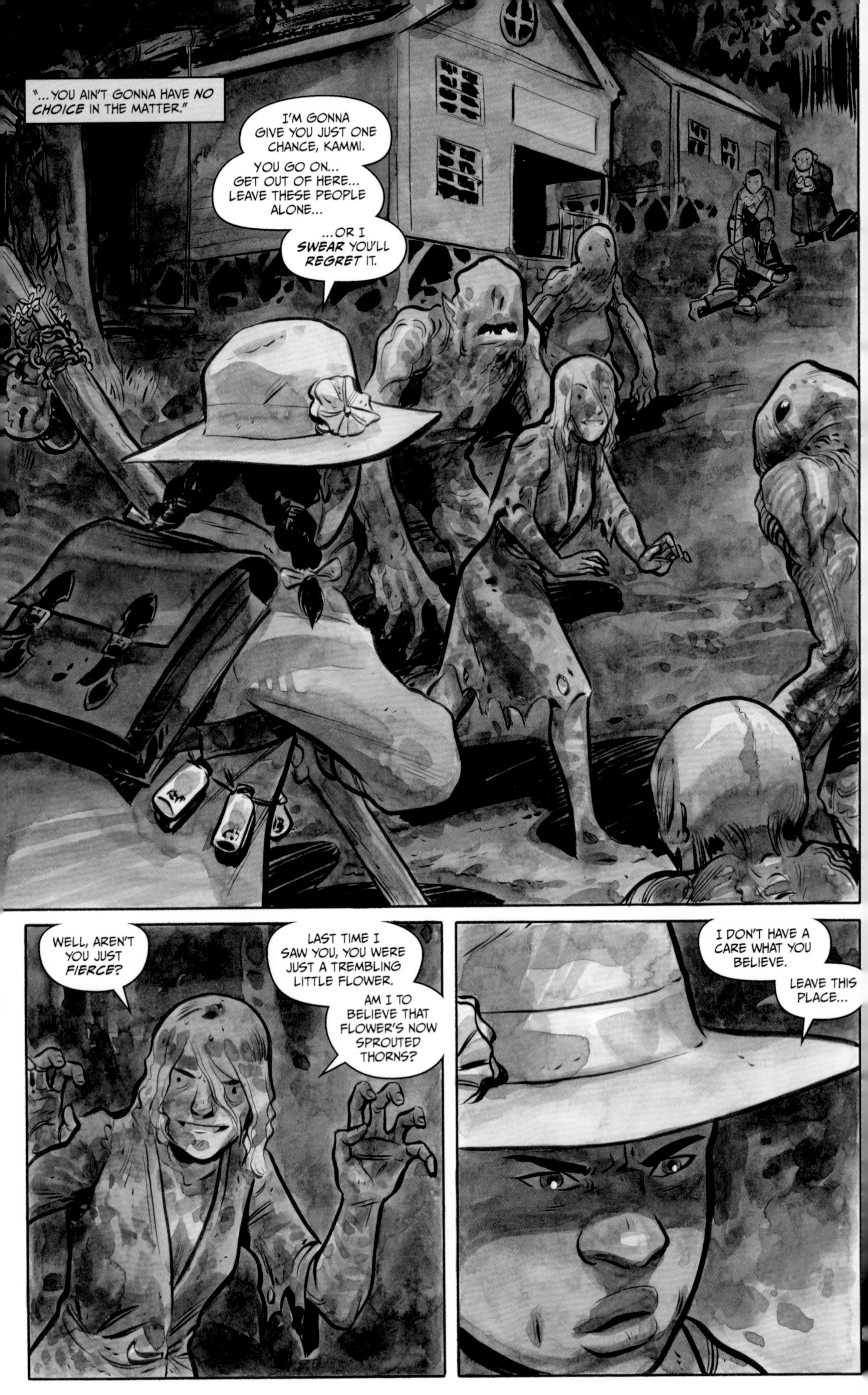
"...YOU AIN'T GONNA HAVE *NO CHOICE* IN THE MATTER."
I'M GONNA GIVE YOU JUST ONE CHANCE, KAMMI.
YOU GO ON... GET OUT OF HERE... LEAVE THESE PEOPLE ALONE...
...OR I *SWEAR* YOU'LL *REGRET* IT.
WELL, AREN'T YOU JUST *FIERCE*?
LAST TIME I SAW YOU, YOU WERE JUST A TREMBLING LITTLE FLOWER.
AM I TO BELIEVE THAT FLOWER'S NOW SPROUTED THORNS?
I DON'T HAVE A CARE WHAT YOU BELIEVE.
LEAVE THIS PLACE...

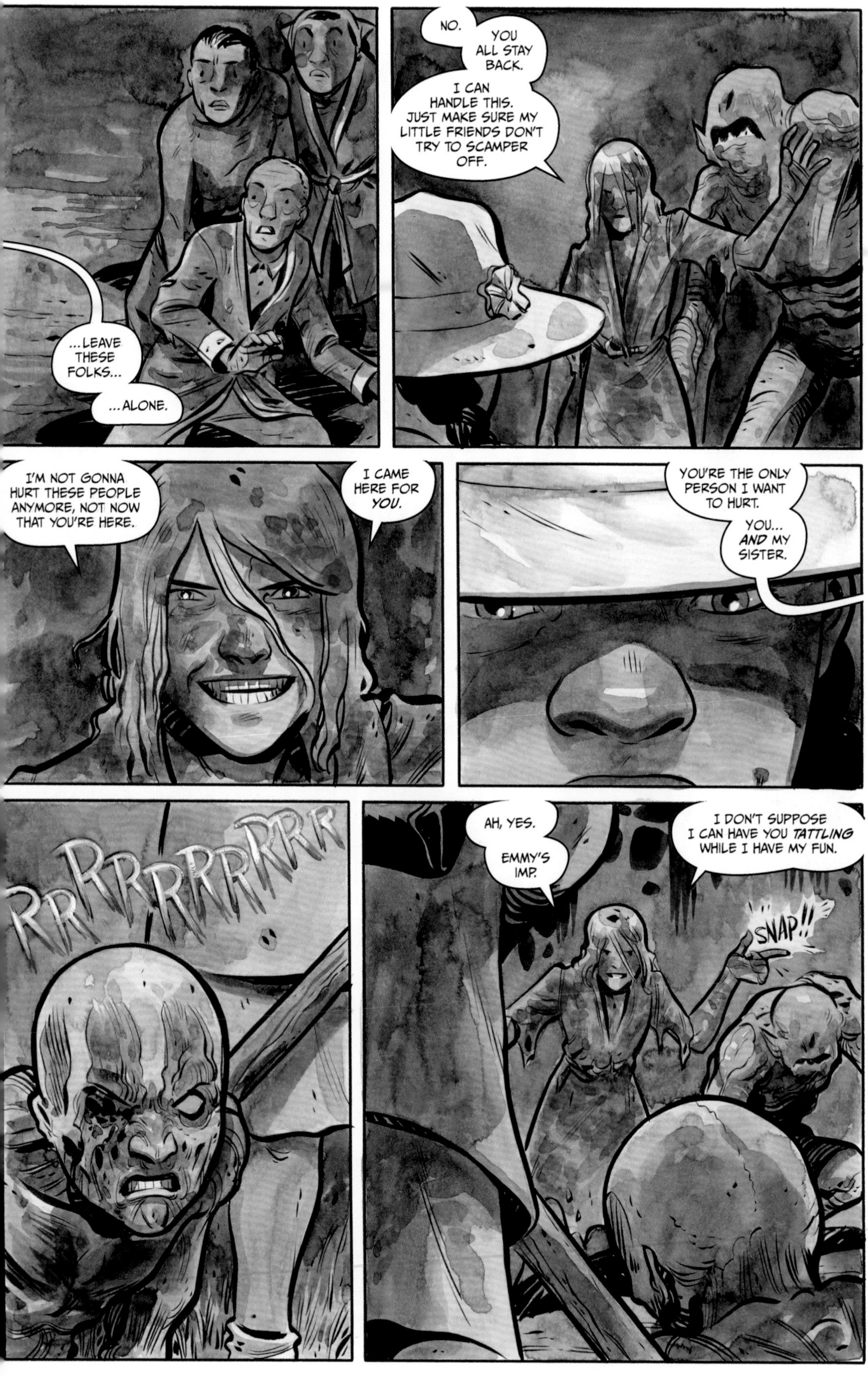
...LEAVE THESE FOLKS...
...ALONE.
NO.
YOU ALL STAY BACK.
I CAN HANDLE THIS. JUST MAKE SURE MY LITTLE FRIENDS DON'T TRY TO SCAMPER OFF.
I'M NOT GONNA HURT THESE PEOPLE ANYMORE, NOT NOW THAT YOU'RE HERE.
I CAME HERE FOR *YOU*.
YOU'RE THE ONLY PERSON I WANT TO HURT.
YOU... *AND* MY SISTER.
RRRRRRRRRRR
AH, YES.
EMMY'S IMP.
I DON'T SUPPOSE I CAN HAVE YOU *TATTLING* WHILE I HAVE MY FUN.
SNAP!!

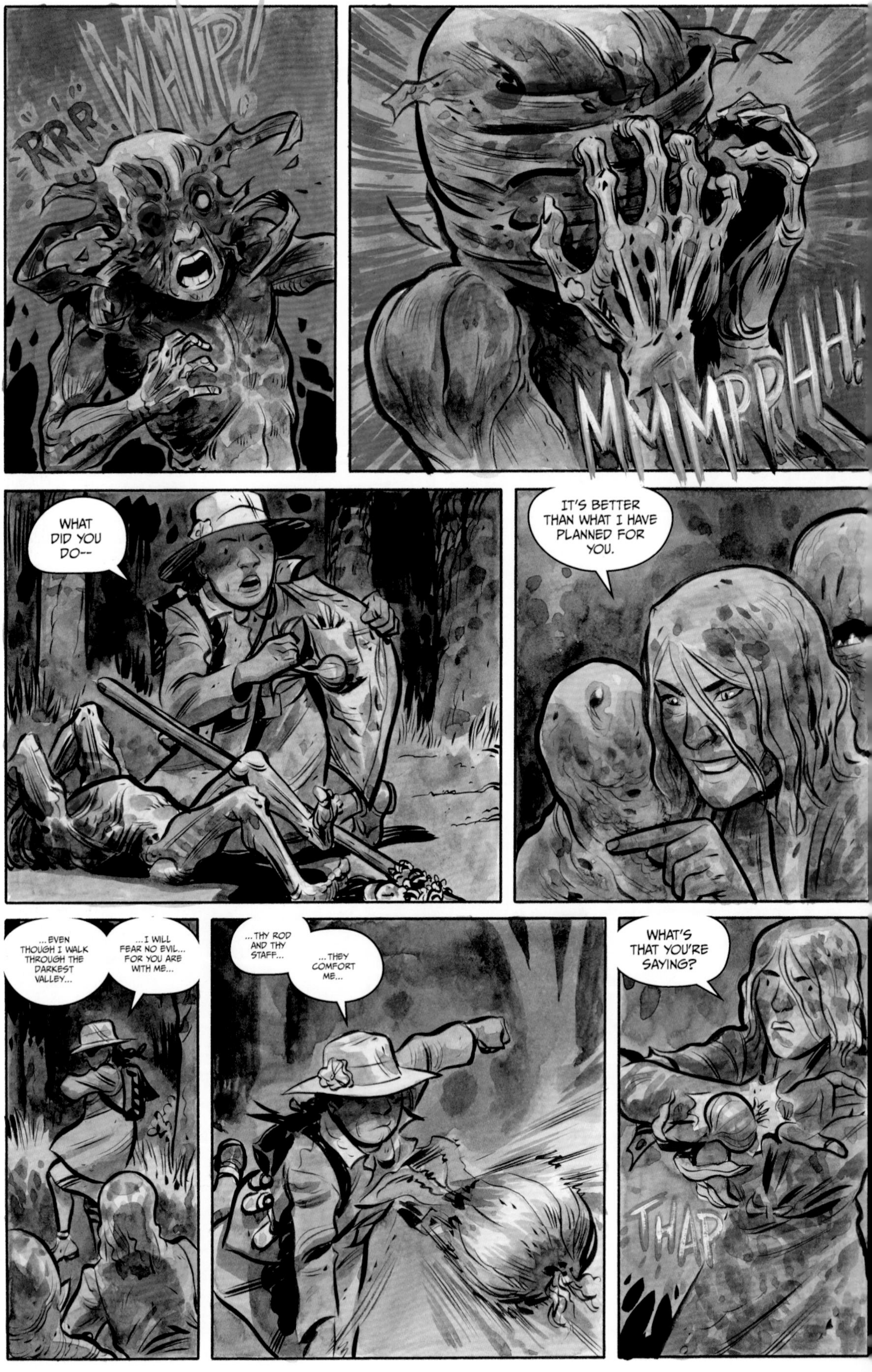
RRR
WHIP!
MMMPPHH!
WHAT DID YOU DO--
IT'S BETTER THAN WHAT I HAVE PLANNED FOR YOU.
...EVEN THOUGH I WALK THROUGH THE DARKEST VALLEY...
...I WILL FEAR NO EVIL... FOR YOU ARE WITH ME...
...THY ROD AND THY STAFF...
...THEY COMFORT ME...
WHAT'S THAT YOU'RE SAYING?
THAP

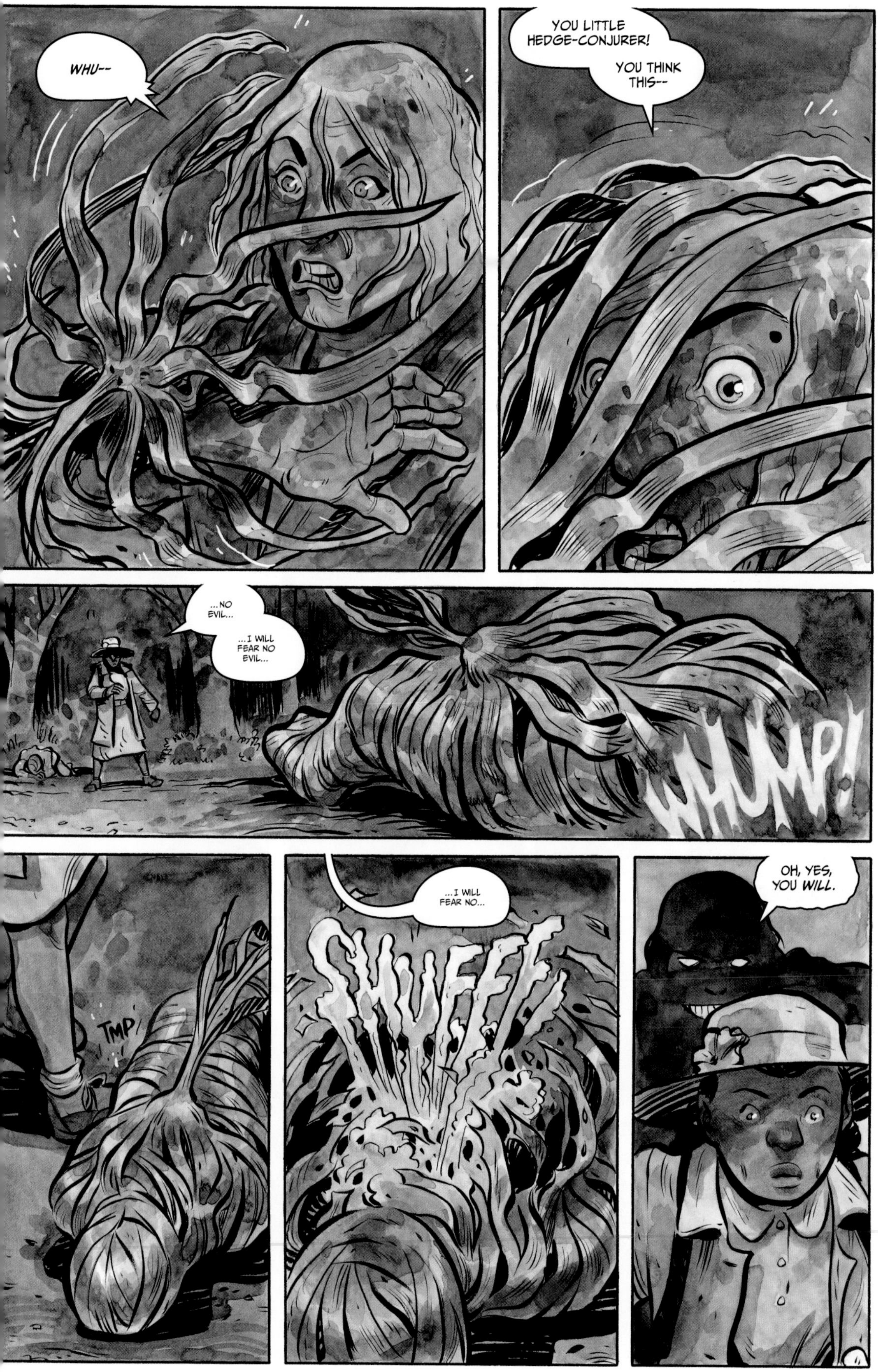
WHU--
YOU LITTLE HEDGE-CONJURER!
YOU THINK THIS--
...NO EVIL...
...I WILL FEAR NO EVIL...
WHUMP!
TMP
...I WILL FEAR NO...
SHUFF
OH, YES, YOU *WILL*.

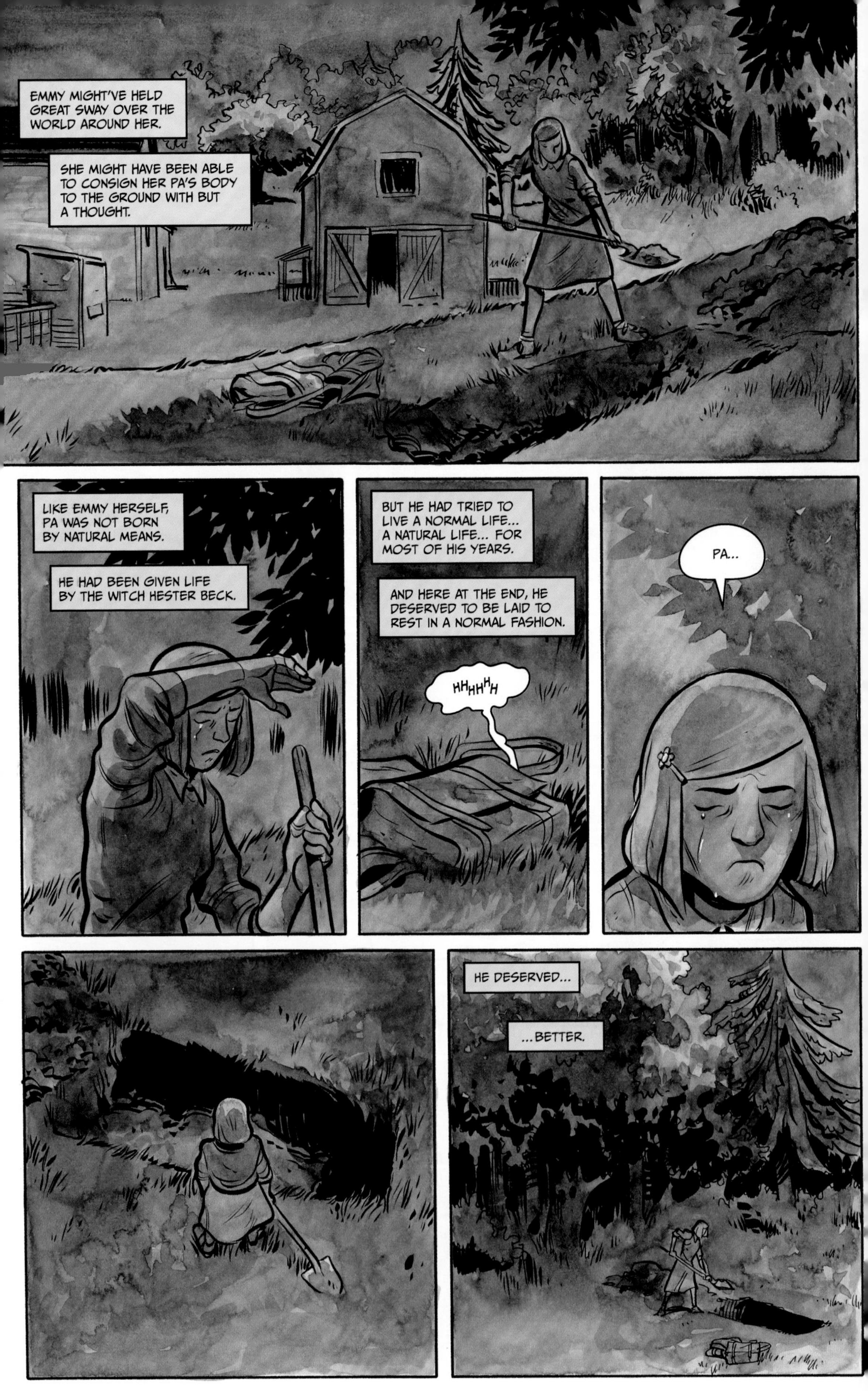
EMMY MIGHT'VE HELD GREAT SWAY OVER THE WORLD AROUND HER.
SHE MIGHT HAVE BEEN ABLE TO CONSIGN HER PA'S BODY TO THE GROUND WITH BUT A THOUGHT.
LIKE EMMY HERSELF, PA WAS NOT BORN BY NATURAL MEANS.
HE HAD BEEN GIVEN LIFE BY THE WITCH HESTER BECK.
BUT HE HAD TRIED TO LIVE A NORMAL LIFE... A NATURAL LIFE... FOR MOST OF HIS YEARS.
AND HERE AT THE END, HE DESERVED TO BE LAID TO REST IN A NORMAL FASHION.
HHHHHH
PA...
HE DESERVED...
...BETTER.

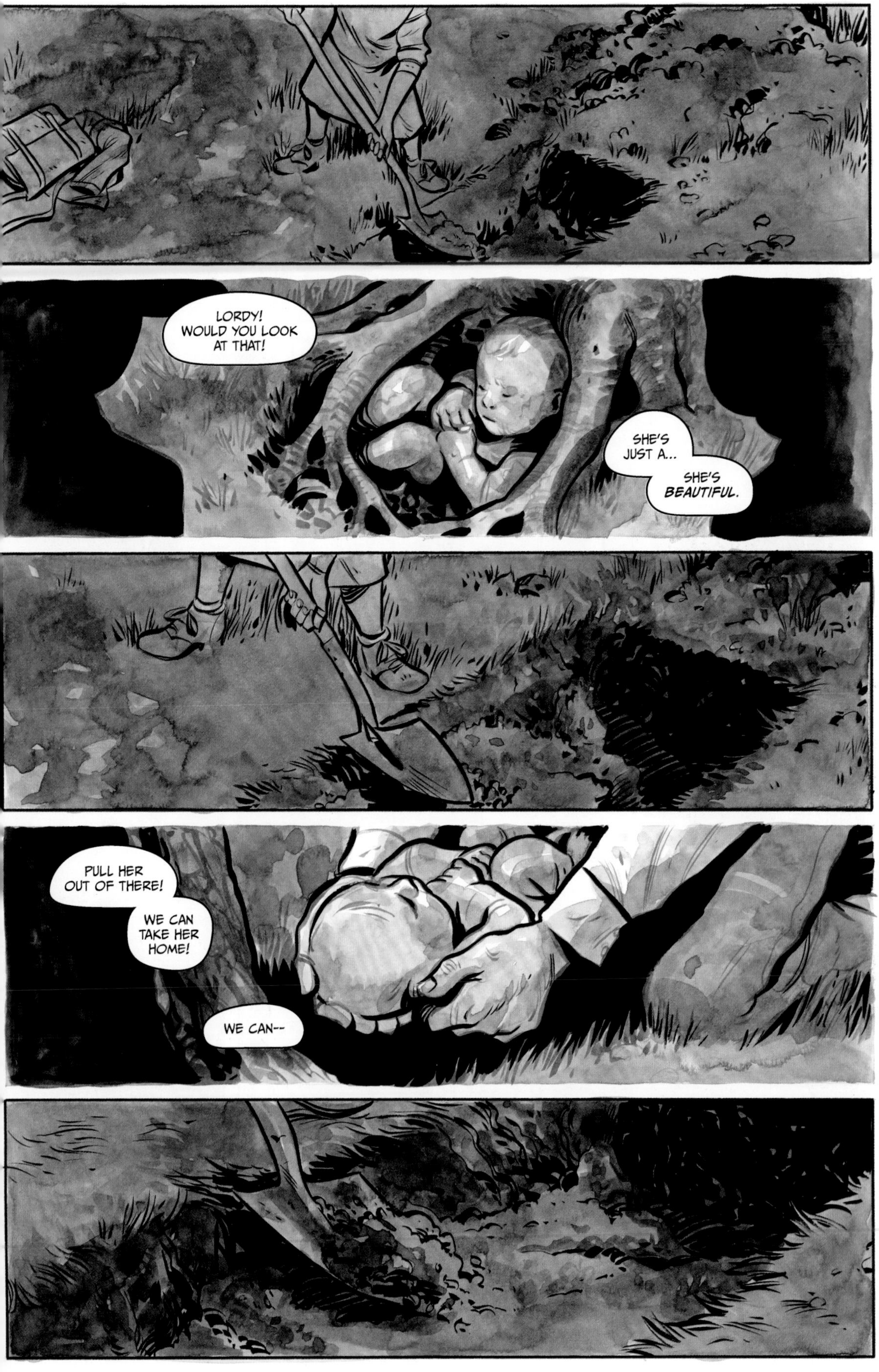
LORDY! WOULD YOU LOOK AT THAT!
SHE'S JUST A...
SHE'S *BEAUTIFUL.*
PULL HER OUT OF THERE!
WE CAN TAKE HER HOME!
WE CAN--

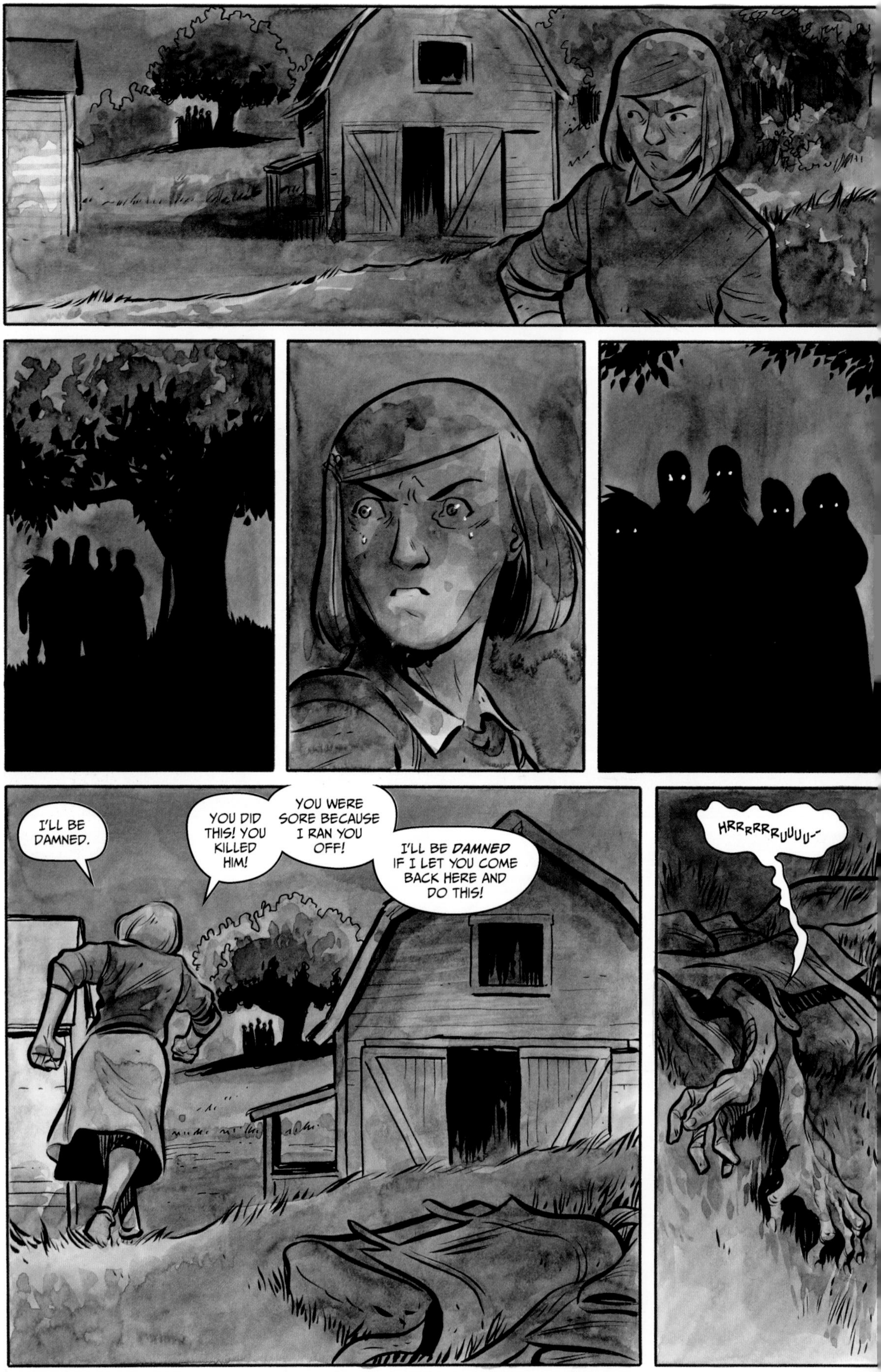
I'LL BE DAMNED.
YOU DID THIS! YOU KILLED HIM!
YOU WERE SORE BECAUSE I RAN YOU OFF!
I'LL BE *DAMNED* IF I LET YOU COME BACK HERE AND DO THIS!
HRRRRRRUUUU--

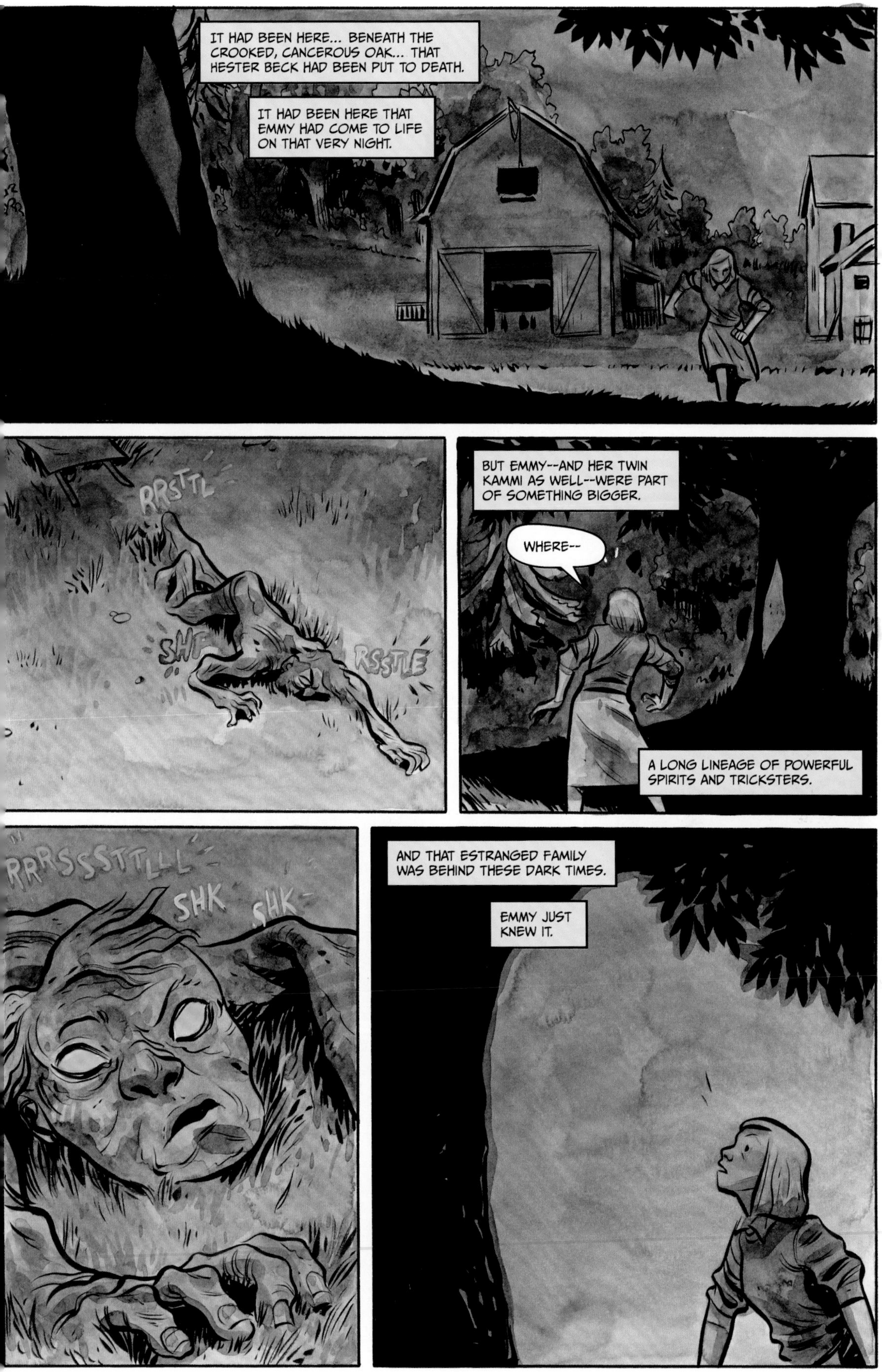
IT HAD BEEN HERE... BENEATH THE CROOKED, CANCEROUS OAK... THAT HESTER BECK HAD BEEN PUT TO DEATH.
IT HAD BEEN HERE THAT EMMY HAD COME TO LIFE ON THAT VERY NIGHT.
RRSTTL
SHF
RSSTLE
BUT EMMY--AND HER TWIN KAMMI AS WELL--WERE PART OF SOMETHING BIGGER.
WHERE--
A LONG LINEAGE OF POWERFUL SPIRITS AND TRICKSTERS.
RRRSSSTTLLL
SHK
SHK
AND THAT ESTRANGED FAMILY WAS BEHIND THESE DARK TIMES.
EMMY JUST KNEW IT.

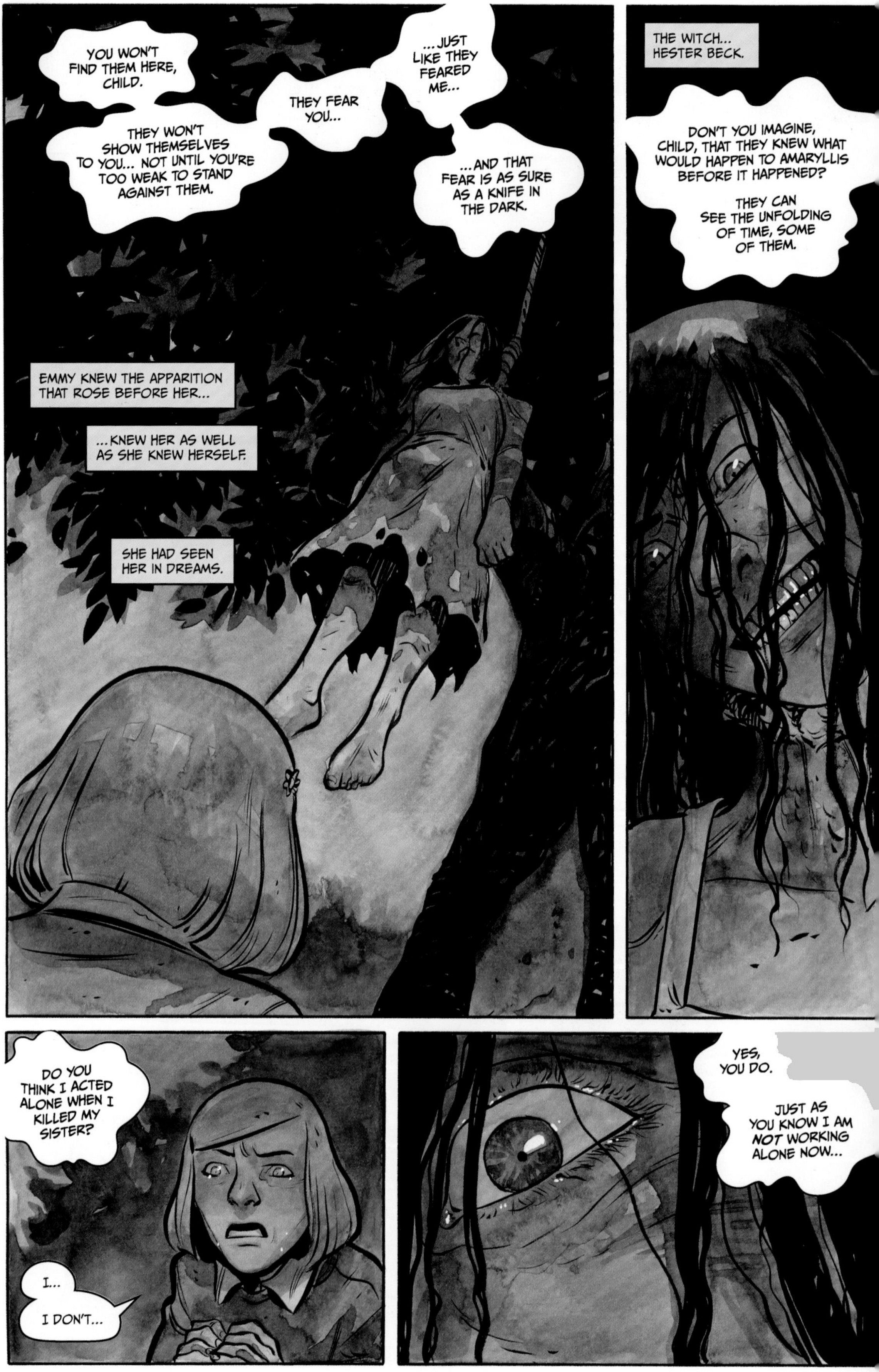
YOU WON'T FIND THEM HERE, CHILD.
THEY WON'T SHOW THEMSELVES TO YOU... NOT UNTIL YOU'RE TOO WEAK TO STAND AGAINST THEM.
THEY FEAR YOU...
...JUST LIKE THEY FEARED ME...
...AND THAT FEAR IS AS SURE AS A KNIFE IN THE DARK.
EMMY KNEW THE APPARITION THAT ROSE BEFORE HER...
...KNEW HER AS WELL AS SHE KNEW HERSELF.
SHE HAD SEEN HER IN DREAMS.
THE WITCH... HESTER BECK.
DON'T YOU IMAGINE, CHILD, THAT THEY KNEW WHAT WOULD HAPPEN TO AMARYLLIS BEFORE IT HAPPENED?
THEY CAN SEE THE UNFOLDING OF TIME, SOME OF THEM.
DO YOU THINK I ACTED ALONE WHEN I KILLED MY SISTER?
I...
I DON'T...
YES, YOU DO.
JUST AS YOU KNOW I AM *NOT* WORKING ALONE NOW...

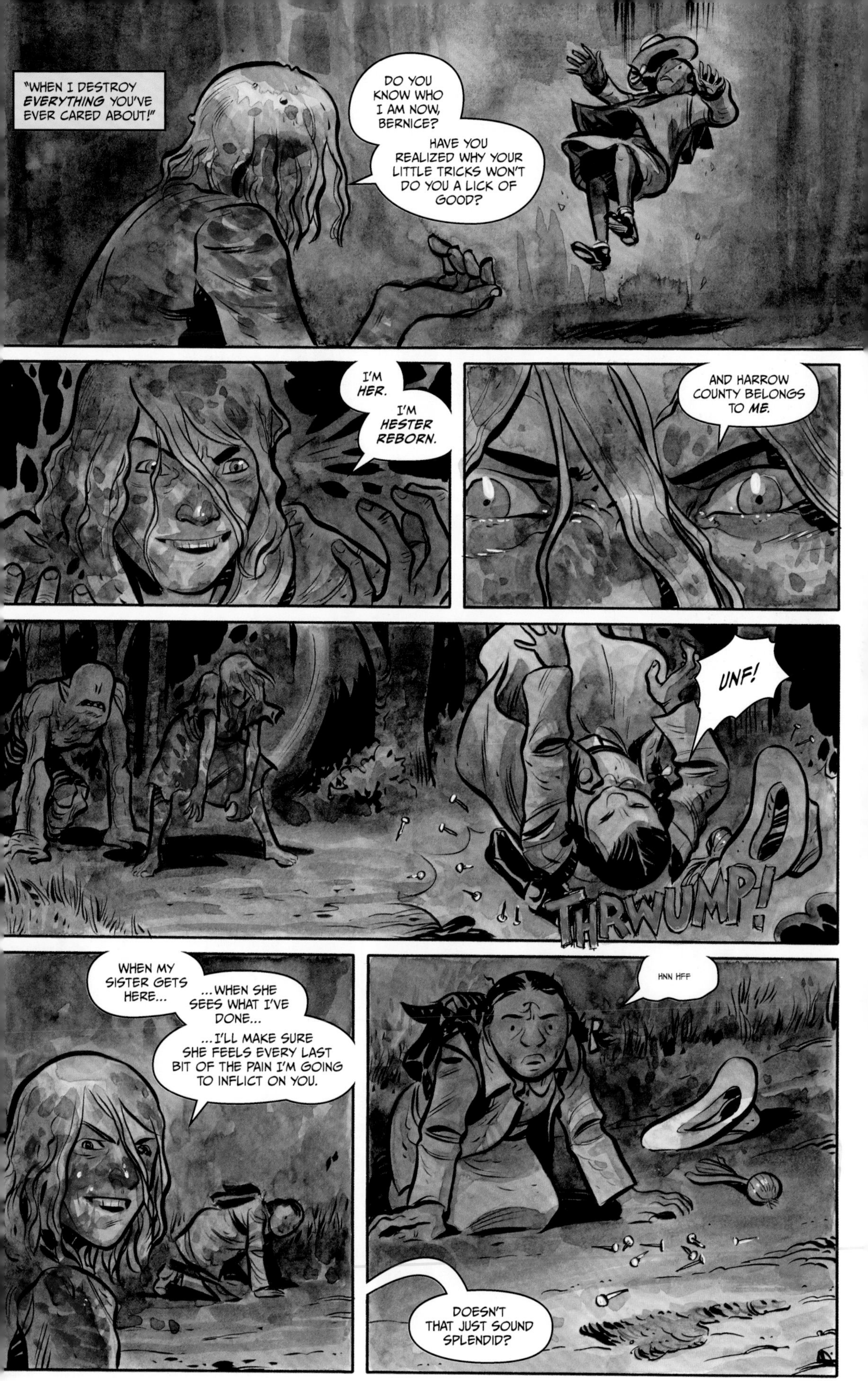
"WHEN I DESTROY *EVERYTHING* YOU'VE EVER CARED ABOUT!"
DO YOU KNOW WHO I AM NOW, BERNICE?
HAVE YOU REALIZED WHY YOUR LITTLE TRICKS WON'T DO YOU A LICK OF GOOD?
I'M *HER*.
I'M *HESTER REBORN*.
AND HARROW COUNTY BELONGS TO *ME*.
UNF!
THRWUMP!
WHEN MY SISTER GETS HERE...
...WHEN SHE SEES WHAT I'VE DONE...
...I'LL MAKE SURE SHE FEELS EVERY LAST BIT OF THE PAIN I'M GOING TO INFLICT ON YOU.
HNN HFF
DOESN'T THAT JUST SOUND SPLENDID?

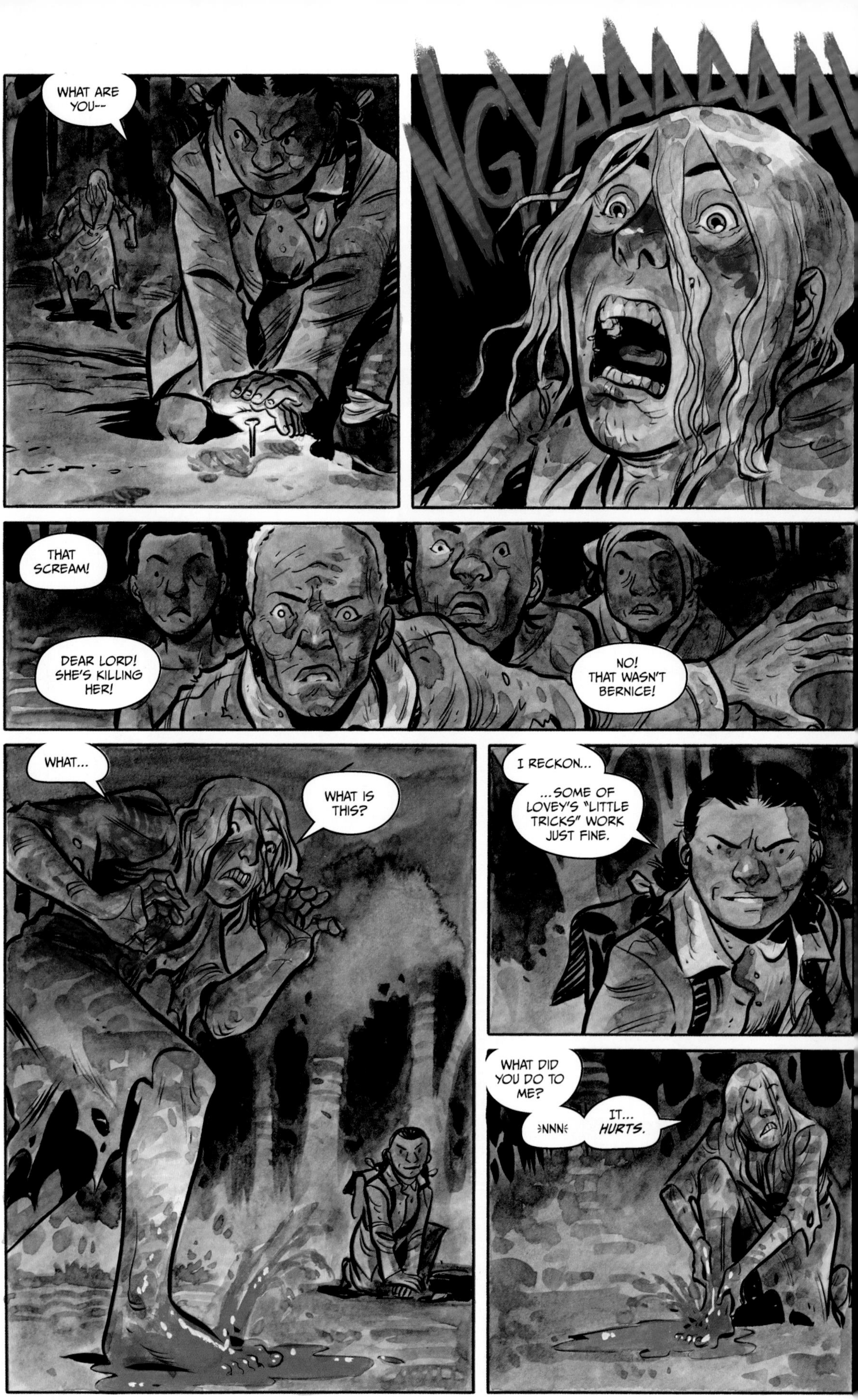
WHAT ARE YOU--
NGYAAAAAA
THAT SCREAM!
DEAR LORD! SHE'S KILLING HER!
NO! THAT WASN'T BERNICE!
WHAT...
WHAT IS THIS?
I RECKON...
...SOME OF LOVEY'S "LITTLE TRICKS" WORK JUST FINE.
WHAT DID YOU DO TO ME?
NNN
IT... *HURTS*.

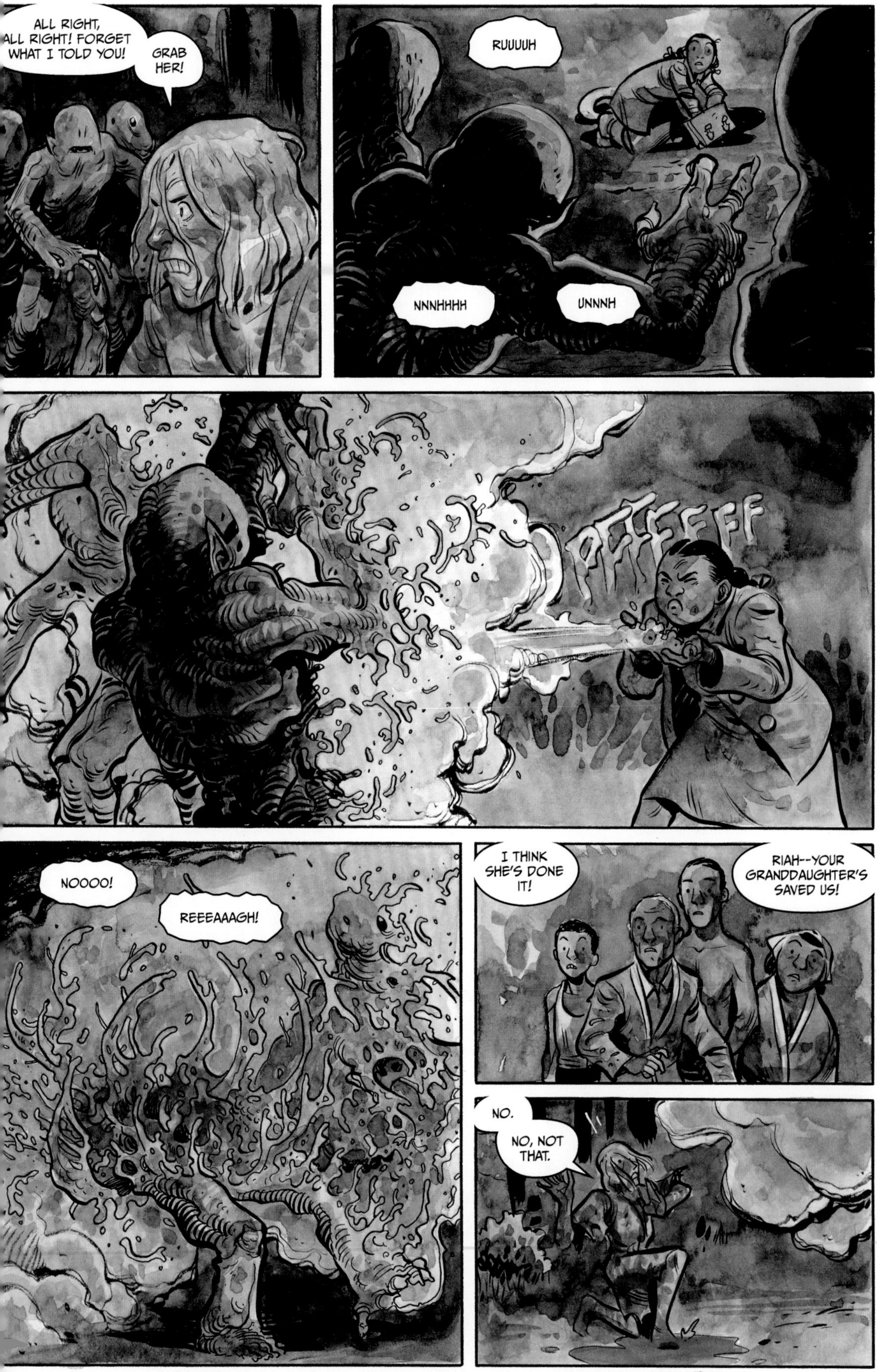
ALL RIGHT, ALL RIGHT! FORGET WHAT I TOLD YOU!
GRAB HER!
RUUUUH
NNNHHHH
UNNNH
PFFFFFF
NOOOO!
REEEAAAGH!
I THINK SHE'S DONE IT!
RIAH--YOUR GRANDDAUGHTER'S SAVED US!
NO.
NO, NOT THAT.

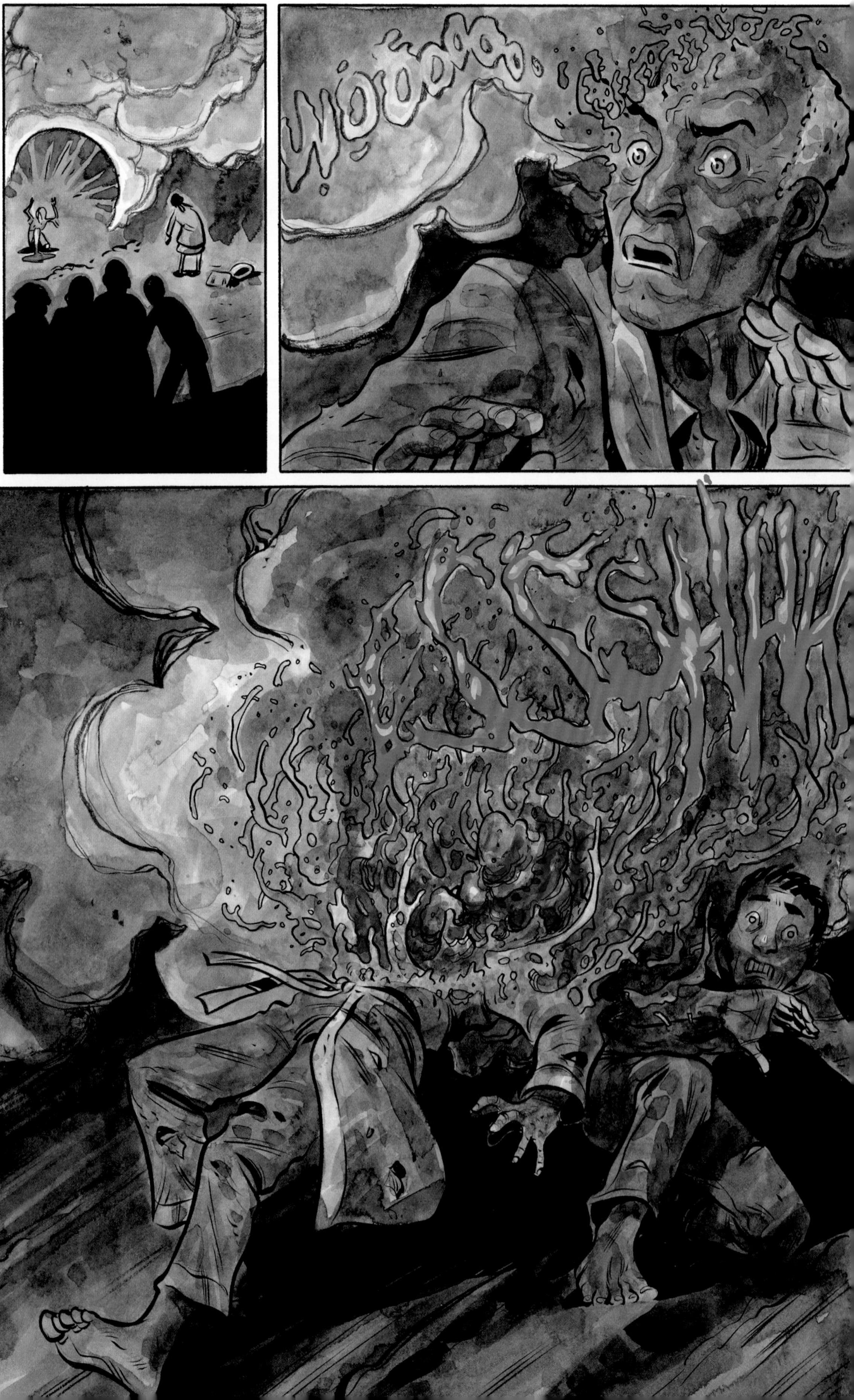
WOOOOOOO

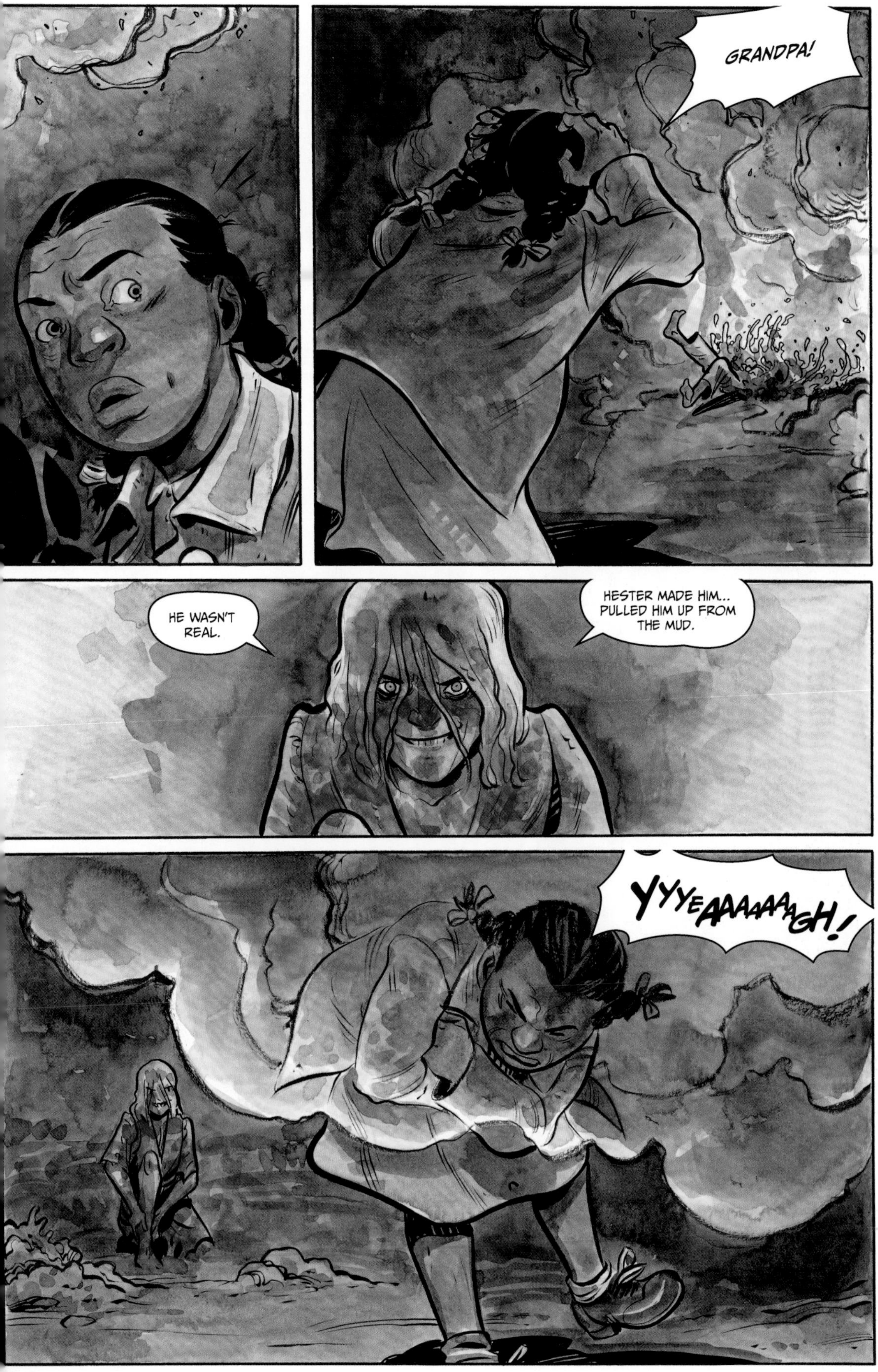
GRANDPA!
HE WASN'T REAL.
HESTER MADE HIM... PULLED HIM UP FROM THE MUD.
YYYEAAAAAAAGH!

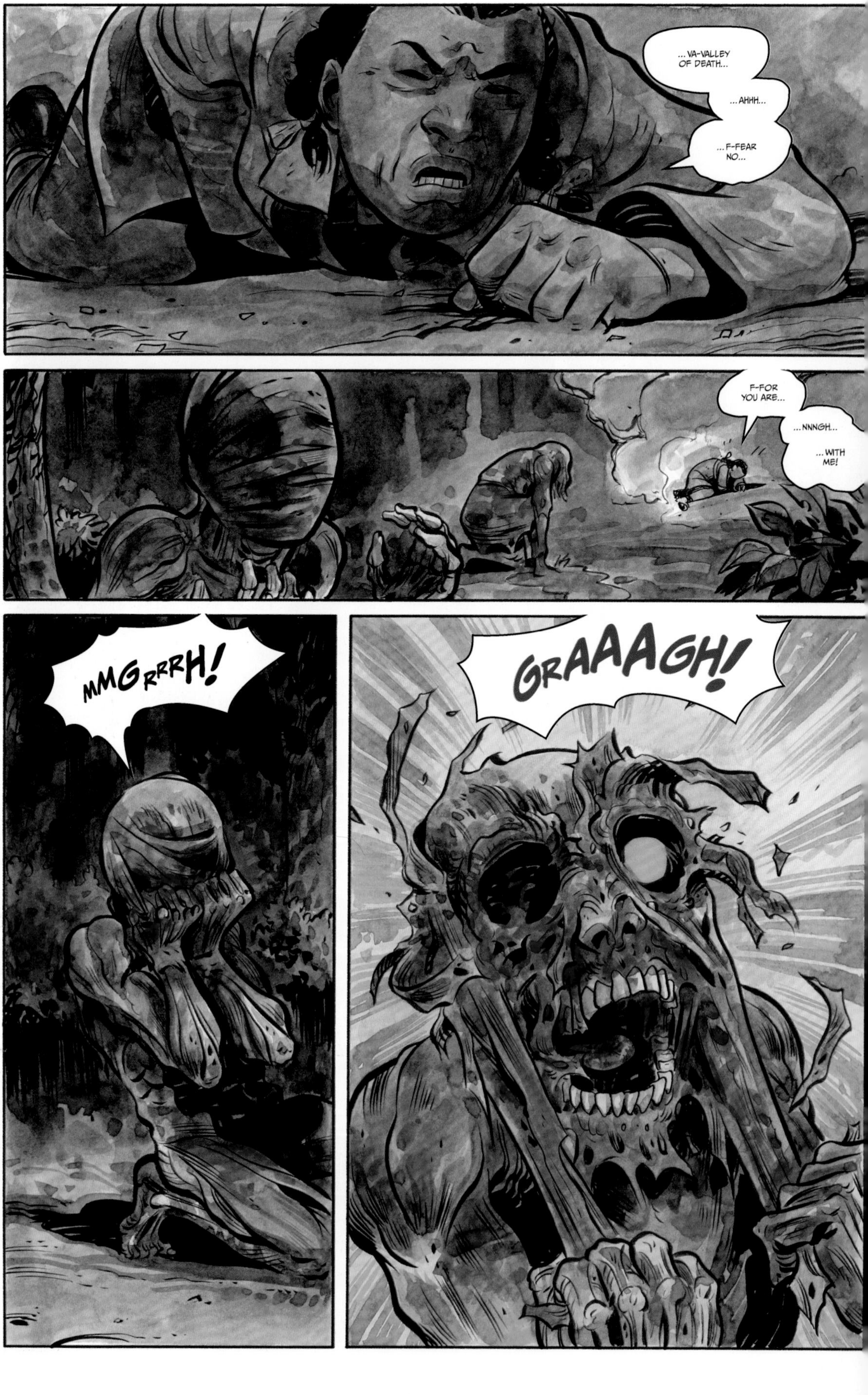
...VA-VALLEY OF DEATH...
...AHHH...
...F-FEAR NO...
F-FOR YOU ARE...
...NNNGH...
...WITH ME!
MMGRRRH!
GRAAAGH!

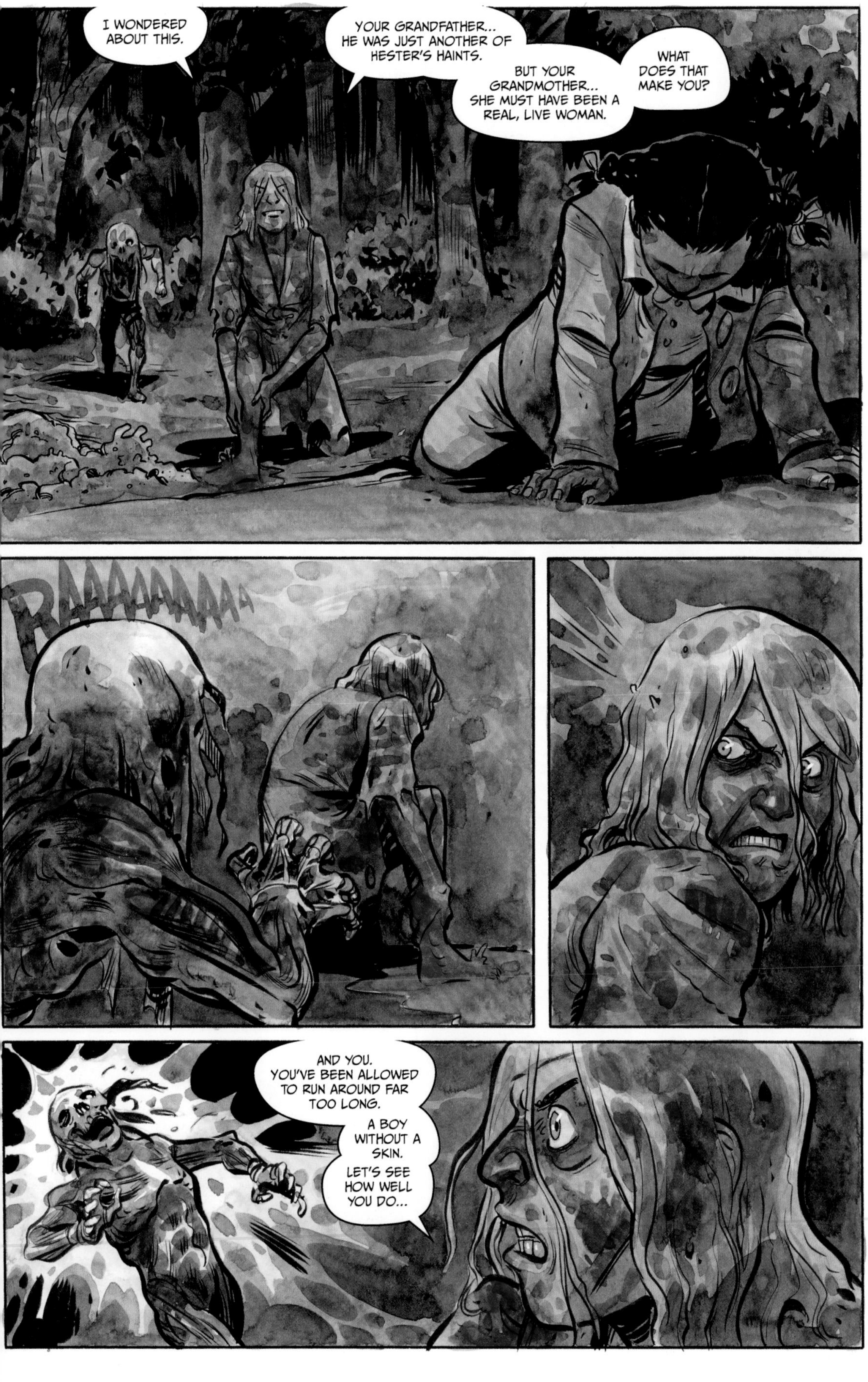
I WONDERED ABOUT THIS.
YOUR GRANDFATHER... HE WAS JUST ANOTHER OF HESTER'S HAINTS.
BUT YOUR GRANDMOTHER... SHE MUST HAVE BEEN A REAL, LIVE WOMAN.
WHAT DOES THAT MAKE YOU?
RAAAAAAAAa
AND YOU. YOU'VE BEEN ALLOWED TO RUN AROUND FAR TOO LONG.
A BOY WITHOUT A SKIN.
LET'S SEE HOW WELL YOU DO...

...WITHOUT BONES!

GRRRKKSSSSHAK

GLORSLUP

SPLOOOSH

"DON'T TELL ME ABOUT BEING AFRAID."

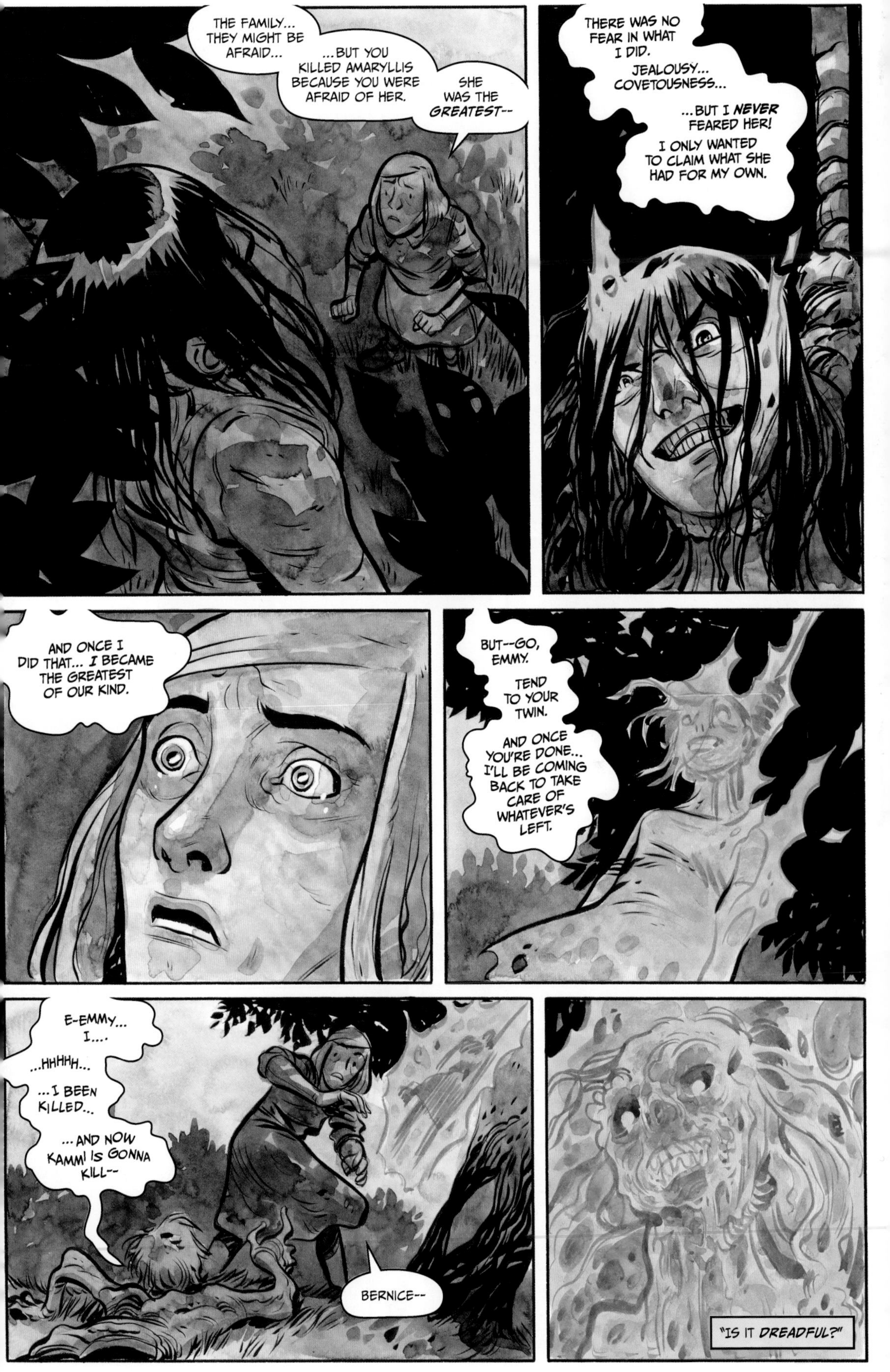
THE FAMILY... THEY MIGHT BE AFRAID...
...BUT YOU KILLED AMARYLLIS BECAUSE YOU WERE AFRAID OF HER.
SHE WAS THE *GREATEST*--
THERE WAS NO FEAR IN WHAT I DID.
JEALOUSY... COVETOUSNESS...
...BUT I *NEVER* FEARED HER!
I ONLY WANTED TO CLAIM WHAT SHE HAD FOR MY OWN.
AND ONCE I DID THAT... I BECAME THE GREATEST OF OUR KIND.
BUT--GO, EMMY.
TEND TO YOUR TWIN.
AND ONCE YOU'RE DONE... I'LL BE COMING BACK TO TAKE CARE OF WHATEVER'S LEFT.
E-EMMY... I....
...HHHHH...
...I BEEN KILLED...
...AND NOW KAMMI IS GONNA KILL--
BERNICE--
"IS IT *DREADFUL?*"

I CAN ONLY IMAGINE THAT IT IS.

BEING HALF FLESH AND HALF HAINT.

NOW I'VE SET THE TWO PARTS OF YOU AGAINST ONE ANOTHER.

NNNGGH!

AAAGH!

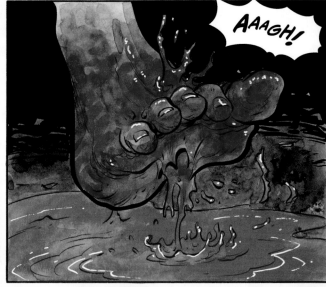

THE HAINT PART OF YOU...

...IT'S SO HUNGRY...

...GONNA EAT WHAT'S REAL.

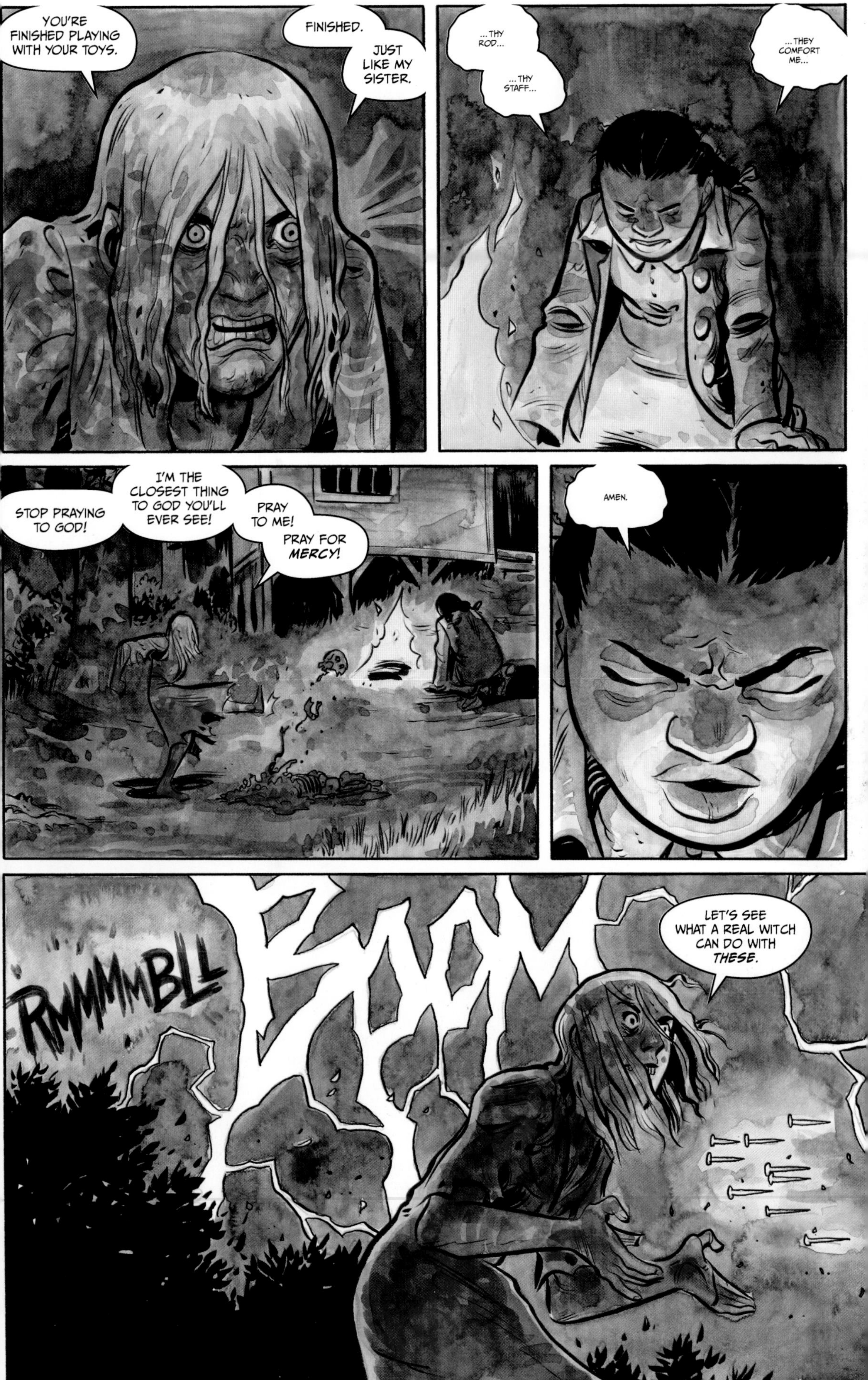
YOU'RE FINISHED PLAYING WITH YOUR TOYS.
FINISHED.
JUST LIKE MY SISTER.
...THY ROD...
...THY STAFF...
...THEY COMFORT ME...
STOP PRAYING TO GOD!
I'M THE CLOSEST THING TO GOD YOU'LL EVER SEE!
PRAY TO ME!
PRAY FOR *MERCY*!
AMEN.
RMMMMBLL
BOOM
LET'S SEE WHAT A REAL WITCH CAN DO WITH *THESE*.

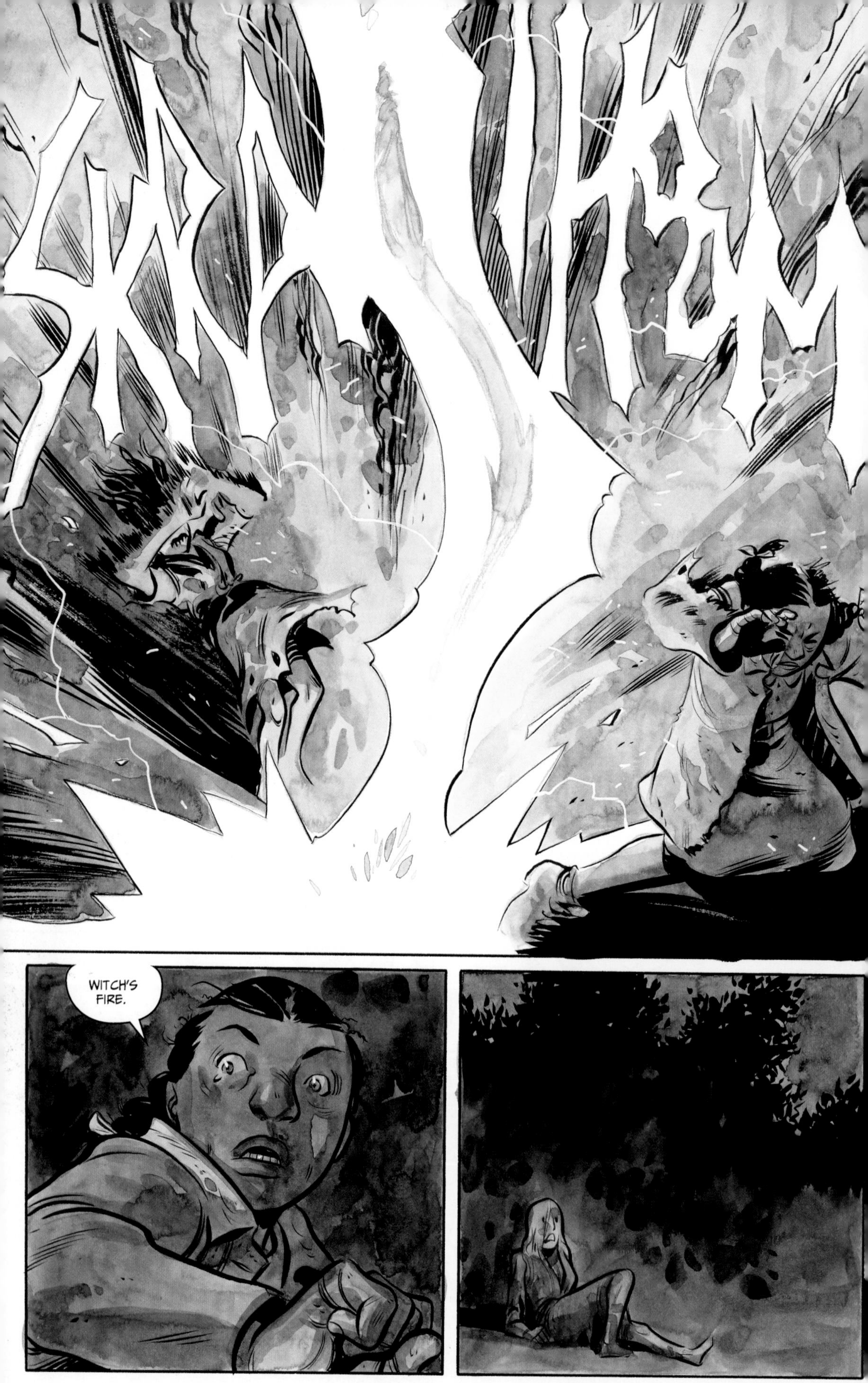
WITCH'S FIRE.

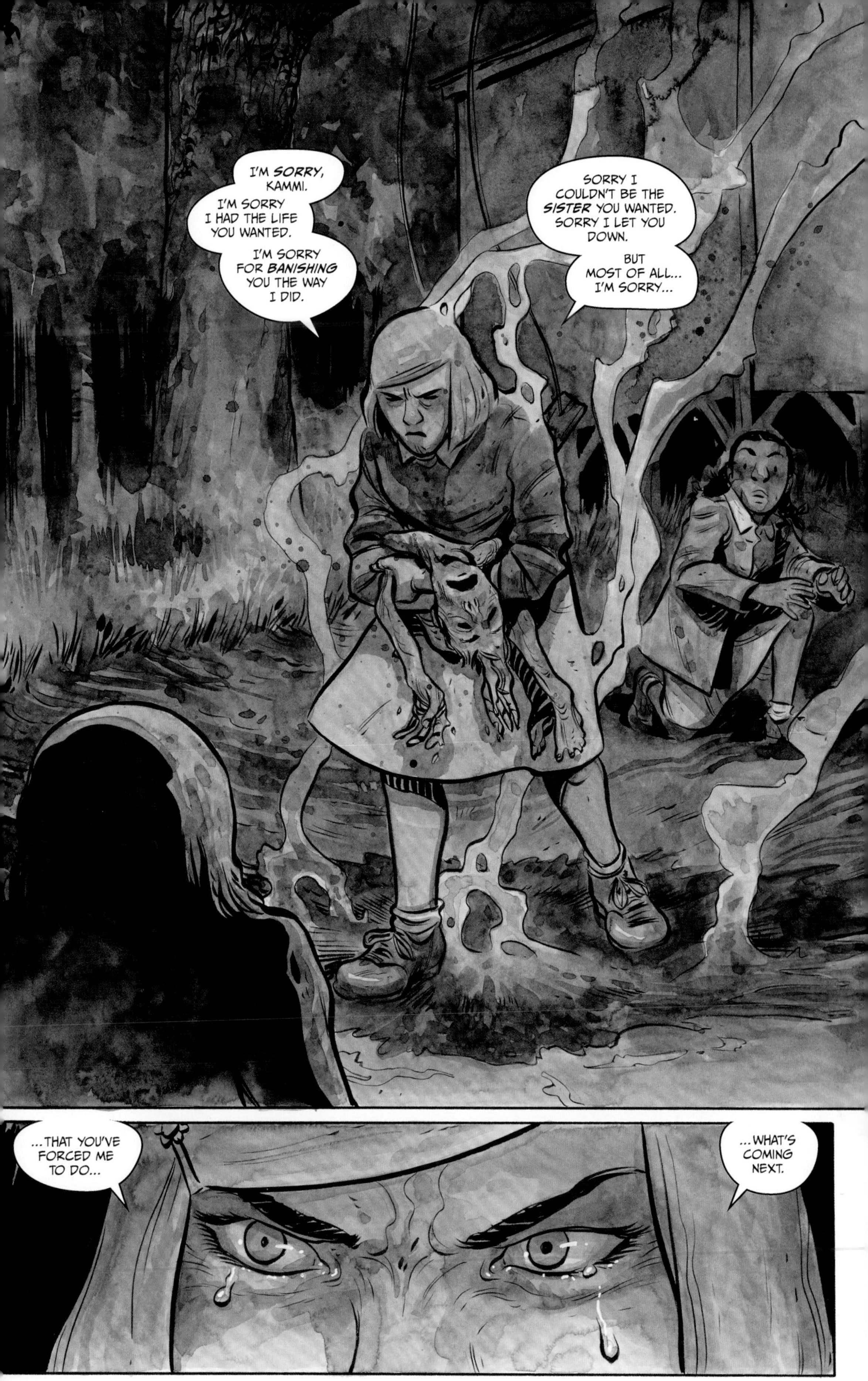
I'M SORRY, KAMMI.
I'M SORRY I HAD THE LIFE YOU WANTED.
I'M SORRY FOR BANISHING YOU THE WAY I DID.
SORRY I COULDN'T BE THE SISTER YOU WANTED. SORRY I LET YOU DOWN.
BUT MOST OF ALL... I'M SORRY...
...THAT YOU'VE FORCED ME TO DO...
...WHAT'S COMING NEXT.

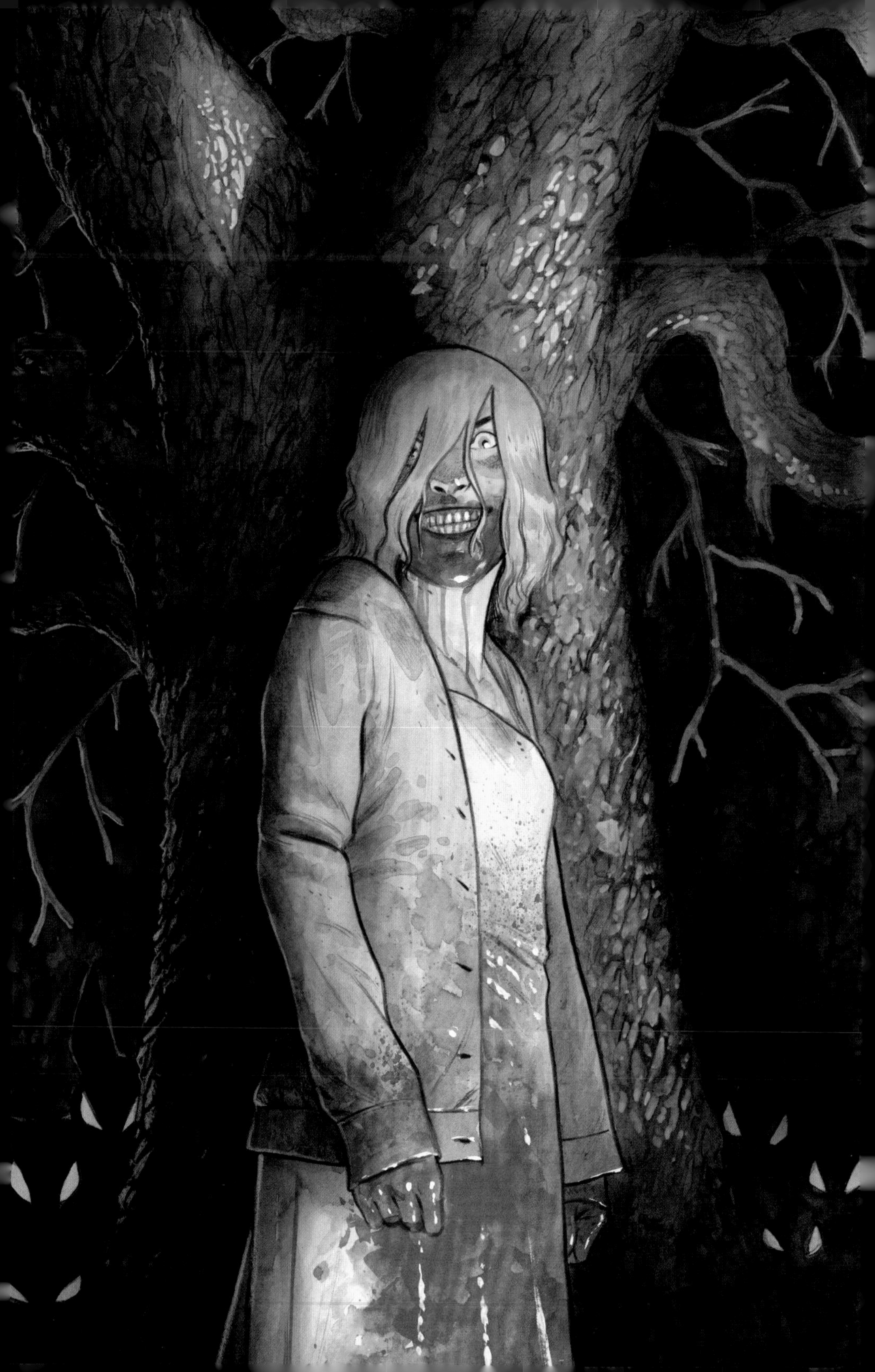

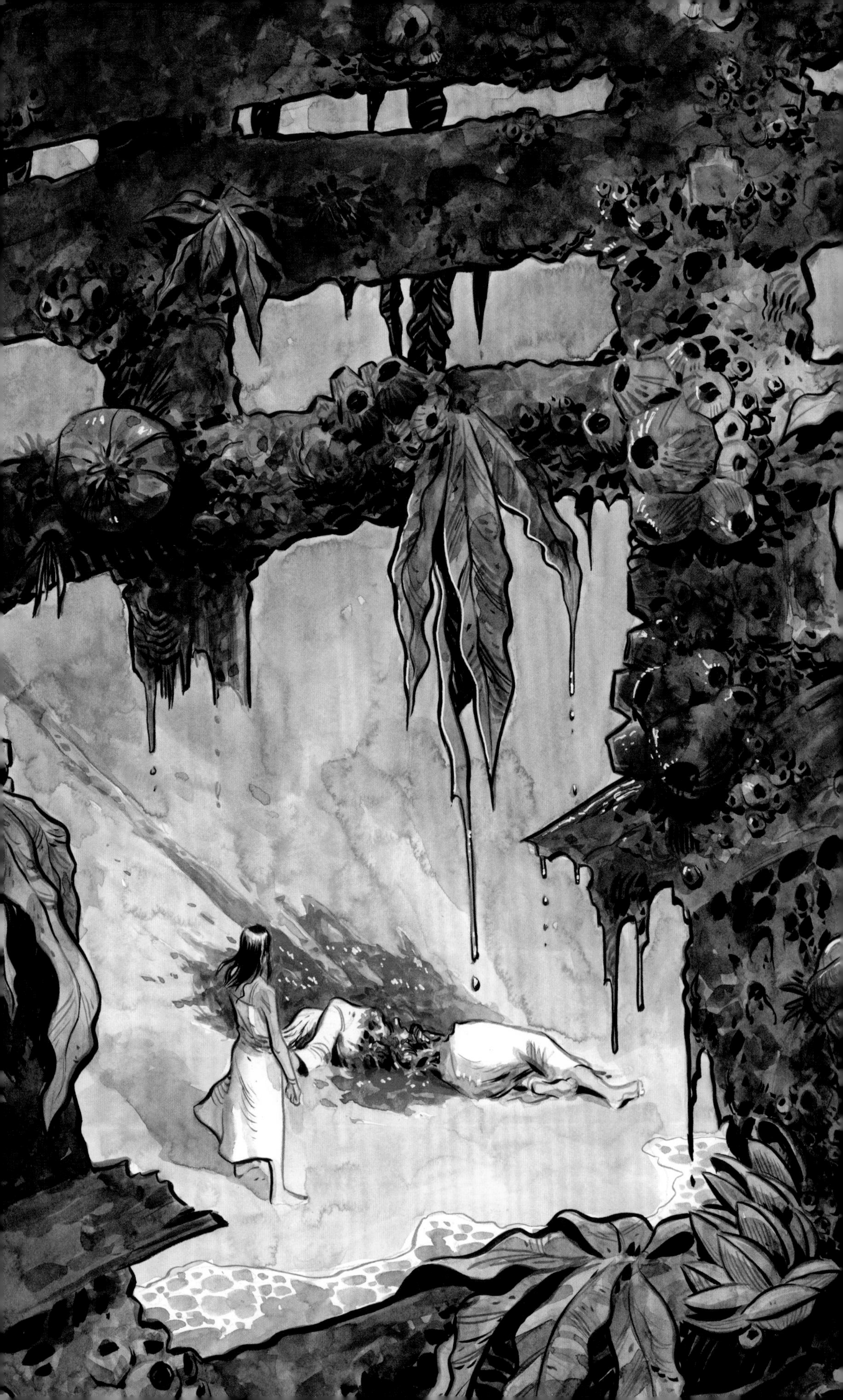

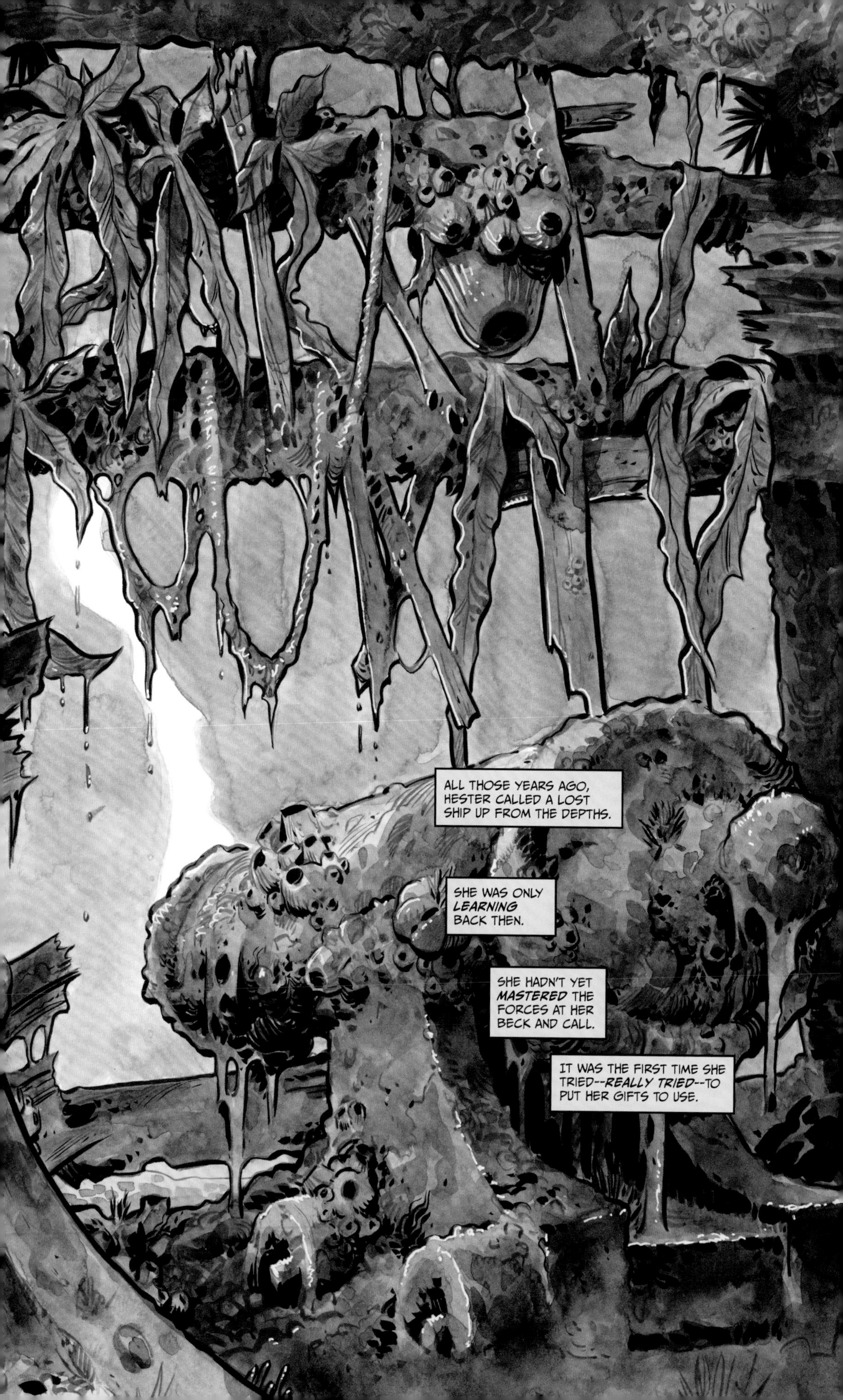
ALL THOSE YEARS AGO, HESTER CALLED A LOST SHIP UP FROM THE DEPTHS.
SHE WAS ONLY *LEARNING* BACK THEN.
SHE HADN'T YET *MASTERED* THE FORCES AT HER BECK AND CALL.
IT WAS THE FIRST TIME SHE TRIED--*REALLY TRIED*--TO PUT HER GIFTS TO USE.

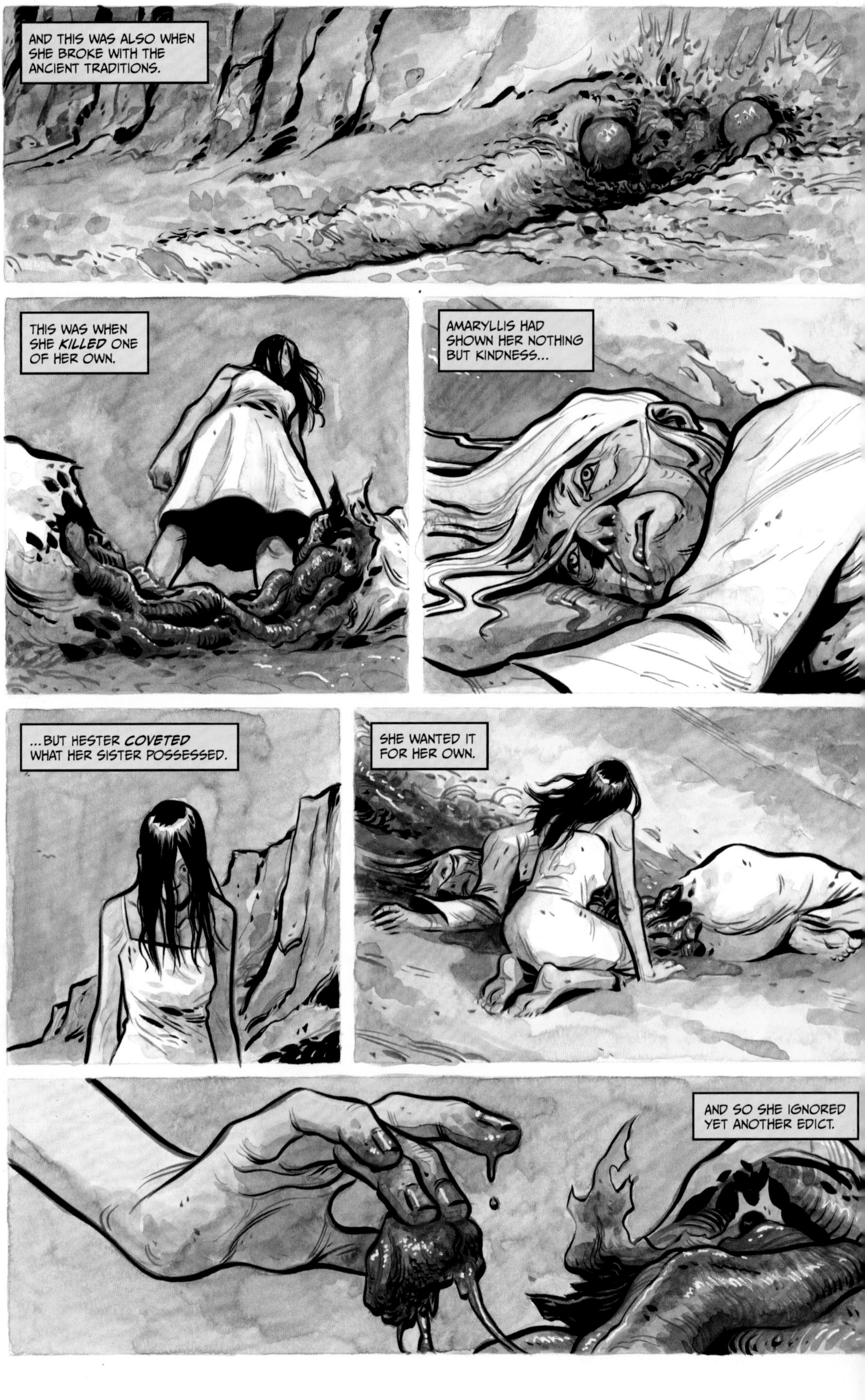
AND THIS WAS ALSO WHEN SHE BROKE WITH THE ANCIENT TRADITIONS.
THIS WAS WHEN SHE *KILLED* ONE OF HER OWN.
AMARYLLIS HAD SHOWN HER NOTHING BUT KINDNESS...
...BUT HESTER *COVETED* WHAT HER SISTER POSSESSED.
SHE WANTED IT FOR HER OWN.
AND SO SHE IGNORED YET ANOTHER EDICT.

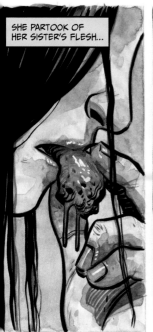

SHE PARTOOK OF HER SISTER'S FLESH...

MM.

NNNMMM!

MMMMMM!

...AND CLAIMED AMARYLLIS'S POWER AS HER OWN.

"I CONSIDERED LETTING YOU LIVE..."

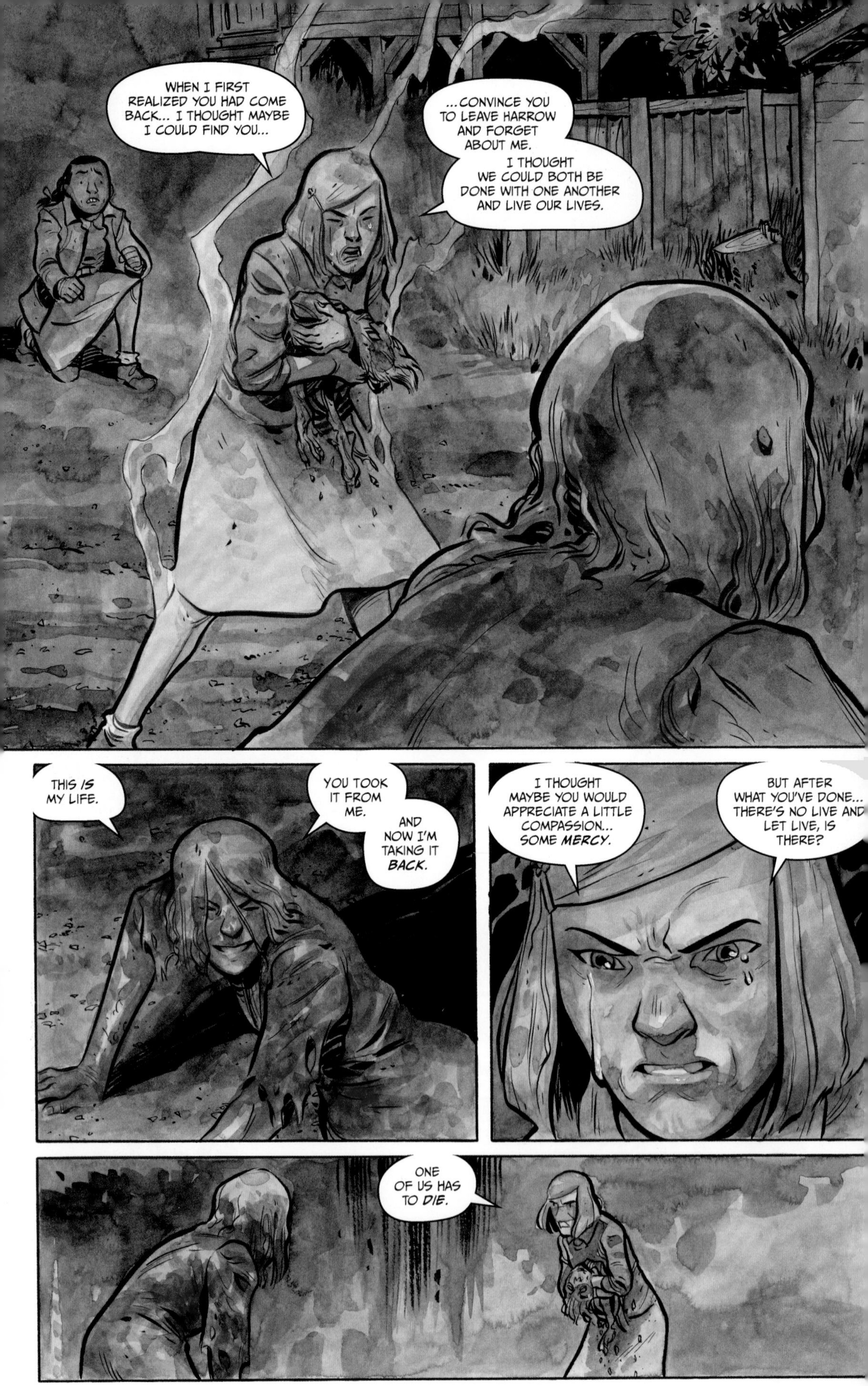

WHEN I FIRST REALIZED YOU HAD COME BACK... I THOUGHT MAYBE I COULD FIND YOU...
...CONVINCE YOU TO LEAVE HARROW AND FORGET ABOUT ME.
I THOUGHT WE COULD BOTH BE DONE WITH ONE ANOTHER AND LIVE OUR LIVES.
THIS *IS* MY LIFE.
YOU TOOK IT FROM ME.
AND NOW I'M TAKING IT *BACK*.
I THOUGHT MAYBE YOU WOULD APPRECIATE A LITTLE COMPASSION... SOME *MERCY*.
BUT AFTER WHAT YOU'VE DONE... THERE'S NO LIVE AND LET LIVE, IS THERE?
ONE OF US HAS TO *DIE*.

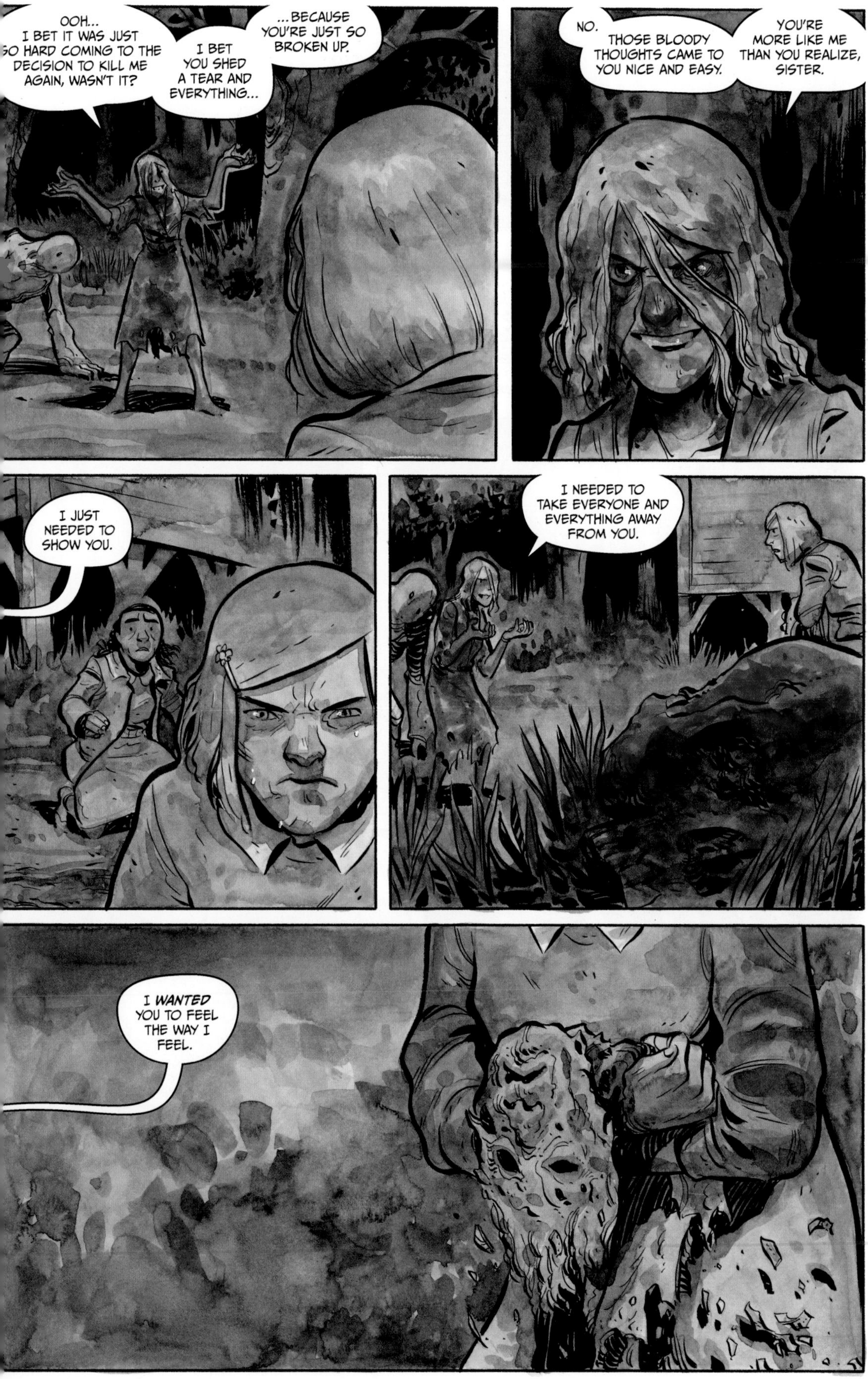
OOH... I BET IT WAS JUST SO HARD COMING TO THE DECISION TO KILL ME AGAIN, WASN'T IT?
I BET YOU SHED A TEAR AND EVERYTHING...
...BECAUSE YOU'RE JUST SO BROKEN UP.
NO.
THOSE BLOODY THOUGHTS CAME TO YOU NICE AND EASY.
YOU'RE MORE LIKE ME THAN YOU REALIZE, SISTER.
I JUST NEEDED TO SHOW YOU.
I NEEDED TO TAKE EVERYONE AND EVERYTHING AWAY FROM YOU.
I *WANTED* YOU TO FEEL THE WAY I FEEL.

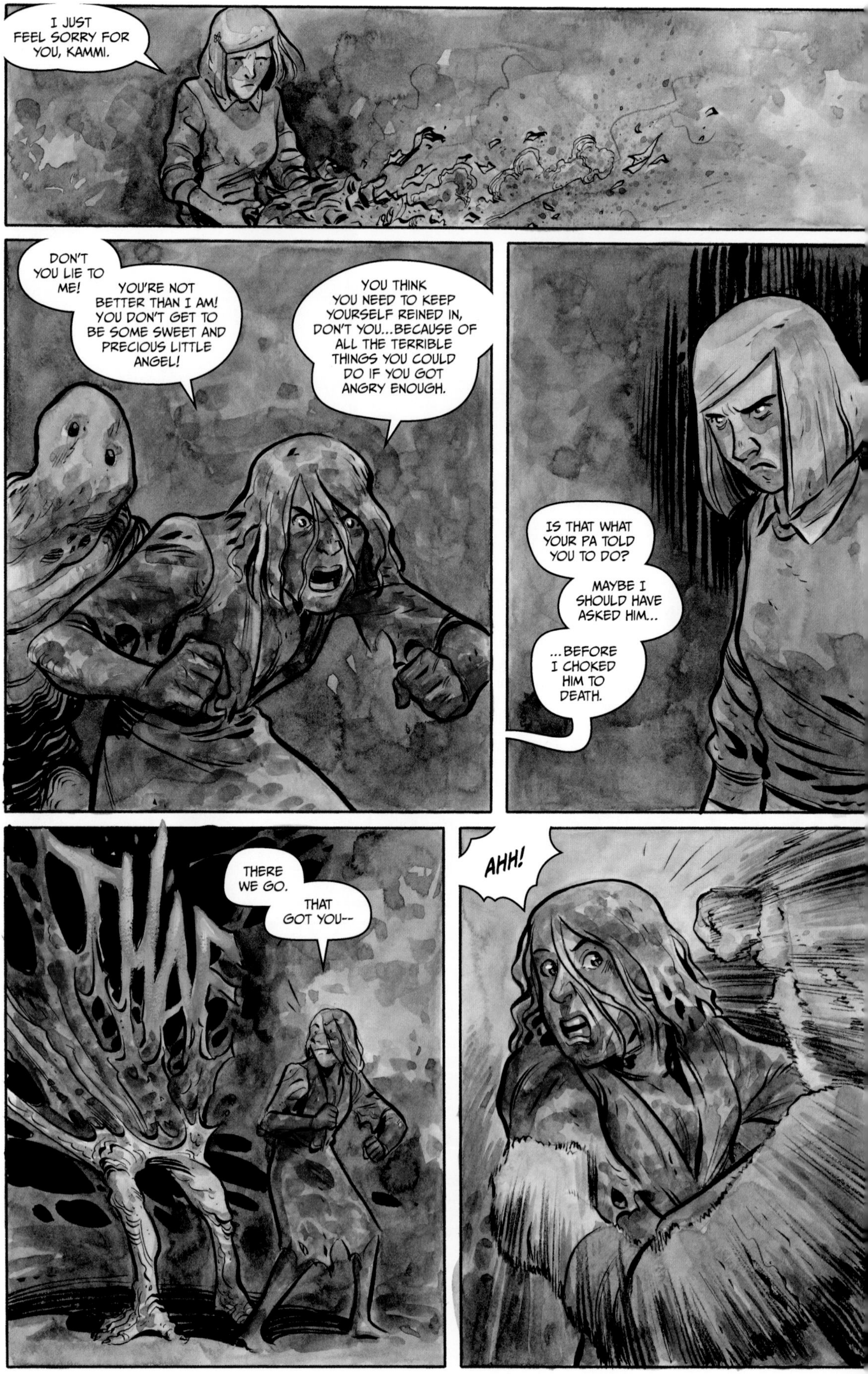

I JUST FEEL SORRY FOR YOU, KAMMI.
DON'T YOU LIE TO ME!
YOU'RE NOT BETTER THAN I AM! YOU DON'T GET TO BE SOME SWEET AND PRECIOUS LITTLE ANGEL!
YOU THINK YOU NEED TO KEEP YOURSELF REINED IN, DON'T YOU...BECAUSE OF ALL THE TERRIBLE THINGS YOU COULD DO IF YOU GOT ANGRY ENOUGH.
IS THAT WHAT YOUR PA TOLD YOU TO DO?
MAYBE I SHOULD HAVE ASKED HIM...
...BEFORE I CHOKED HIM TO DEATH.
THAK
THERE WE GO.
THAT GOT YOU--
AHH!

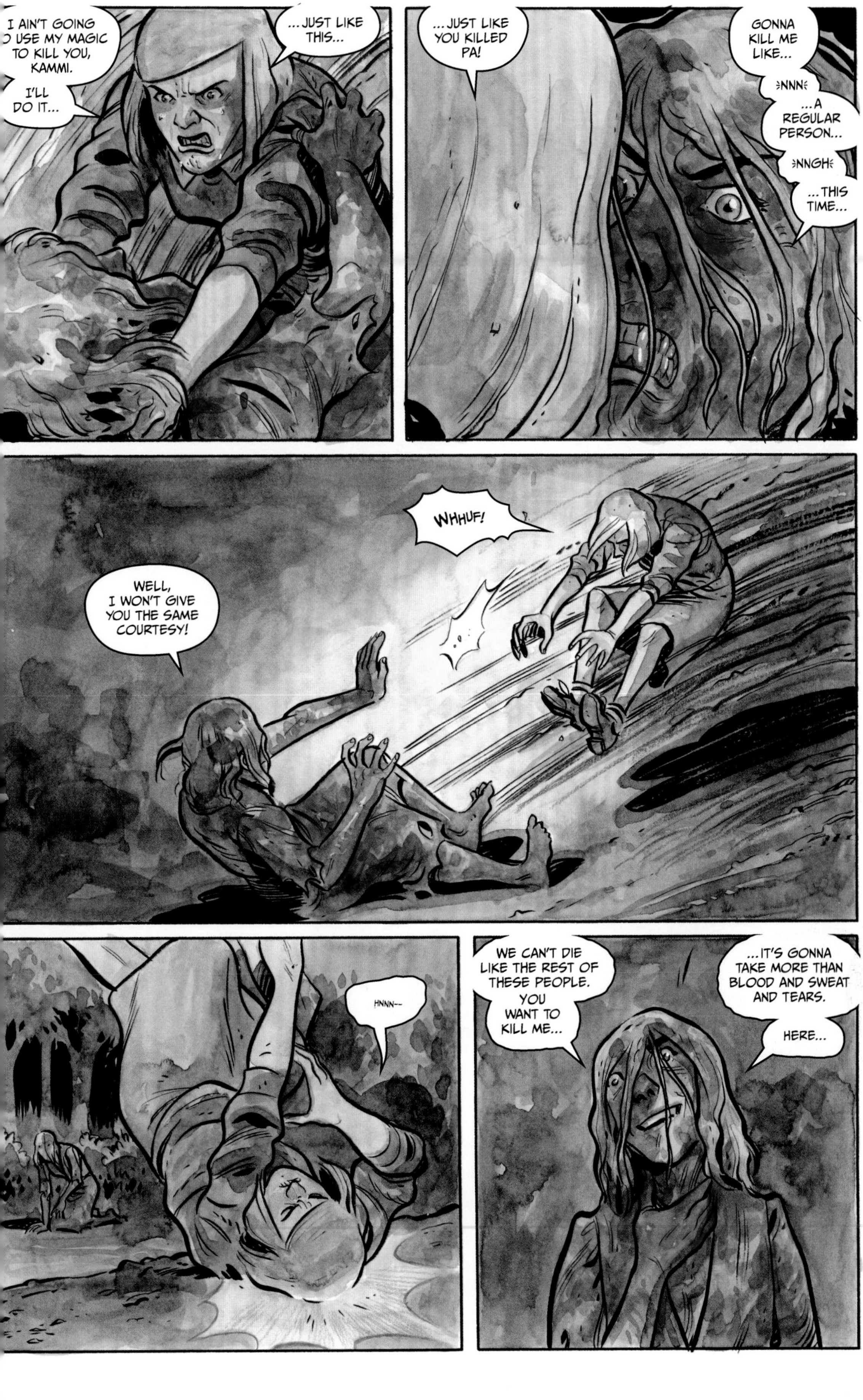
I AIN'T GOING TO USE MY MAGIC TO KILL YOU, KAMMI.
I'LL DO IT...
...JUST LIKE THIS...
...JUST LIKE YOU KILLED PA!
GONNA KILL ME LIKE...
NNN
...A REGULAR PERSON...
NNGH
...THIS TIME...
WHHUF!
WELL, I WON'T GIVE YOU THE SAME COURTESY!
HNNN--
WE CAN'T DIE LIKE THE REST OF THESE PEOPLE.
YOU WANT TO KILL ME...
...IT'S GONNA TAKE MORE THAN BLOOD AND SWEAT AND TEARS.
HERE...

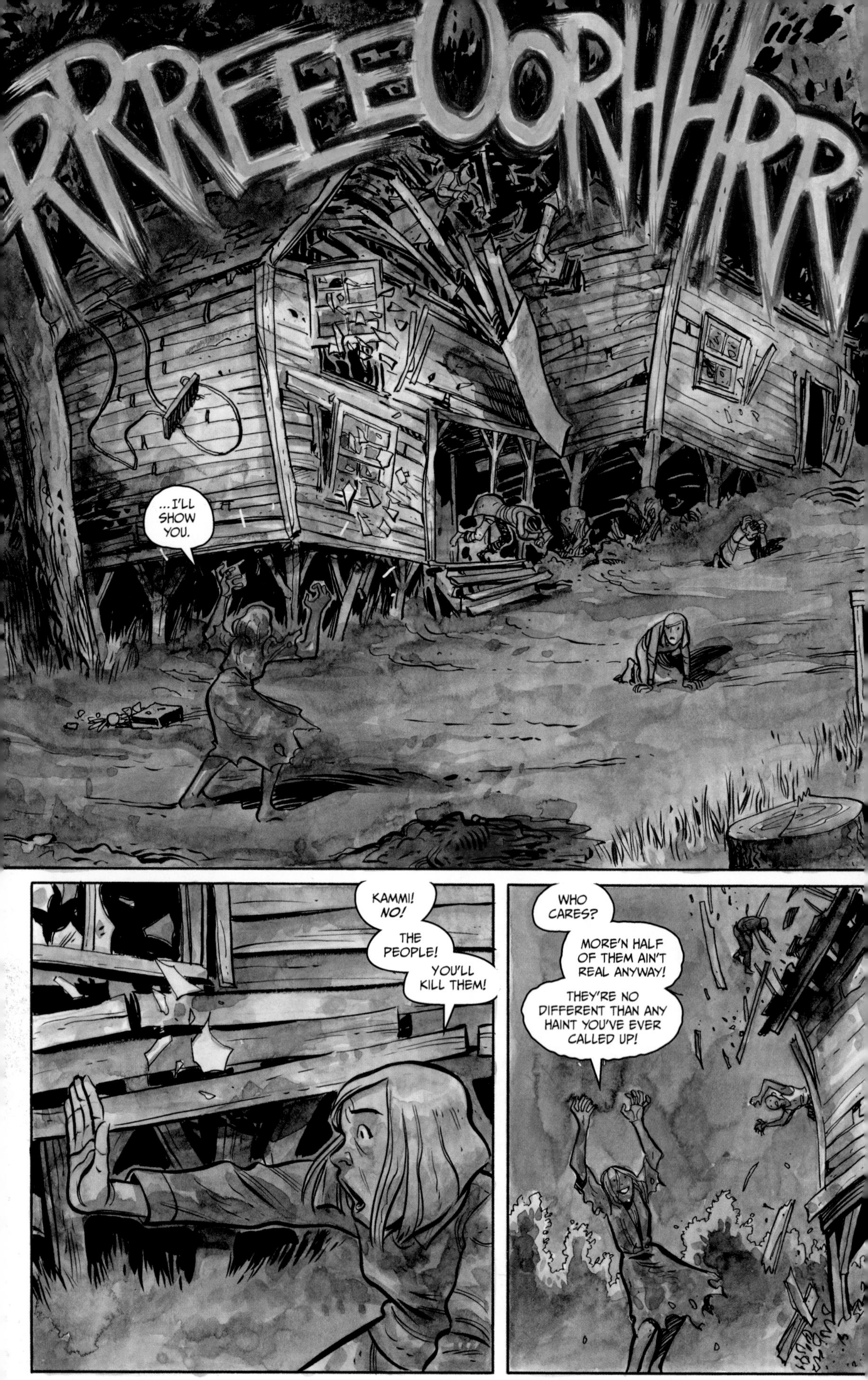
RRREEEOORHHRR
...I'LL SHOW YOU.
KAMMI! NO!
THE PEOPLE!
YOU'LL KILL THEM!
WHO CARES?
MORE'N HALF OF THEM AIN'T REAL ANYWAY!
THEY'RE NO DIFFERENT THAN ANY HAINT YOU'VE EVER CALLED UP!

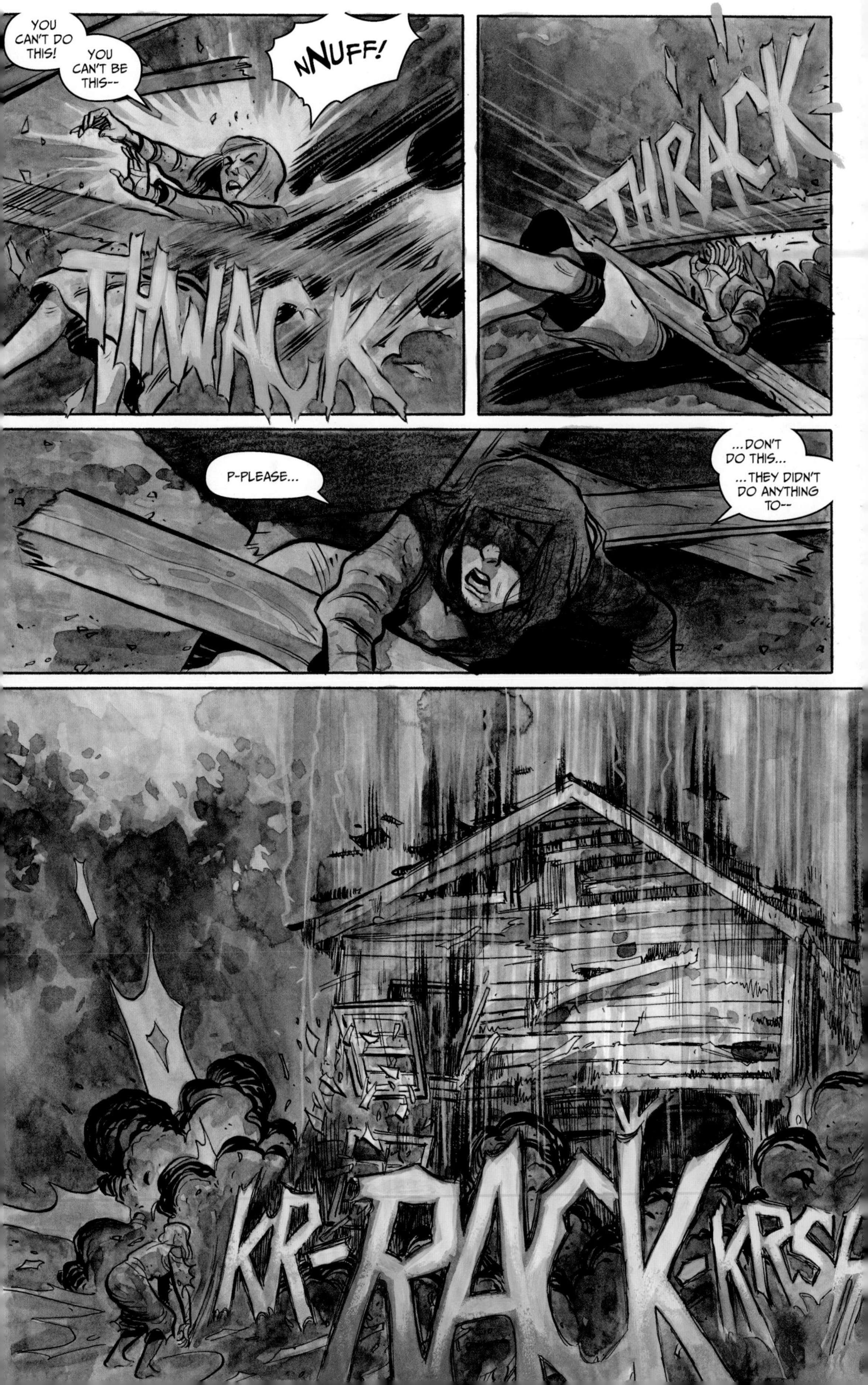

YOU CAN'T DO THIS!
YOU CAN'T BE THIS--
NNUFF!
THWACK
THRACK
P-PLEASE...
...DON'T DO THIS...
...THEY DIDN'T DO ANYTHING TO--
KR-RACK
KRSH

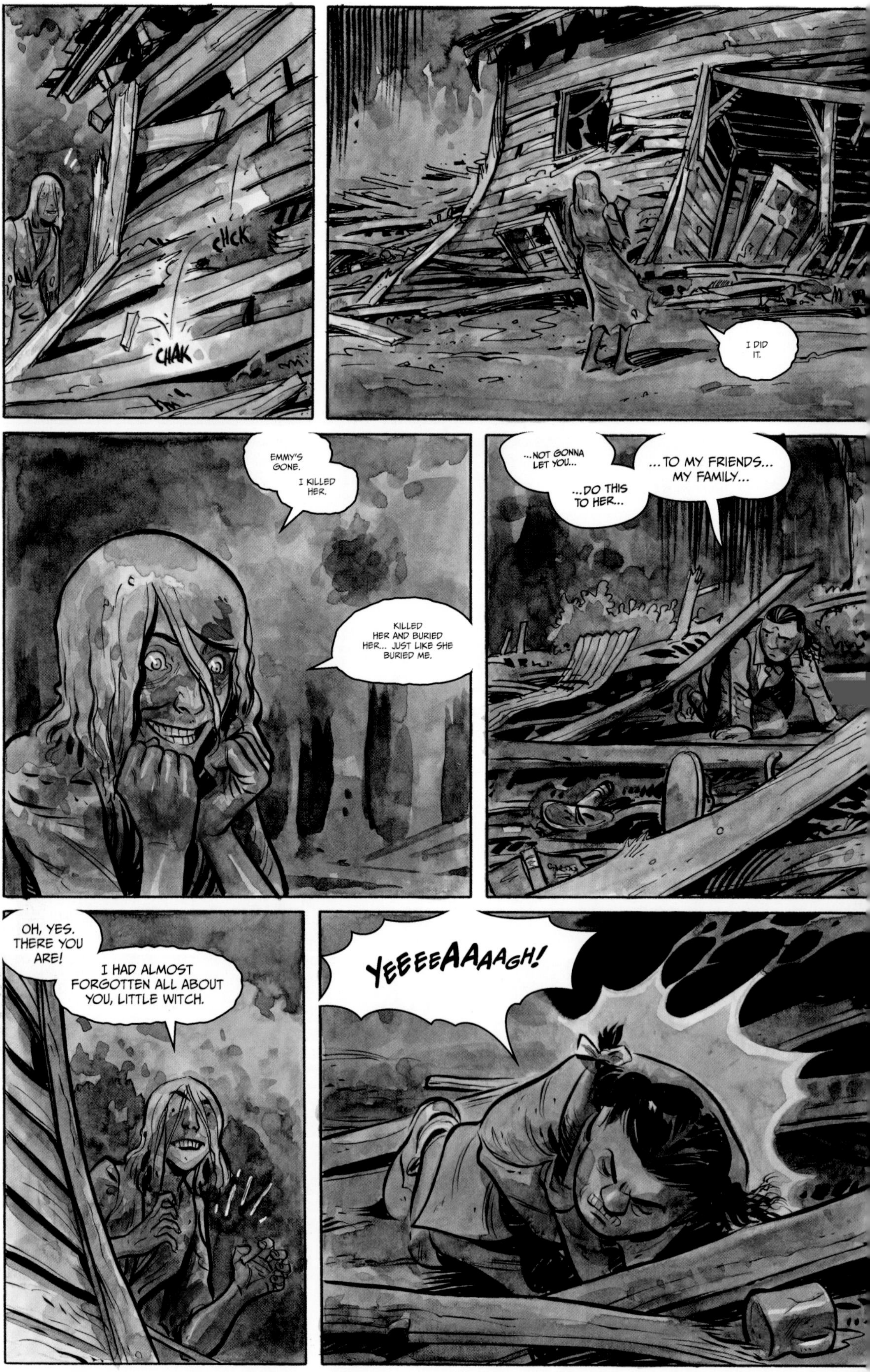
CHCK
CHAK
I DID IT.
EMMY'S GONE.
I KILLED HER.
KILLED HER AND BURIED HER... JUST LIKE SHE BURIED ME.
...NOT GONNA LET YOU...
...DO THIS TO HER...
...TO MY FRIENDS... MY FAMILY...
OH, YES. THERE YOU ARE!
I HAD ALMOST FORGOTTEN ALL ABOUT YOU, LITTLE WITCH.
YEEEEAAAAGH!

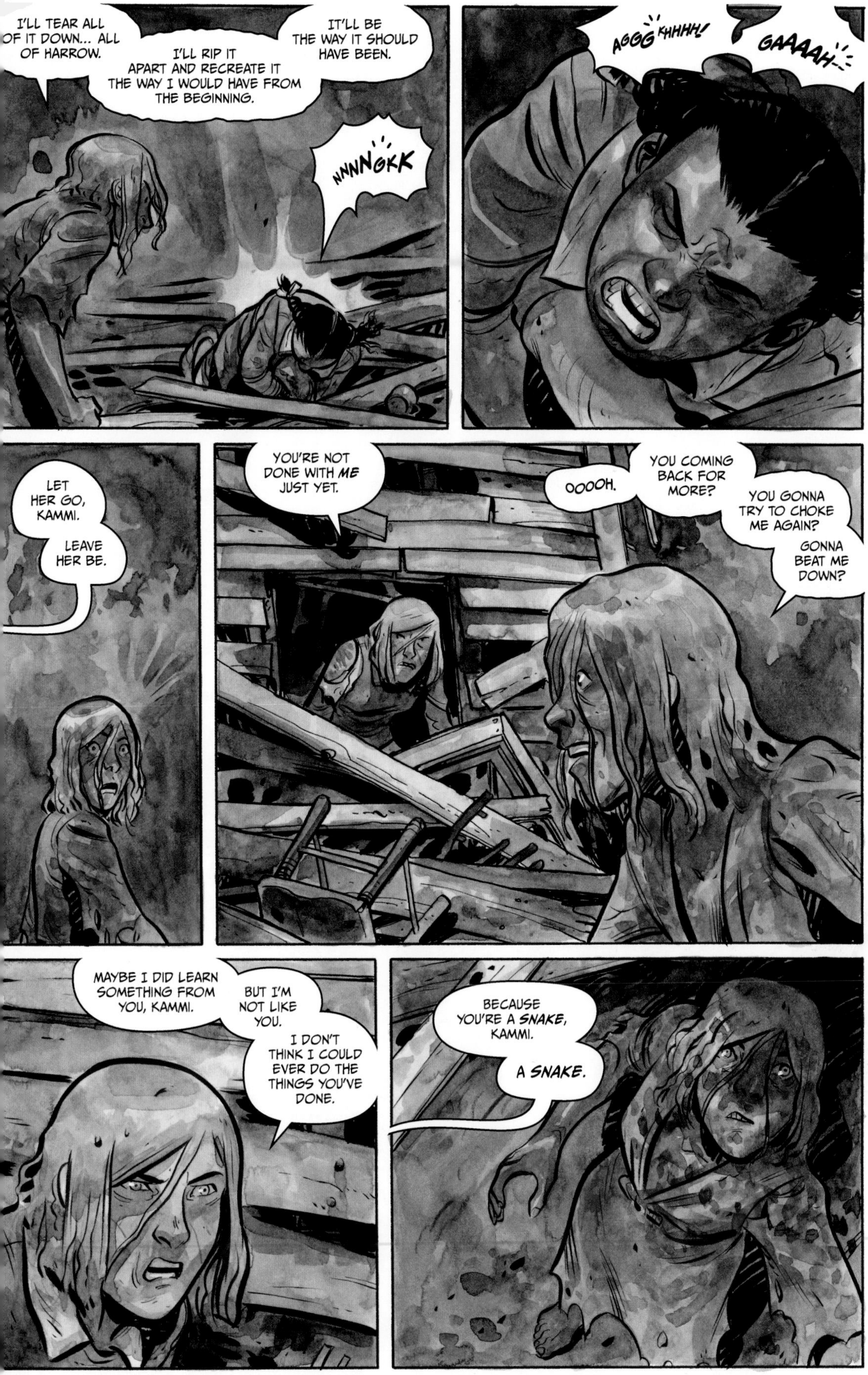

I'LL TEAR ALL OF IT DOWN... ALL OF HARROW.
I'LL RIP IT APART AND RECREATE IT THE WAY I WOULD HAVE FROM THE BEGINNING.
IT'LL BE THE WAY IT SHOULD HAVE BEEN.
NNNNGKK
AGGGKHHHH!
GAAAAAH
LET HER GO, KAMMI.
LEAVE HER BE.
YOU'RE NOT DONE WITH *ME* JUST YET.
OOOOH.
YOU COMING BACK FOR MORE?
YOU GONNA TRY TO CHOKE ME AGAIN?
GONNA BEAT ME DOWN?
MAYBE I DID LEARN SOMETHING FROM YOU, KAMMI.
BUT I'M NOT LIKE YOU.
I DON'T THINK I COULD EVER DO THE THINGS YOU'VE DONE.
BECAUSE YOU'RE A *SNAKE*, KAMMI.
A *SNAKE*.

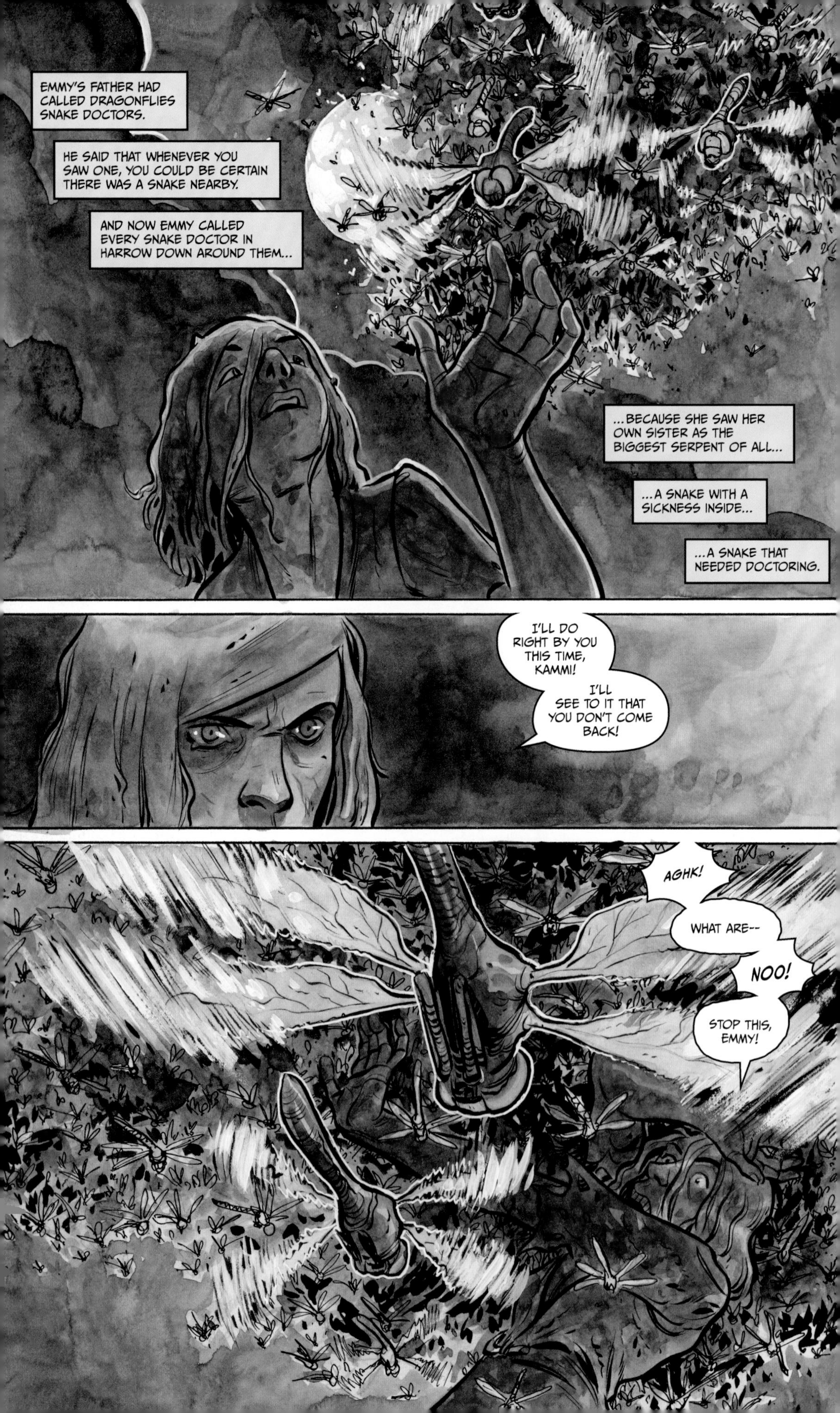
EMMY'S FATHER HAD CALLED DRAGONFLIES SNAKE DOCTORS.
HE SAID THAT WHENEVER YOU SAW ONE, YOU COULD BE CERTAIN THERE WAS A SNAKE NEARBY.
AND NOW EMMY CALLED EVERY SNAKE DOCTOR IN HARROW DOWN AROUND THEM...
...BECAUSE SHE SAW HER OWN SISTER AS THE BIGGEST SERPENT OF ALL...
...A SNAKE WITH A SICKNESS INSIDE...
...A SNAKE THAT NEEDED DOCTORING.
I'LL DO RIGHT BY YOU THIS TIME, KAMMI!
I'LL SEE TO IT THAT YOU DON'T COME BACK!
AGHK!
WHAT ARE--
NOO!
STOP THIS, EMMY!

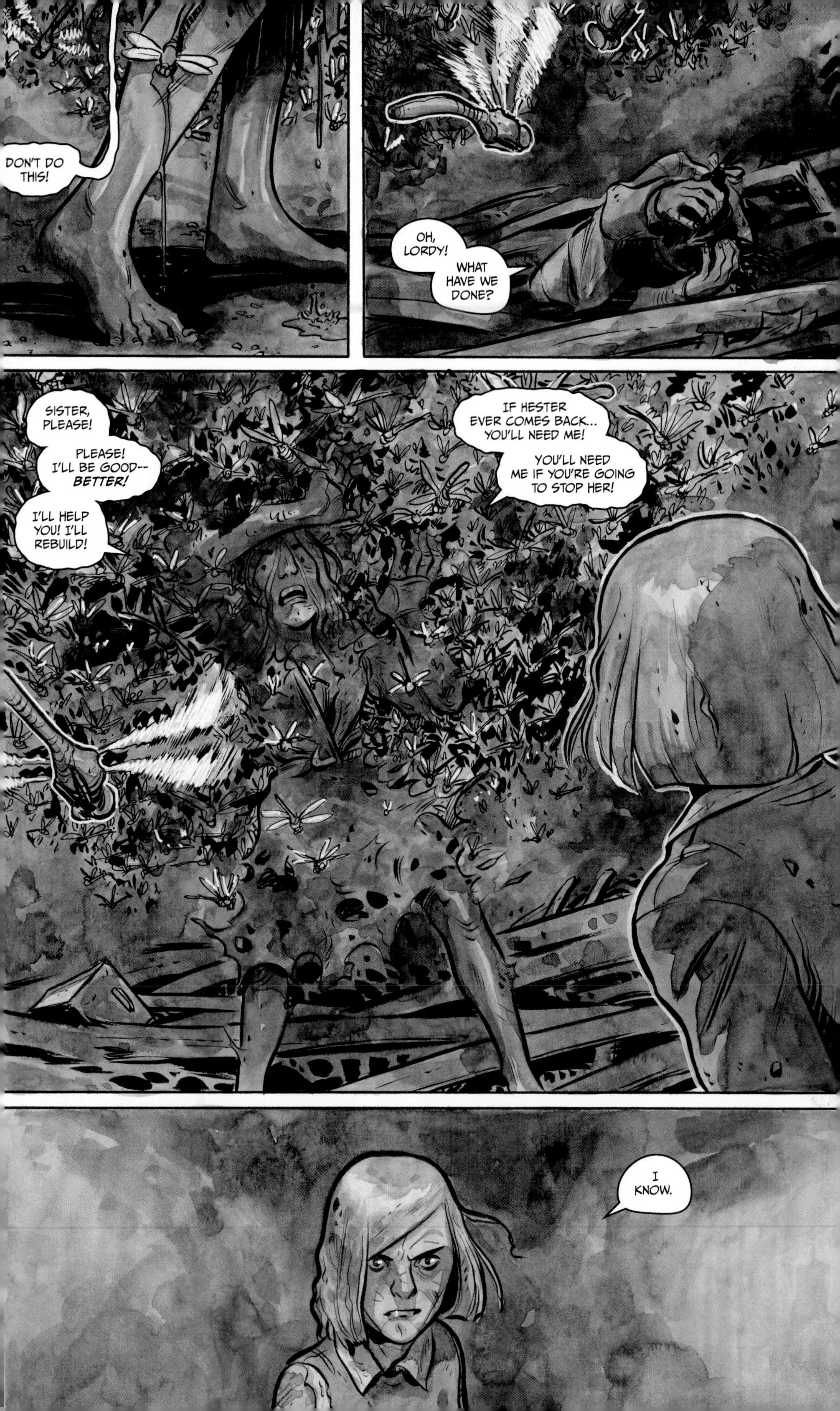
DON'T DO THIS!
OH, LORDY!
WHAT HAVE WE DONE?
SISTER, PLEASE!
PLEASE! I'LL BE GOOD-- *BETTER!*
I'LL HELP YOU! I'LL REBUILD!
IF HESTER EVER COMES BACK... YOU'LL NEED ME!
YOU'LL NEED ME IF YOU'RE GOING TO STOP HER!
I KNOW.

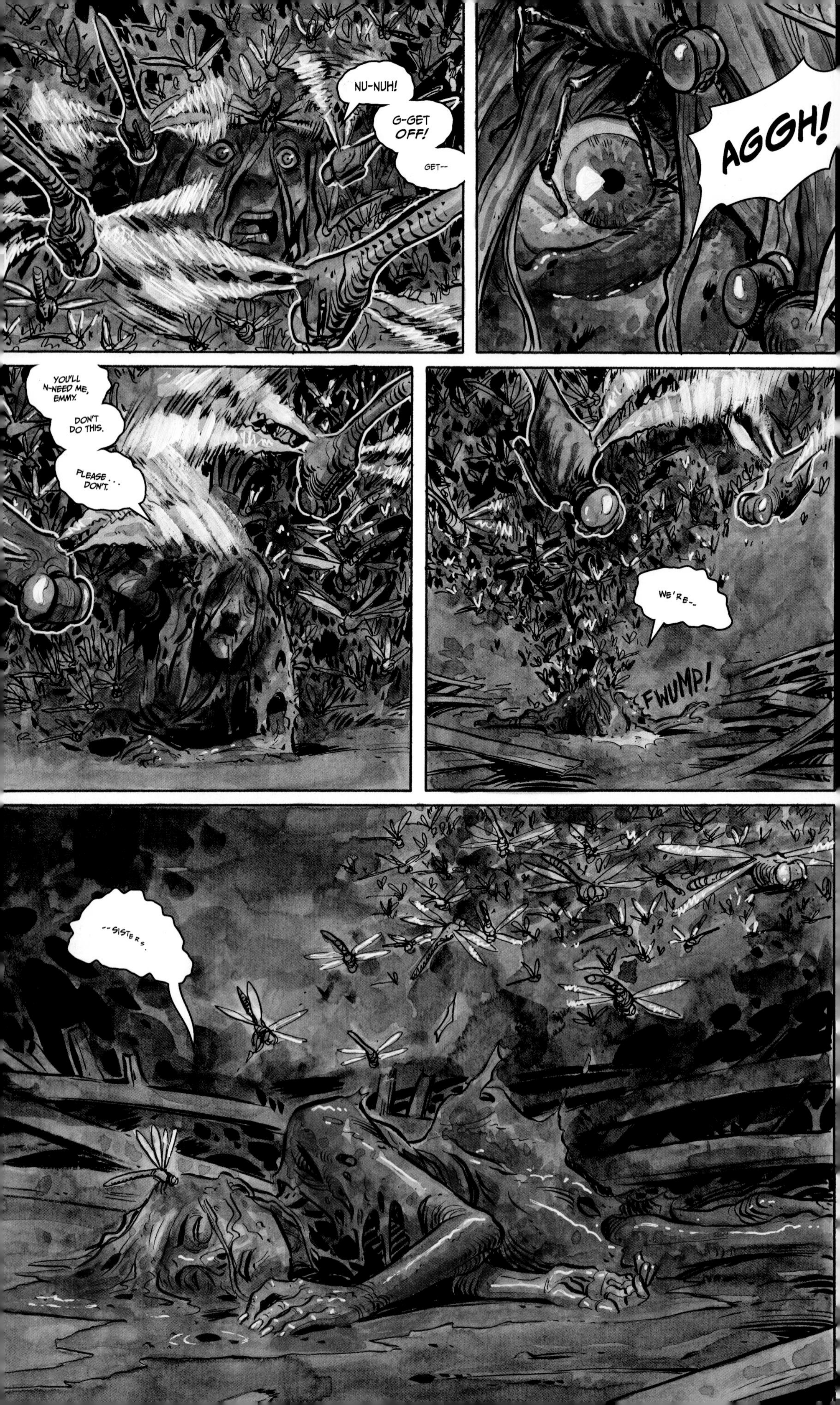
NU-NUH!
G-GET OFF!
GET--
AGGH!
YOU'LL N-NEED ME, EMMY.
DON'T DO THIS.
PLEASE . . . DON'T.
WE'RE--
FWUMP!
--SISTERS.

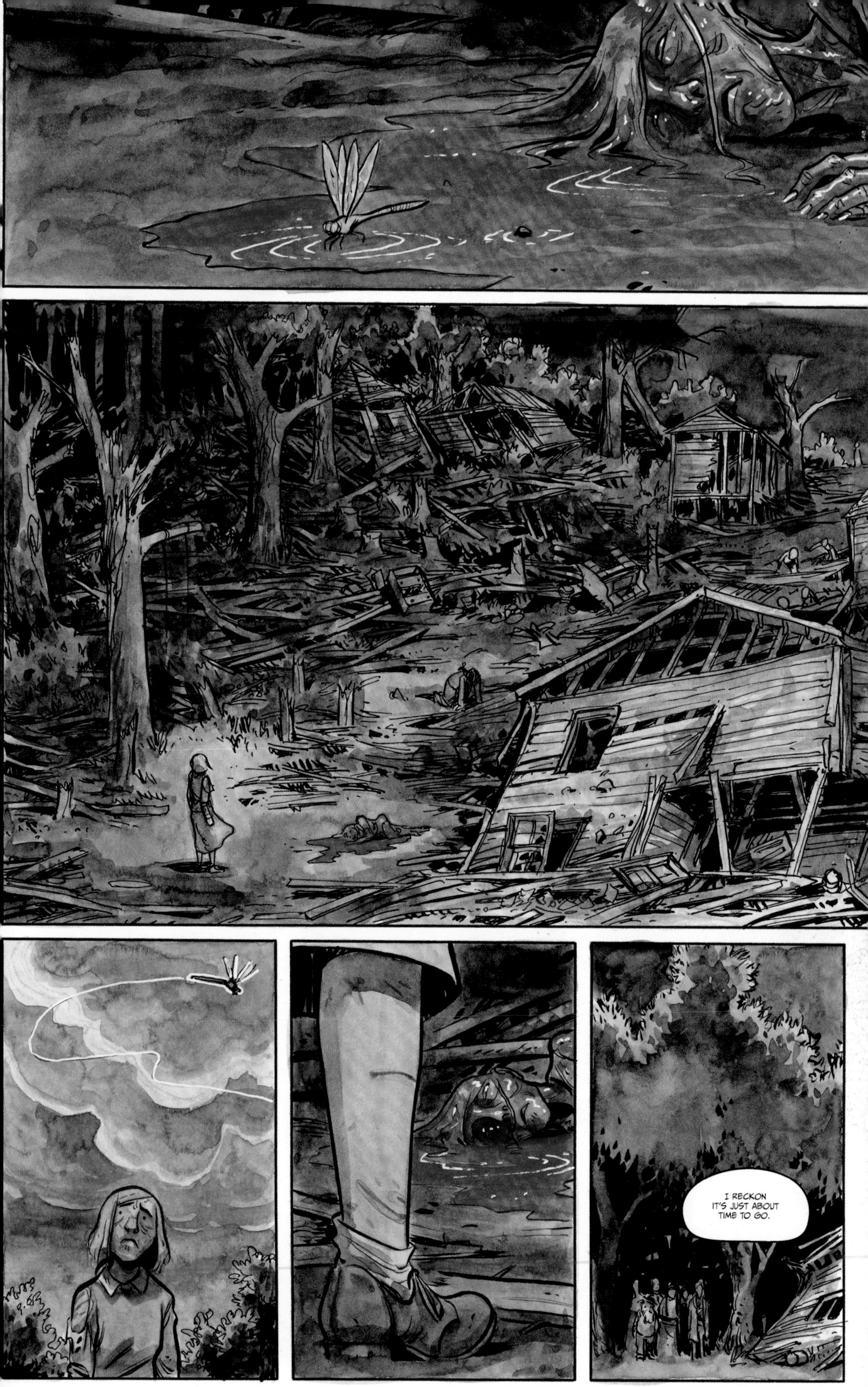
I RECKON IT'S JUST ABOUT TIME TO GO.

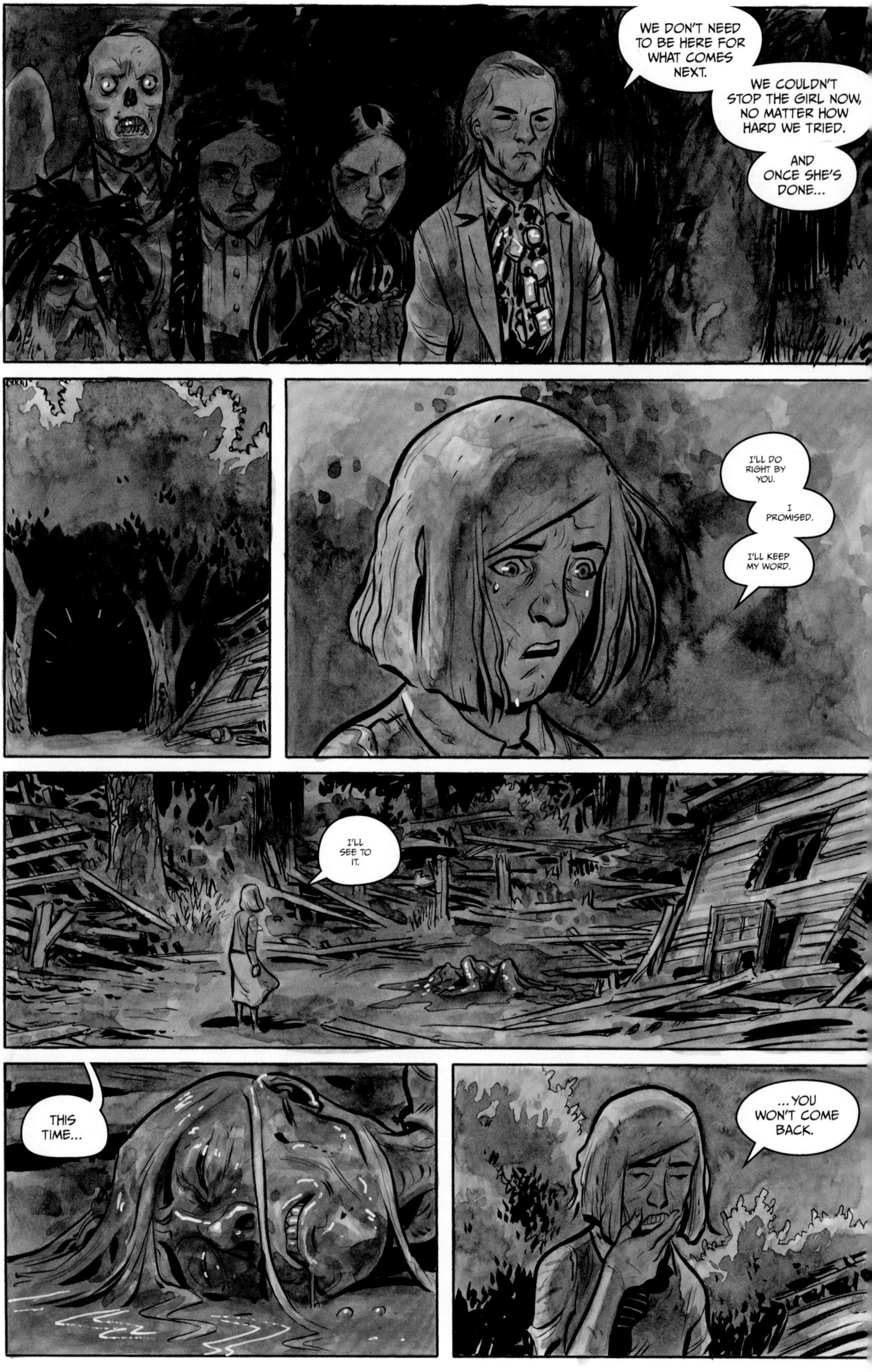
WE DON'T NEED TO BE HERE FOR WHAT COMES NEXT.
WE COULDN'T STOP THE GIRL NOW, NO MATTER HOW HARD WE TRIED.
AND ONCE SHE'S DONE...
I'LL DO RIGHT BY YOU.
I PROMISED.
I'LL KEEP MY WORD.
I'LL SEE TO IT.
THIS TIME...
...YOU WON'T COME BACK.

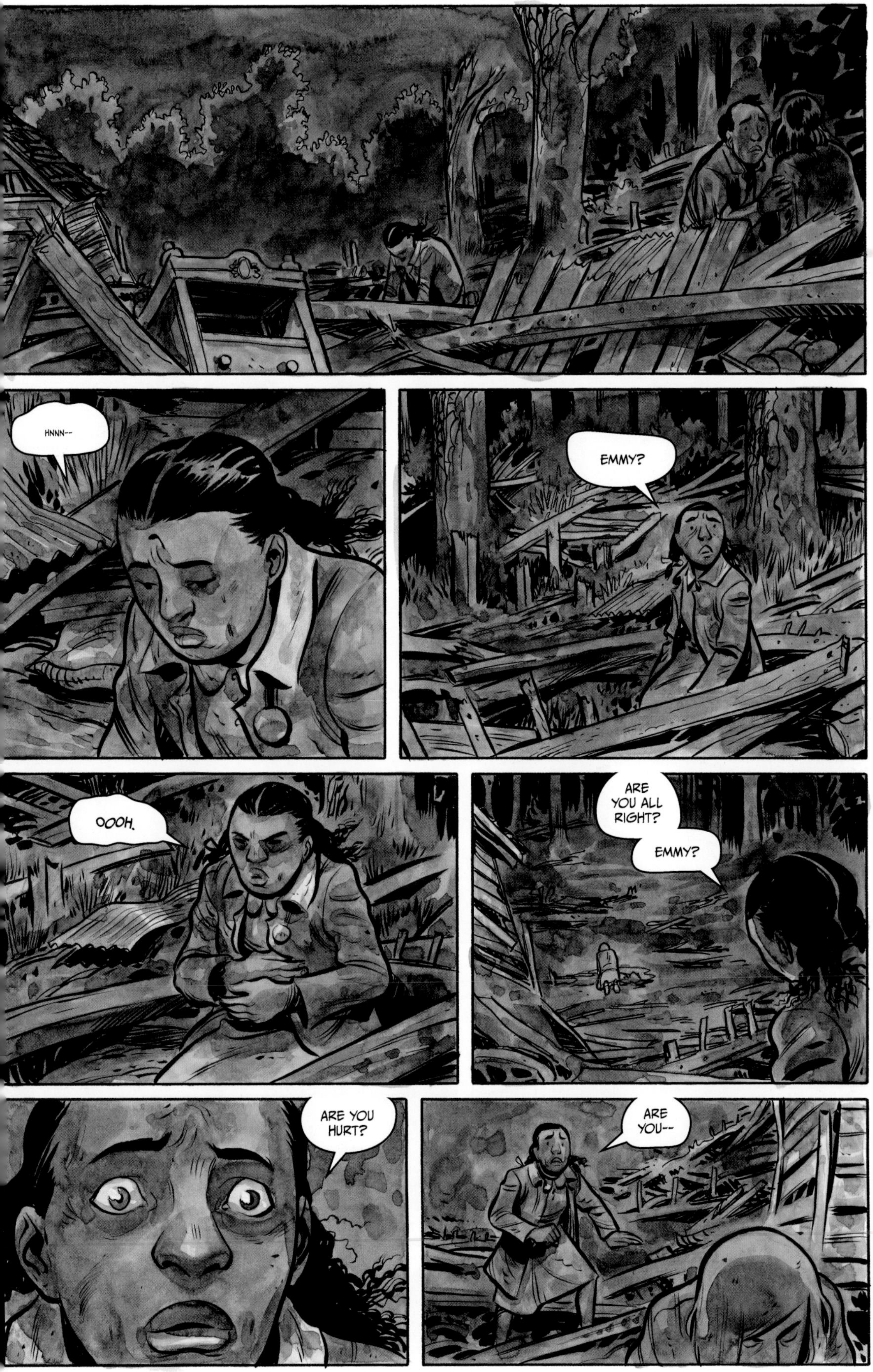
HNNN--
EMMY?
OOOH.
ARE YOU ALL RIGHT?
EMMY?
ARE YOU HURT?
ARE YOU--

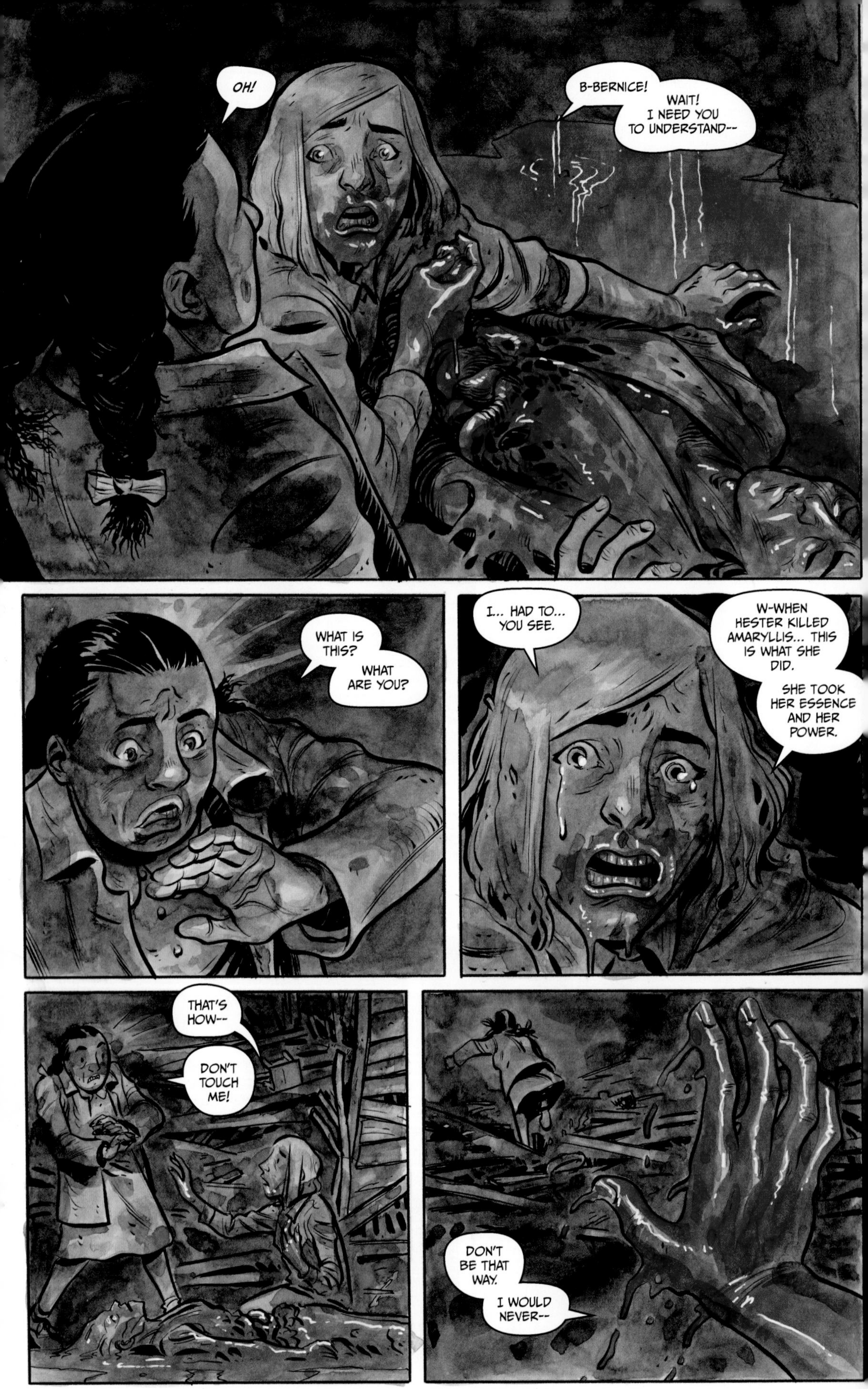
OH!
B-BERNICE!
WAIT! I NEED YOU TO UNDERSTAND--
WHAT IS THIS?
WHAT ARE YOU?
I... HAD TO... YOU SEE.
W-WHEN HESTER KILLED AMARYLLIS... THIS IS WHAT SHE DID.
SHE TOOK HER ESSENCE AND HER POWER.
THAT'S HOW--
DON'T TOUCH ME!
DON'T BE THAT WAY.
I WOULD NEVER--

BERNICE.

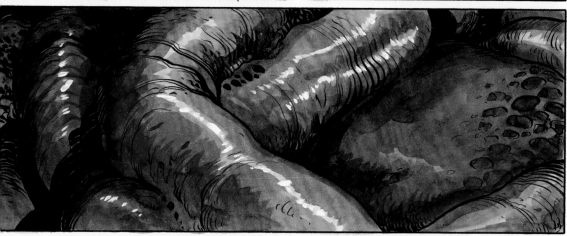

BUT... EVEN AFTER THE AWFUL THING SHE HAD DONE... EMMY KNEW HER TROUBLES WERE FAR FROM OVER.

A STORM WAS BREWING... A STORM THAT HAD STARTED A-RUMBLING ON THE DAY SHE WAS BORN.

RMMₕMMₕBBLLEEₑ

AND SOON ENOUGH, THE CLOUDS WOULD COME...

...THE RAIN WOULD POUR DOWN IN SHEETS...

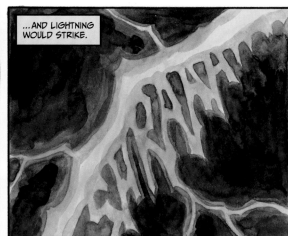

...AND LIGHTNING WOULD STRIKE.

EIGHTEEN YEARS AGO, THE WITCH HESTER BECK HAD BEEN LYNCHED FROM THE BRANCHES OF THAT OLD TREE.

PRAYERS HAD BEEN SPOKEN BEFORE HER TWITCHING AND KICKING BODY.

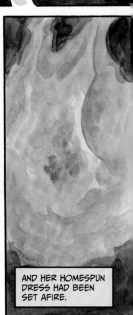

AND HER HOMESPUN DRESS HAD BEEN SET AFIRE.

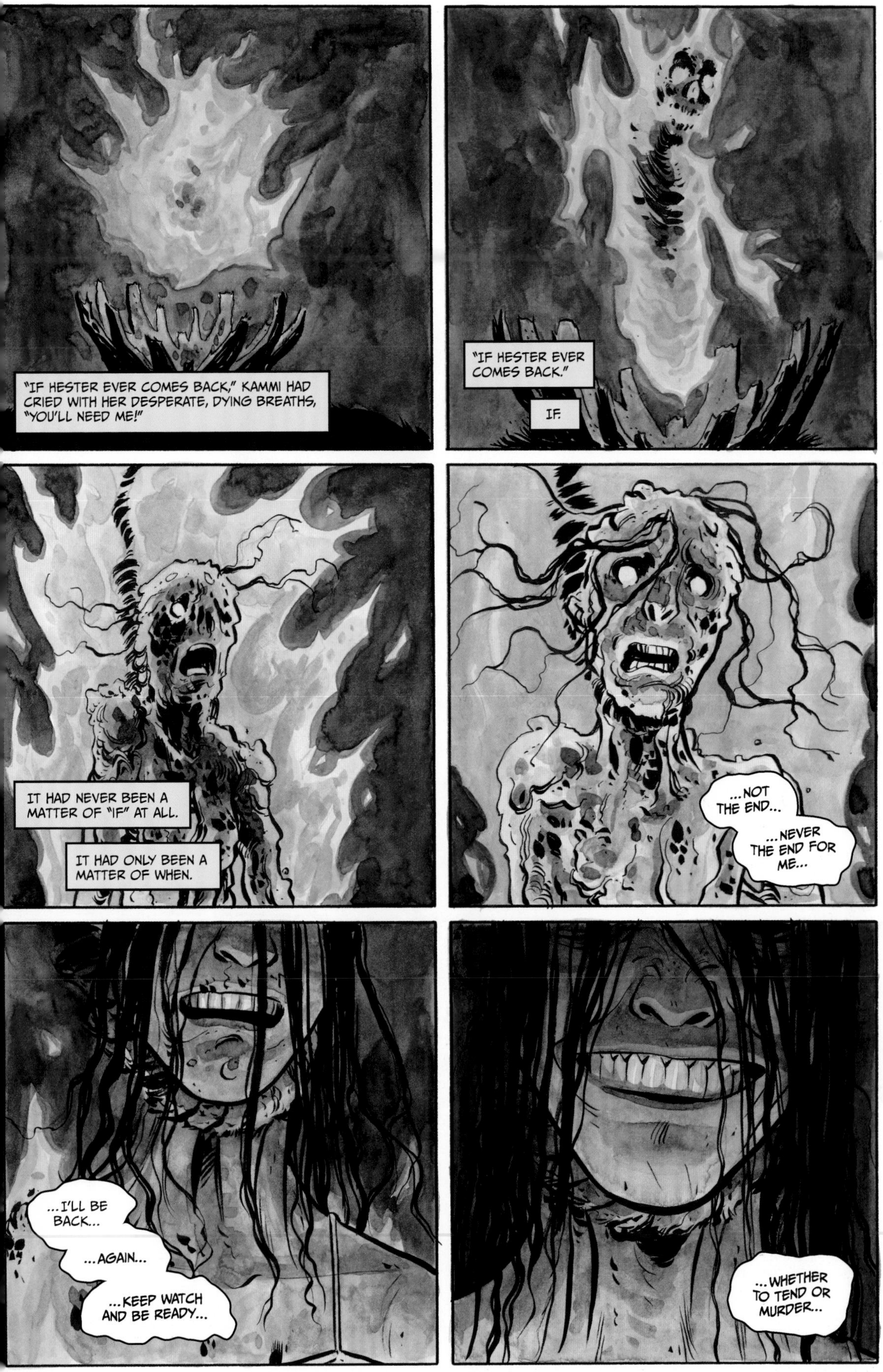
"IF HESTER EVER COMES BACK," KAMMI HAD CRIED WITH HER DESPERATE, DYING BREATHS, "YOU'LL NEED ME!"
"IF HESTER EVER COMES BACK."
IF.
IT HAD NEVER BEEN A MATTER OF "IF" AT ALL.
IT HAD ONLY BEEN A MATTER OF WHEN.
...NOT THE END...
...NEVER THE END FOR ME...
...I'LL BE BACK...
...AGAIN...
...KEEP WATCH AND BE READY...
...WHETHER TO TEND OR MURDER...

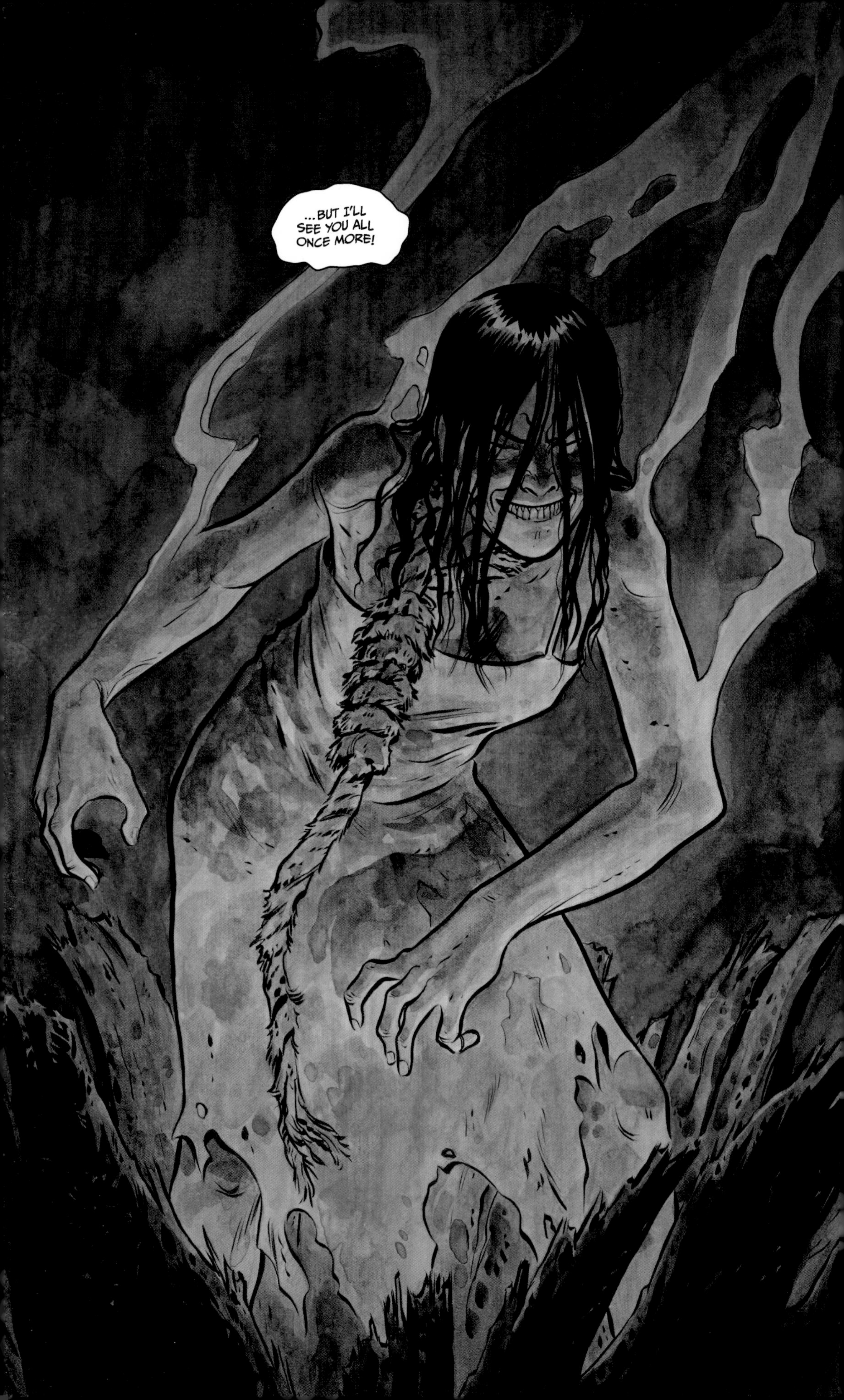
...BUT I'LL SEE YOU ALL ONCE MORE!

HARROW
◄ SKETCHBOOK ►
COUNTY

NOTES BY
DANIEL CHABON

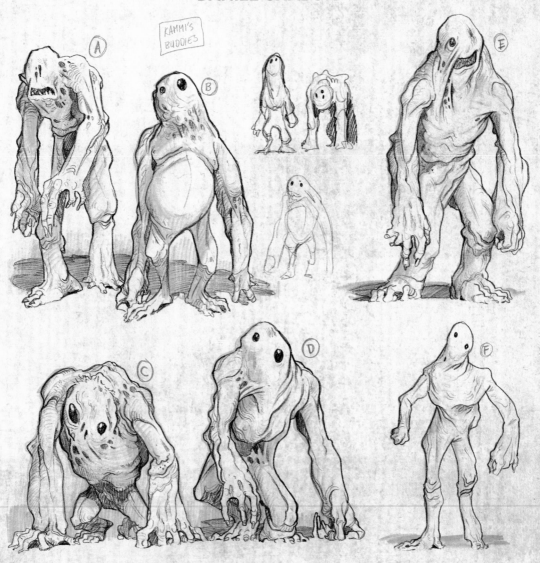

KAMMI'S BUDDIES

Featured here are some character designs for some of Kammi's monster allies.

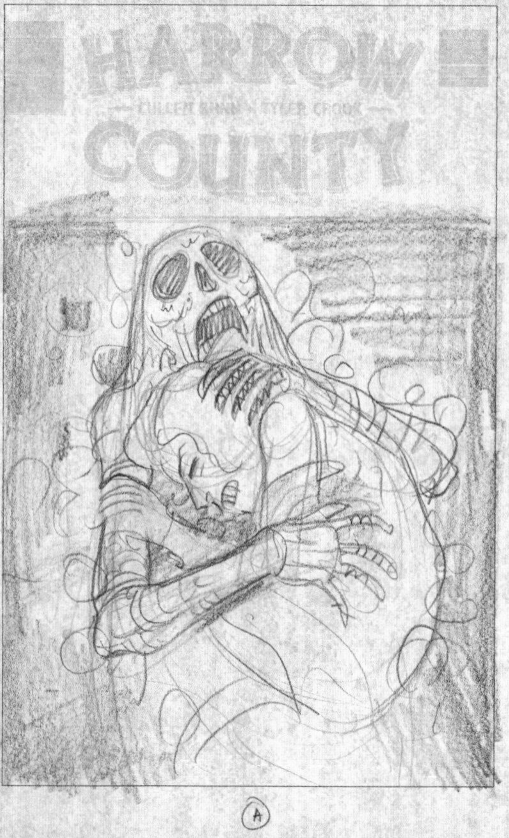
HARROW
CULLEN BUNN • TYLER CROOK
COUNTY

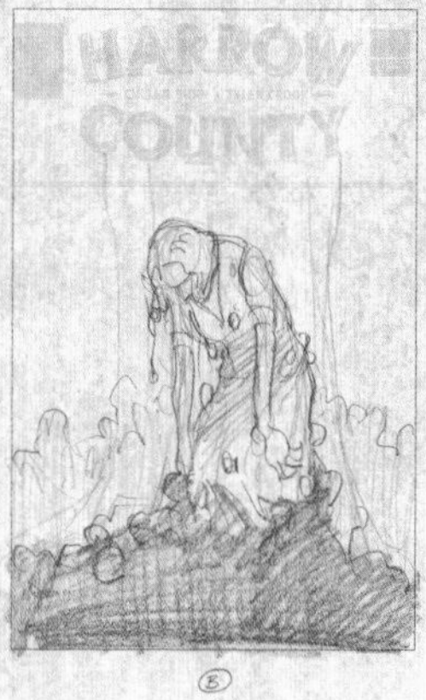
HARROW
COUNTY

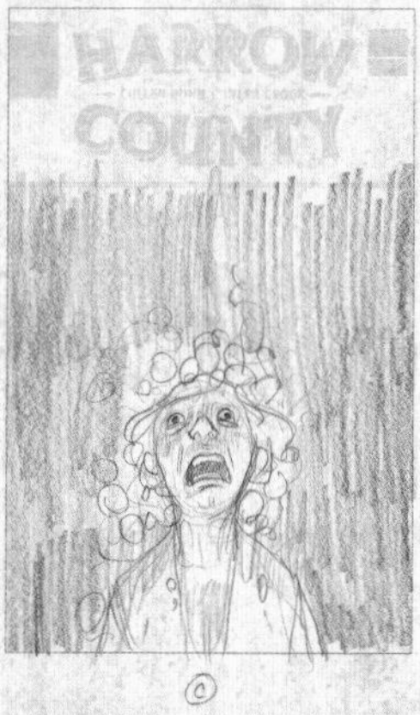
HARROW
COUNTY

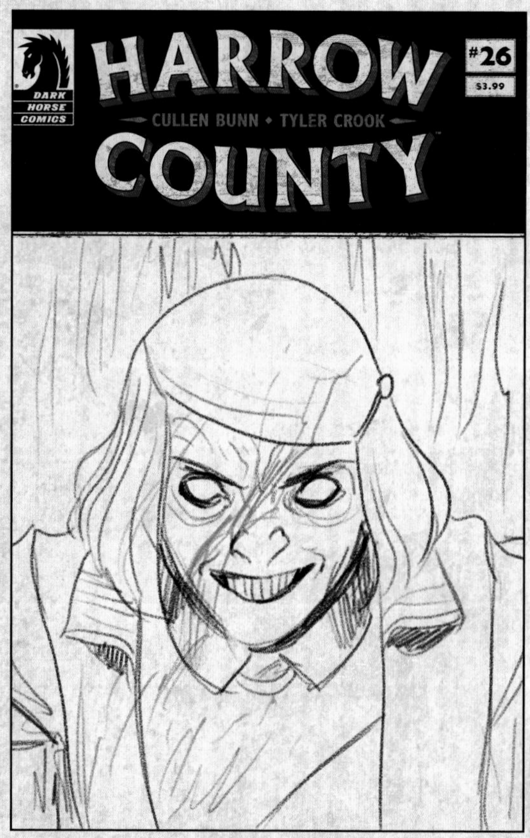
DARK HORSE COMICS
HARROW
#26
$3.99
CULLEN BUNN • TYLER CROOK
COUNTY

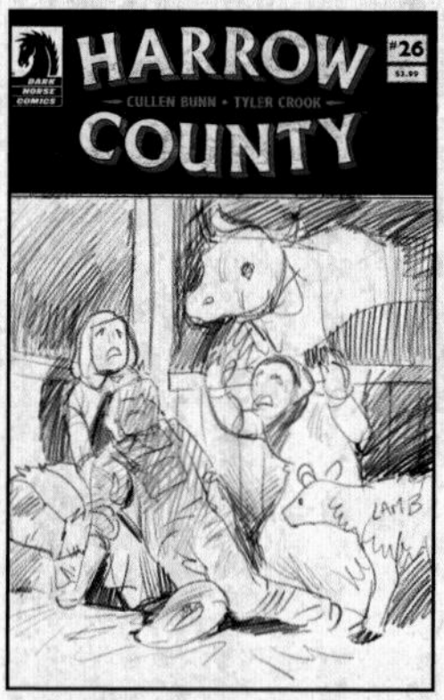
HARROW
#26
CULLEN BUNN • TYLER CROOK
COUNTY
LAMB

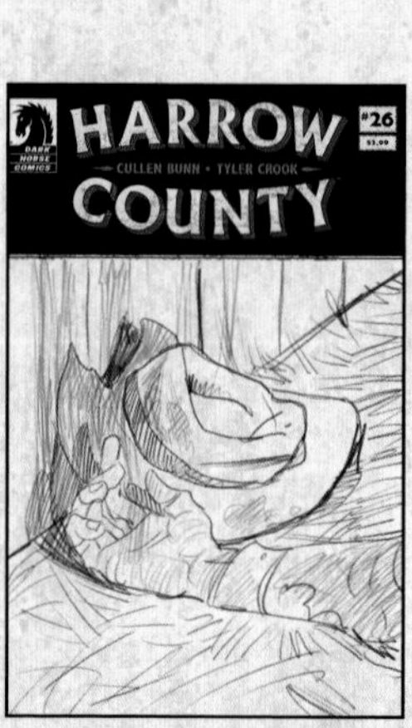
HARROW
#26
CULLEN BUNN • TYLER CROOK
COUNTY

This page features cover sketches for the issues #25 and #26 covers.

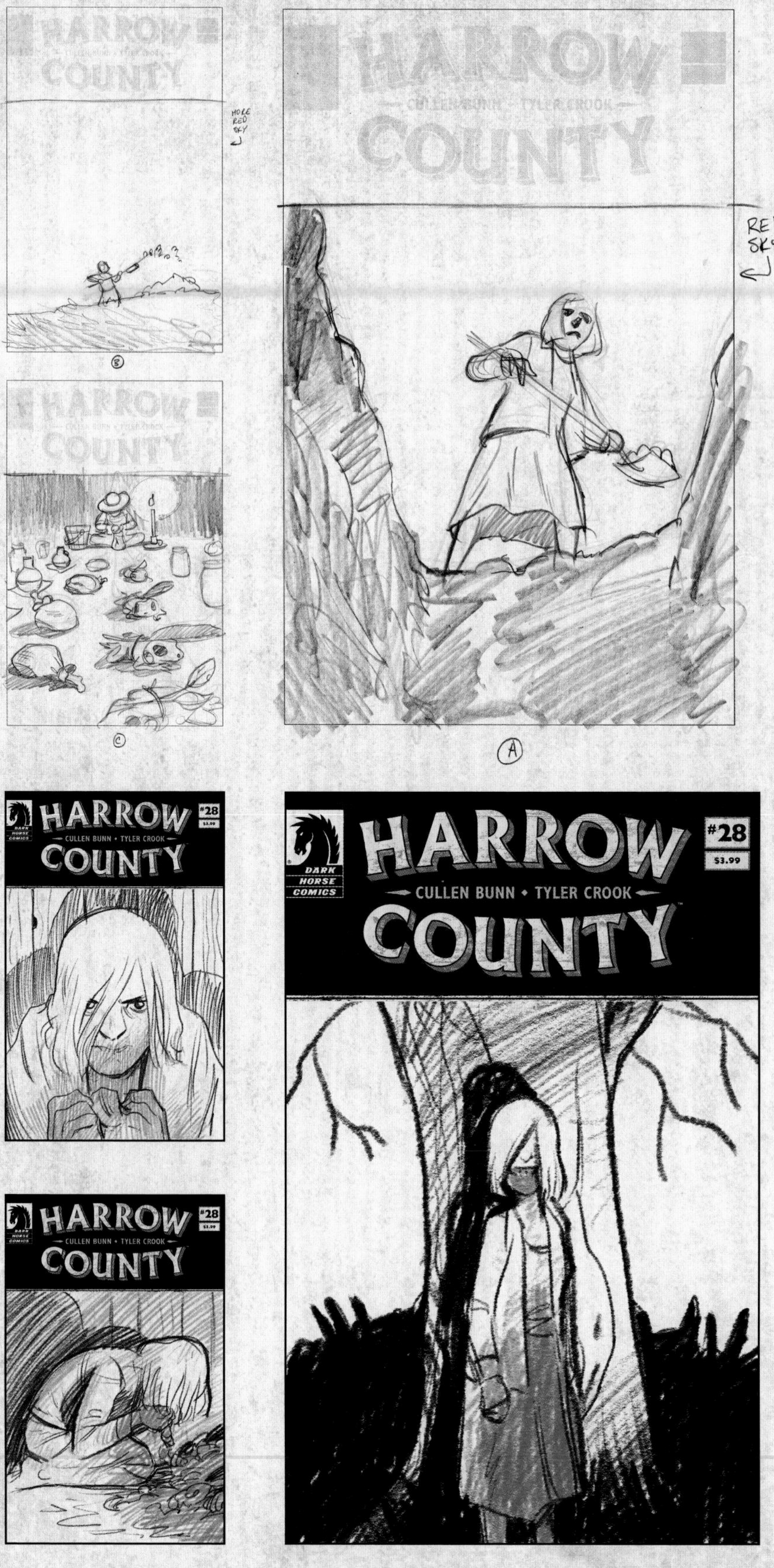

MORE RED SKY
RED SKY
HARROW COUNTY
CULLEN BUNN • TYLER CROOK
#28
$3.99
DARK HORSE COMICS

Here are the cover sketches for the issues #27 and #28 covers.

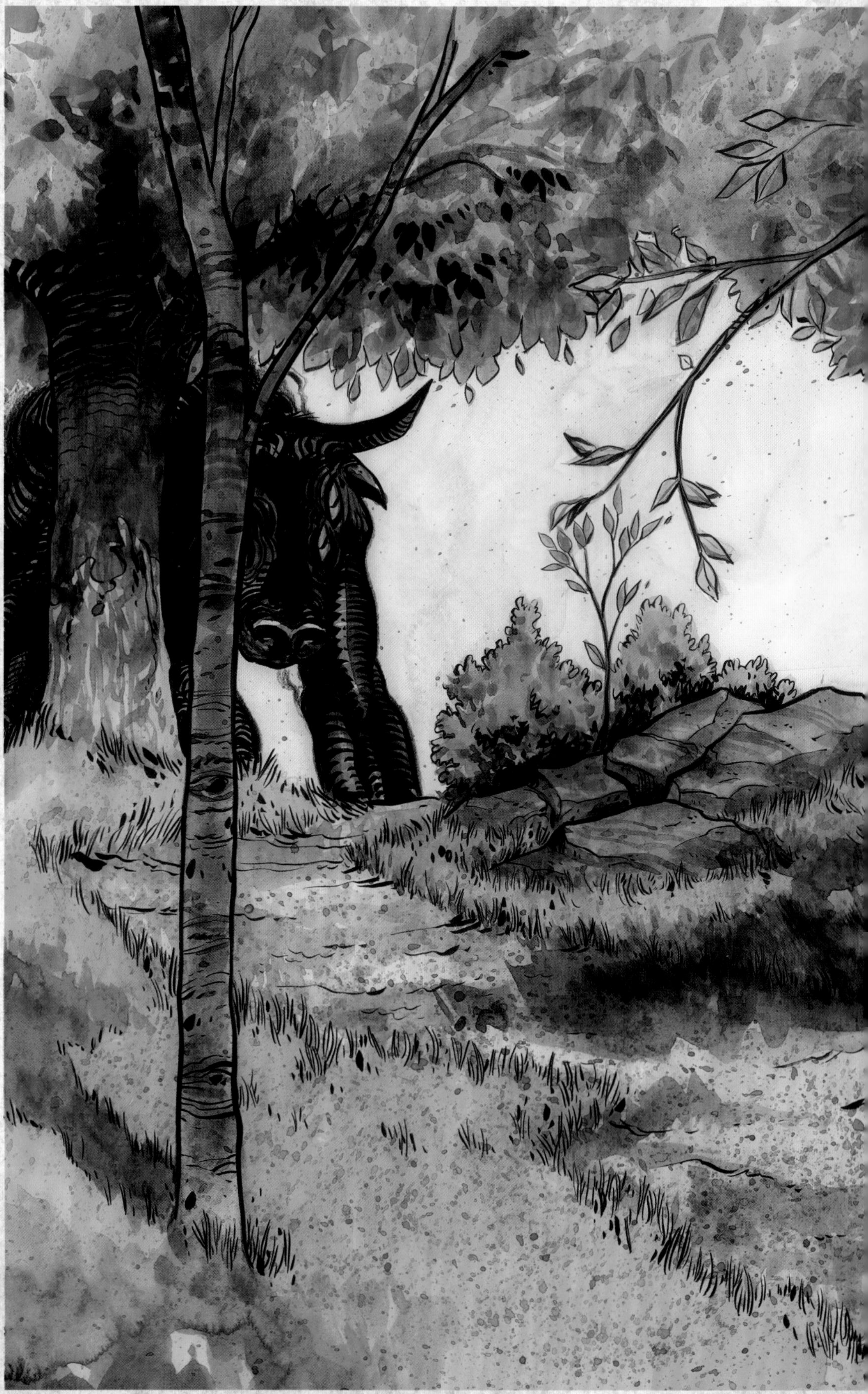

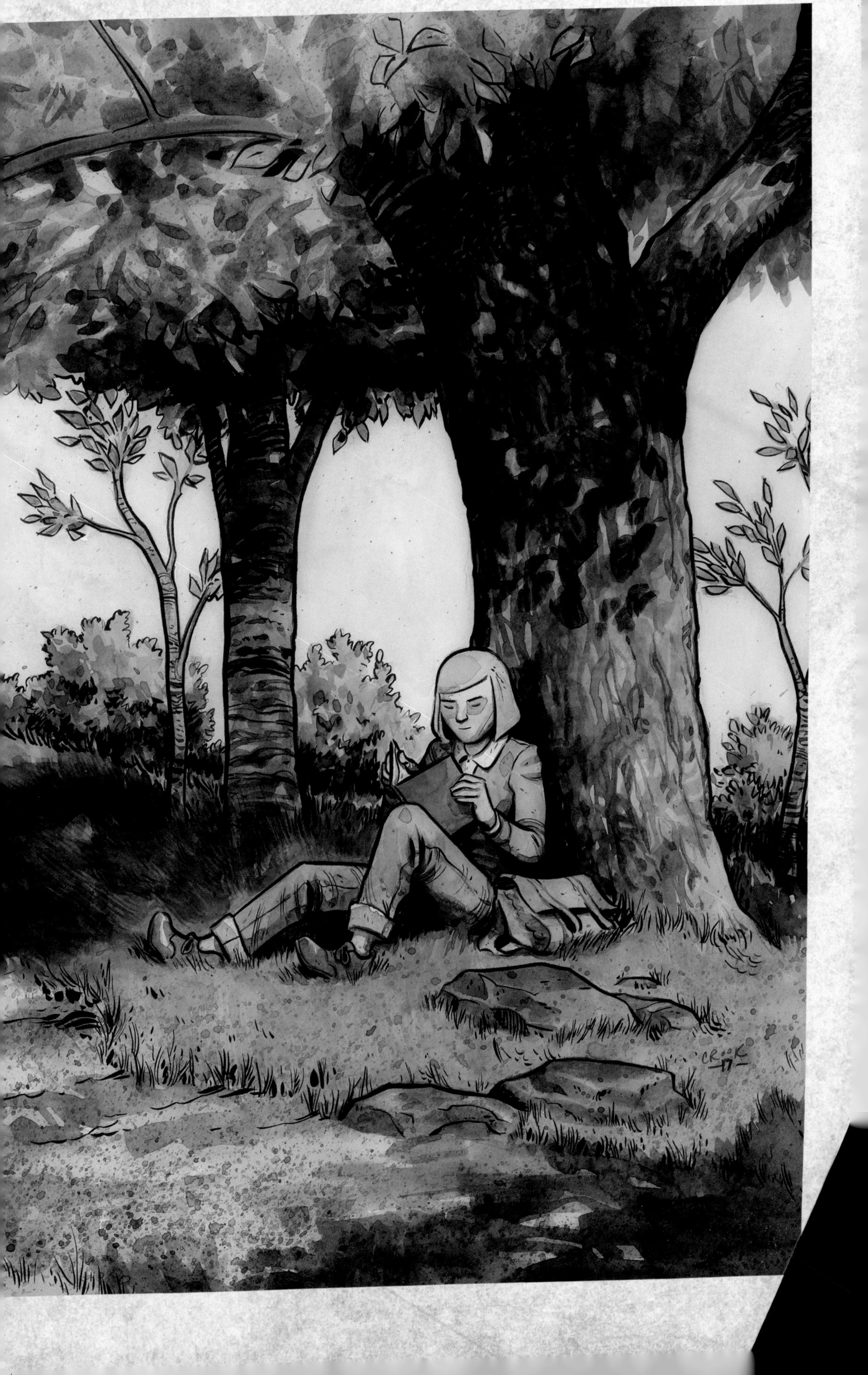
CROOK
17